Walking Along the Paths of Buddhist Epistemology

Cataloging in Publication Data — DK
[Courtesy: D.K. Agencies (P) Ltd. <docinfo@dkagencies.com>]

Chattopadhyay, Madhumita, 1961-
Walking along the paths of Buddhist epistemology / Madhumita Chattopadhyay.
p. cm.
Includes bibliographical references (p.)
Includes index.
ISBN 812460441X

1. Knowledge, Theory of (Buddhism). 2. Philosophy, Buddhist. I. Title.

DDC 181.043 22

ISBN 81-246-0441-X
First published in India in 2007

Published by:
D.K. Printworld (P) Ltd.
Regd. Office: 'Sri Kunj', F-52, Bali Nagar
Ramesh Nagar Metro Station
New Delhi-110 015
Phones: (011) 2545 3975; 2546 6019; *Fax*: (011) 2546 5926
E-mail: dkprintworld@vsnl.net
Website: www.dkprintworld.com

in collaboration with
Jadavpur University
Kolkata (West Bengal)

Printed by: D.K. Printworld (P) Ltd., New Delhi

Preface

THE book Walking along the Paths of Buddhist Epistemology is the result of a project undertaken by the author to make the basic doctrines of Buddhist epistemology available to students who are interested in Buddhist studies but who do not have sufficient knowledge of Sanskrit language to go through the original texts themselves. The idea of writing a book on this topic was the thought of my teacher Prof. Arindam Chakraborty of the Department of Philosophy, Hawaii University, USA when he got the information that the author was going to offer a course on Buddhist epistemology to students of the Graduate level at Western Michigan University, USA, as a Fulbright Visiting Scholar in the Fall Semester 2004. The students at the Graduate level were totally novices in the area of Buddhist epistemology. For them, Buddhism was a philosophy which deals with transcendental matters like *nirvāṇa, sūnya,* etc. and had nothing to do with epistemology or logic which is concerned more with empirical/worldly subjects. So in each class I had to face lots of questions regarding the relevance of Buddhist studies to empirical issues — how Buddhism tries to deal with the ordinary ways of knowing that this is a table, this is a substance, etc. So I had a twofold task, answering to the queries of my students and showing that Buddhist epistemology has relevance to the modern day epistemological discussions. This is the background story of this book.

I am really indebted to Prof. Arindam Chakrabory not only for his inspiration but also for giving me time to discuss philosophical issues with him. Since my student life I felt that whenever I was stumbled by any philosophical problem, he was the only person who, with his profound knowledge of both Western and Indian philosophy, could help me most by giving suggestions or referring to texts where I could find answers to those problems. Words are not sufficient to express my gratitude to him.

I would be failing in my duty if I do not mention the name of Prof. Shoryu Katsura, ex-Professor, Department of Indian Philosophy, Hiroshima University, Hiroshima, Japan who opened before me a new way of dealing with different Buddhist texts like the *Pramāṇavārttikā* along with its commentaries. I am really thankful to him for his guidance and teaching. Along with Prof. S. Katsura, I want to mention the contributions of my Japanese friends, especially, Y. Honda, Watanabe, Yoshie Kobayashie and Prof. H. Ogawa, who not only made our stay in Japan very comfortable, but still now help me a lot by providing books and articles which are not easily available in Calcutta. I want to thank them all for their kind help. I also want to mention the name of Prof. Tim Light, Department of Religious Studies, Western Michigan University, Kalamazoo, USA, who in spite of his age and busy schedule used to regularly attend my classes at WMU, and his active participation in the class enabled me to think a lot on the subject. Thanks are due specially to him and also to all my students who made my class a lively one.

It would be wrong on my part if I forget to mention the contributions of my teachers, colleagues, friends and students at Calcutta who have helped me a lot in the form of giving me inspiration and encouraging me to complete the work in a short period. In this context I want to pay my homage to the departed soul of late Pandit Srimohan Tarkavedantatirtha who first opened the doors of the wonderful world of Indian philosophy before me by teaching me the kernels of Vedānta, Nyāya and Buddhist schools of thought.

Among my wellwishers I first want to thank Prof. Sekhar Ghosh of University of Burdwan who always provides support to me like my guardian. This time he voluntarily took upon himself the task of giving my English some polish wherever necessary. In this context I want to mention the names of Prof. Sandhya Basu, of Rabindra Bharati University and Prof. Rita Gupta of Viswa Bharati University, who though not my direct teachers always treat me as their student and spread their hands of help and co-operation to me whenever needed. Prof. Sandhya Basu being an expert in the area of Western epistemology, kindly had gone through the concluding chapter of the book and it is out of her suggestions that some changes have been made for its betterment. Prof. Rita Gupta, an expert in the area of Buddhist philosophy went through the entire manuscript and suggested appropriate changes for its improvement. I have tried to incorporate their suggestions as far as possible. I express my respect and gratitude to both these teachers. I want to pay respect to another teacher of mine, Professor Prabal Kumar Sen who with his encyclopaedic knowledge on Indian philosophy would often quote *śloka*s from different texts some of which I tried to add in my books in the relevant contexts. Dr Prayas Sarker and Prof. Ratna Datta Sharma, of the Department of Philosophy, Jadavpur University had voluntarily taken the task of going through some chapters of this book and gave their valued opinions. I am thankful to them for their observations. Finally I must mention the contributions of my students, both at the P.G. and M.Phil levels at Jadavpur University with whom I shared some of my thoughts on Buddhism and waited for their observations. I wish them success in life.

Shri Susheel Mittal of D.K. Printworld has undertaken the entire responsibility of getting the book published. Mere words of thanks are not sufficient for him. I wish him a healthy and prosperous life.

Last but not the least I must mention the contributions of my family members, especially my husband, my daughter Mriduchhanda and her nephew Swarnendu who had shown patience at moments when I was engaged in my studies. They deserve love and best wishes from me. My parents are no more with me in their gross physical body, but they would have been the happiest persons to see the book published. I offer my *praṇāma*s to them and seek their blessings.

Madhumita Chattopadhyay

Contents

Abbreviations

AK	—	*Abhidharmakośa*
AKBh	—	*Abhidharmakośabhāṣya*
AS/EA	—	*Asiatische Studien/Etudes Asiatiques*
DhP	—	*Dharmottara Pradīpa*
HB	—	*Hetubindu*
HBT	—	*Hetubinduṭīkā*
JIP	—	*Journal of Indian Philosophy*
NB	—	*Nyāyabindu*
NBT	—	*Nyāyabinduṭīkā*
NBVT	—	*Nyāyabinduṭīkā of Vinītadeva*
NVT	—	*Nyāyavārttikatātparyaṭīkā*
PS	—	*Pramāṇasamuccaya*
PSV	—	*Pramāṇasamuccayavṛtti*
PV	—	*Pramāṇavārttikam*
PVV	—	*Pramāṇavārttikavṛtti* of Manorathanandi
PVBh	—	*Pramāṇavārttikabhāṣya* of Prajñākaragupta
PVSV	—	*Pramāṇavārttikasvavṛtti*
PVSVT	—	*Pramāṇavārttikasvavṛttiṭīkā* of Karṇakagomin

SV	—	*Ślokavārttika*
TBh	—	*Tarkabhāṣā*
TS	—	*Tattvasaṁgrahaḥ*
TSP	—	*Tattvasaṁgrahapañjikā*
VP	—	*Vākyapadīyam*
WZKS	—	*Wiener Zeitschrift für die Kunde Südasiens*

Introduction

It has been the task of the human race from the dawn of civilization to attain knowledge of entities in the universe, which they did not know. But once the direction of this investigation is changed from the outer world to itself, i.e. towards knowledge itself, several problems crop up. Though knowledge seems to be quite obvious, quite natural phenomenon, a deep thinking into this "obvious" matter reveals its really problematic character. In this respect philosophers of both the Western tradition and the Indian tradition share the same experience. Our concern, here, in this monograph is to present the discussion made by one particular school of Classical Indian philosophy, namely Buddhism, specially the Sautrāntika-Yogācāra school of Buddhism, regarding knowledge.

The English term "knowledge" has many equivalents in Indian languages: scholars mention more than seventy Sanskrit words. We feel almost lost. But the word which is most frequently used seems to be *jñāna* (*ñāna* in Pāli). At the outset we must state that the Sanskrit term *jñāna,* though philologically cognate with the English word "knowledge" through its similarity with the Greek *gnosis,* has a very different meaning in Indian philosophy. The sense in which the term *jñāna* is used is in one sense wider and in another sense narrower than the sense in which the term "knowledge" is used in Western philosophy. It is wider because *jñāna* is used to denote not only true but also false cognitions, doubt, belief, assumption, and also the usual perception, introspection; it denotes non-propositional states like sensing (*anubhava*). It is narrower in the sense that *jñāna* is used only in the episodic sense while "knowledge" is used in Western philosophy both in the dispositional as well as in episodic senses.

Since *jñāna* can be true (*yathārtha*) as well as false (*ayathārtha*) there may be a suggestion that if *jñāna* is qualified by *yathārtha*, it can be treated as equivalent to knowledge, as knowledge is always true. In reply it would be said that this suggestion is not acceptable, as knowledge is not merely true belief, but justified true belief, so, *yathārtha jñāna* or *samyag jñāna* or *pramāṇa* as the Buddhists hold them, will be equivalent to knowledge if it also possesses or contains the feature of justification. To put it distinctively, is there any notion of justification in addition to truth found in the notion of *samyag jñāna* or *pramāṇa* so that it can be regarded as equivalent to knowledge in the sense of justified true belief? In the Western tradition the "justification" aspect has been interpreted differently in the internalist and the externalist tradition. For the internalist to know that **p** one must be able to give one's justification for believing that **p**, while the externalist will require that one be in a situation that gives one justification for the belief that **p;** one need not be able to cite the reasons that provide such justification. In the background of this debate between internalism and externalism, we can say that the Buddhist philosophers were externalists in orientation, since they tried to account for the occurrence of cognition not in terms of any justification in the mind of the individual, but in terms of the success of the activity led by that knowledge. On a hot summer day when I am extremely thirsty, no assurance in my mind of the object in front of me that it is pure drinking water will quench my thirst. It is the actual capacity of the object to quench my thirst and give me satisfaction at that moment of crisis, that will convince me that I really know the object as water and no one can challenge me in this regard. Thus for the Buddhist, success of telic function of the object is the ultimate determinant for something's being judged as "known."

Now let us consider a situation. Suppose on a hot summer afternoon after a hard day's work, I happened to be passing through a shopping mall. Suddenly I saw through the window of the juice parlour a glass full of pineapple juice well decorated with ice and cherry, which at once increased my thirst. Wishing to quench my thirst I went to the shop, ordered for that juice, got it and I was satisfied. So here the telic function of the object is achieved. But can I claim that I *knew* it was a glass of pineapple juice? Certainly, not. For, the object by which I was guided to action and the object which served the telic function are not the same. The object by which I was guided to have the drink was actually an iconic model of the glass made of wax while the object which satisfied me by quenching my thirst was the glass filled with actual pineapple juice. Certainly the glass made of wax and the glass filled with fruit juice are not the same. No one will claim that success of the telic function of an object is the only determinant of *jñāna*. What else is then required?

The first thing all the Indian philosophers, including the Buddhists, highlight is that in order to be *pramāṇa*, knowledge must be **trustworthy**, must be true revealer or reporter of what there is in reality. In fact, the feature of *pramāṇa* to lead to successful activity is very much related to the feature of trustworthiness. Why? Just as in our ordinary life, we regard a man to be trustworthy and dependable, only when guided by his words and we can attain success in our practical life;

similarly is the case here. A piece of *pramāṇa* is trustworthy if it leads to success in practical activity, and we are successful in our practical activity only because the knowledge that reveals the object is trustworthy. So these two aspects "trustworthiness" and "success" in telic function are two sides of the same coin for the Buddhists.

But the Buddhists are not satisfied with only these two functions of *jñāna;* they require something more. Their point is that *pramāṇa* is required for serving some practical purpose. If that practical purpose is already served by one object which is revealed by a piece of knowledge, do we need to be involved in the same practical purpose served by the same object again through a second piece of knowledge? Let us make the point a bit clear. Suppose, someone is hungry. She needs some food to satisfy her hunger. Looking through her visual sense organs she is sure that what is lying in front of her is a piece of bread that can satisfy her hunger. She takes up the bread and eats and it serves her purpose. So, by the two characteristics stated above we can say that she has knowledge *pramāṇa* that the object in front of her is a piece of bread. Once she possesses this knowledge, does she need to know again by other means that it is a piece of bread? While the schools of Indian philosophy, like the Nyāya one, believe that if she has a "desire to infer," then although she possesses a certain knowledge regarding the object, she may be involved in another piece of knowledge regarding the same object. But the Buddhists are very firm on this issue. Since, for them, workability or serving practical purposes or success in mundane life is the ultimate deciding factor with regard to knowledge, they hold that *pramāṇa* is always regarding something new. Since that which is known has already led to successful activity there is no sense in repeating the same activity. Accordingly knowledge cannot be of anything already known. So, for the Buddhists, *pramāṇa* or *samyag jñāna* is a trustworthy awareness that illuminates an unknown object. An individual who determines an object by means of such *pramāṇa* and acts on the basis of that knowledge is not deceived about that object's telic function. Thus it can be said that the Buddhists in their analysis of knowledge emphasize on three aspects — novelty, certainty and pragmatic workability.

It may be argued by the non-Buddhists that this sort of interpretation is not really Buddhist in spirit for this certainly was not the intention of Buddhism. If we look into the history of Buddhism we will find that at its earliest stage when Lord Buddha established Buddhism as a religion, his prime concern was something soteriological, namely removal of human suffering and showing human beings the way to liberation. Anything other than human suffering did not draw his attention. Even metaphysical speculations concerning problems not related to human suffering and the attainment of enlightenment — such as whether the world is infinite or finite, whether the soul and the body are identical or different from each other, etc. — were not encouraged. Only the attainment of *bodhi* and finding out the way or path for that attainment were encouraged by Lord Buddha in his different dialogues and by his followers in the early stage of Buddhism. In view of that, it will be too much to attribute such a systematic account of *pramāṇa* theory to the Buddhists.

We may counter the attack of such a possible opponent in two ways. First, it can be said that indeed it is true that the main concern of early Buddhism was with knowledge in the transcendental level and not of the empirical one. But what they said regarding transcendental knowledge fits in very well with empirical knowledge also. For example, just as in the transcendental sphere, ultimate knowledge or *bodhi* can lead to success in life in the form of attainment of enlightenment by the removal of suffering, the same model applies in the empirical plane as well. There also, before the attainment of the desired object, say for example a bottle of cold drink at the moment of thirst, there is a dissatisfaction which gives rise to some kind of discomfort, some kind of uneasiness which may be described as a sort of suffering. This discomfort or uneasiness or suffering is removed only when the thirst is quenched by attaining the actual glass of cold drink and knowing it as something that is not poisonous or unhealthy, etc. Thus here also it is knowledge regarding the object that removes the discomfort, the suffering. Secondly, just as in the transcendental plane the objective of the ultimate knowledge is to remove human ignorance which is believed to be the root cause of all our suffering, in the empirical plane also scientific rational knowledge aims to remove ignorance. Scientific knowledge serves "curiosity or the love of truth" and such curiosity has been included by Hume in his list of passions as a passion. Though Hume has declared reason to be and "ought only to be" the slave of passions, still our study of social sciences tells us that in the case of scientific knowledge curiosity becomes the slave of reason. By satisfying curiosity human beings come to know more and more new objects and get rid of their ignorance. So removal of ignorance remains the same basic aim in the empirical level as well as in the transcendental level. Thus there is no inconsistency in the original Buddhist framework of knowledge focused mainly towards the transcendental level and the later Buddhist framework of knowledge focusing on the empirical level.

Just as in the Western world we find the skeptics challenging the possibility of knowledge, among the Buddhists also we find the great dialectician Nāgārjuna raising serious doubts about the possibility of acquiring knowledge by pointing out the self-contradictory character of all means of attaining knowledge. But unless knowledge of objects is admitted there is no sense in making philosophical comments on such objects. Accordingly, all subsequent Buddhist philosophers felt the need to provide a solid foundation to the study of empirical knowledge before formulating their own philosophical positions. Consequently, we have the development of Buddhist logic and epistemology concentrating exclusively on empirical knowledge under the auspices of Asaṁga (about CE 405) and Vasubandhu (about CE 410). It was Diṅnāga (about CE 450) who put such epistemology on a solid footing and gave it a distinct character. The task initiated by Diṅnāga was given a successful shape by his brilliant successor Dharmakīrti (about CE 635) in his different masterpieces *Pramāṇavārttika, Nyāyabindu, Pramāṇaviniścayaḥ,* etc.

Without entering into the historical survey of Buddhist epistemology, in this monograph attempt has been made to highlight the philosophical arguments offered mainly by Diṅnāga and Dharmakīrti on the different issues of knowledge. The target group of this monograph is the students of the Graduate Level who want to study Buddhist epistemology deeper than the introductory stage, but who do not have such maturity to go through the details of the original text. Accordingly, the contents of this volume have been designed in such a fashion that the student first comes to know what the Buddhists mean by knowledge, what are the varieties of knowledge according to them, how they explain the validity of knowledge and how do they account for the knowledge of such knowledge. The different chapters are planned to discuss these issues and other related issues as they occur one after another. In the context of knowledge another relevant question that arises is — what is it that we know through *pramāṇa,* is it a positive entity or can it be negative also? Let us put it in concrete terms. Suppose I look at my study table. I see several items scattered on it — books, writing-pad, pen, pencil, eraser, etc. But at the same time I am aware that my favourite flower-vase is not there. So the point is that just as we can regard the books to be the objects of our knowledge, we can regard the absence of the flower-vase also to be the object of our knowledge. But the moment we admit this, the question will arise, how do we apprehend this absence? It is in answer to this question that the Buddhists have to think over their epistemology in a different pattern. In their philosophical framework the concept of absence has a very significant role. Against the realist theory of universals the Buddhist logicians have come up with their theory of *apoha* which has been appropriately translated by Prof. A. Chakraborty as "negative nominalism." On this theory, it seems "flowerness" is replaced by "absence of non-flower-ness" or distinction (mutual absence) from all non-flowers, which sounds like two importantly distinct applications of negations. So unless they can account for the apprehension of negation or absence in their epistemology, they will not be able to account for the doctrine of *apoha* as a substitute for universals in their metaphysics. It is because of this importance that we have taken up the question of knowledge of absence in the last but one chapter. Introduction of the other chapters are self-explanatory and so they are not justified here. In the last chapter our attempt has been to assess the Buddhist epistemology in the light of the debates of contemporary Western epistemology.

If this monograph is of any help to the students to get interested in the ocean of Buddhist epistemology, I shall consider my toil well-spent.

1

Knowledge
What it is?

IN Indian philosophy, pursuit of knowledge or cognition is not considered as a mere theoretical enterprise, but as a pragmatic one. That is, knowledge is pursued not only for the sake of knowledge itself but for some other goal. In fact, all the schools of Indian philosophy consider knowledge as the only means for the attainment of the ultimate goal, viz. liberation. Of course, that knowledge is believed to be something different from ordinary mundane knowledge; it is knowledge of a different level, viz. transcendental knowledge, which in their terminology is *tattva jñāna* that enables the individual to have direct access to Truth or Reality (*tattva*).[1] Even admitting the necessity of such transcendental knowledge, the Indian philosophers could not overlook the importance of empirical, mundane knowledge in our day-to-day life. Accordingly in every school we find discussion of issues like what is knowledge, when is knowledge valid, how can we have knowledge of knowledge, etc. In the Buddhist system also we find that like other orthodox schools, they admit transcendental knowledge to realize the Ultimate Truth; but at the same time they put emphasis on the need of valid cognition in the practical life of an individual. Proper

---

1. . . . *tattvajñānāt niḥśreyasādhigamaḥ* — *NS*, I:1.1.

knowledge or valid cognition helps the individual to realize his end of life (*puruṣārtha*).[2]

The word *puruṣārthaḥ* may be analysed as *puruṣasya arthaḥ* the object of the aim of human life, that which the individual aims at.[3] What does an individual aim at? An end is defined in Indian philosophical system as that for the attainment of which the individual makes an effort.[4] All our efforts are mainly directed towards the attainment of happiness and getting rid of suffering. Hence, the goal of human life is the attainment of the desirable and the rejection of the undesirable.[5] An individual performs an action to get something only when that object is considered to be either acceptable or rejectable. It is via the media of this acceptance and rejection that he attains his end, viz. attainment of pleasure and removal of suffering. For instance, if I am thirsty I require water to quench my thirst. So getting water is my objective. Again if there is a poisonous snake in my room, my first requirement will be to get rid of that snake as soon as possible. So avoiding the snake by any means is my objective. In fact, Indian philosophers believe that all our voluntary actions (which if positive is termed by them as *pravṛtti* and if negative is regarded as *nivṛtti*) are guided by the two options, attainment of the desired object (*hitasya prāpti*) and rejection of the unwanted one (*heyasya parihāra*). So according to the Buddhists the object towards which all human activities are directed is either *heya* (rejectable)

---

2. *yā kācit puruṣārthasiddhiḥ sā samyagjñānanivandhanaiva* ।
— *NBT.* 34.1.

3. *puruṣasya arthaḥ puruṣārthaḥ* । *arthyate ityarthaḥ kāmyata iti yāvat* ।
— *Nyāyabinduṭīkā,* 30.1.

4. *yamarthamadhi-kṛtya pravarttate tat prayojanam* ।
— *Nyāyasūtra,* I.1.24.

5. *hitāhitaprāptiparihāra vuddiśyeti tāveva prayojana yukte* ।
— *Dharmottarapradīpaḥ.*

or *upādeya* (acceptable). It may be noted here that though in other schools of Indian philosophy like for instance in the Nyāya system we find admission of a third variety in addition to these two, namely the *upekṣaṇīya* (ignorable), the Buddhists do not accept such a view. On the contrary they classify the *heya* and *upekṣaṇīya* variety under one head with the argument that both share one feature in common, namely both of them are unacceptable. Accordingly, the Buddhists conclude that there are only two types of objects — those which are acceptable (*upādeya*) and those which are unacceptable and in that sense rejectable (*heya*).[6]

But how can I identify an object as a desirable one or as unwanted? For this valid cognition is required. It is only when the individual has knowledge regarding the proper nature of the object and does not confuse one object for another, he can consider the object to be either desirable or undesirable and be engaged in action. At the moment of my thirst, if I can cognize the object to be water then only I will indulge in that action which will lead me to get that water. Similar is the case with the example of snake. If I know that the object in my room is a snake and not a toy, I will attempt to remove it. Thus, it is established that knowledge regarding the proper nature of the object is the preliminary requirement of all voluntary actions.

This view is shared by all Indian philosophers alike. For example, if we look at Vātsyāyana's commentary on the very first aphorism of Gautama, the founder of the Nyāya School, we will find the same idea — it is through valid cognition that

---

6. *na ca heyopādeyābhyām anyo rāśir asti* । *upekṣaṇīyo hy anupādeyatvāt heya eva* । *tasya siddhiḥ hānam upādānaṁ ca* ।

— *Nyāyabinduṭīkā*, 30.2-3.

the knower coming to know the object desires to get the object or reject it.[7] From this it is clear that for the Indian philosophers, especially for the Buddhists, the value of knowledge is not for its own sake but something pragmatic related to the practical life of the individual.

I

At the outset it may be noticed that we are using the expression "valid cognition" or "valid knowledge" rather than simply "knowledge." This is because unlike the Western epistemologists, Indian philosophers do not regard truth to be a necessary condition of knowledge. Only, one school of Indian philosophy, namely the Mīmāṁsaka, regards all cognition to be valid. All other schools, on the contrary, believe that knowledge can be true as well as false. For example, when I perceive a straight pencil put in water and have the cognition that "this pencil is bent" my cognition is invalid. Since only valid cognition can lead to success in our activities, valid cognition is the basic concern for any philosophical inquiry. As such all philosophical schools have tried to formulate the definition of valid cognition in their own light.

Like other systems, in Buddhism also much emphasis is given for epistemological and logical discussions, i.e. discussion on *pramāṇa,* to provide a solid foundation for the philosophical doctrines. Lord Buddha himself was not much concerned with the question of what is knowledge, what makes a piece of knowledge valid, etc. His main thrust was on transcendental knowledge, the knowledge that would enable the individual to get rid of this world of suffering. But later on, the Buddhist philosophers felt the need of discussing epistemological issues in their philosophical framework. In

7. *pramāṇena khalu ayaṁ jñātā artham upalabhya tamartham abhīpsati jihāsati vā* । — *Vātsyāyanabhāṣya,* on I.1.1.

this respect Diṅnāga and Dharmakīrti exerted probably the greatest influence on the succeeding Buddhist and non-Buddhist philosophers in India. So while delineating the Buddhist notion of epistemology we will mainly rely on the views of these two thinkers as found in their available texts.

We may at the outset spell out some of the fundamental theses of Buddhist epistemology. These are —

1. the doctrine that each type of *pramāṇa* is confined to its specific domain of object (*pramāṇavyavasthā*),
2. the doctrine of two truths where a distinction is drawn between "ultimate" or "fundamental" truth (*paramārtha satya*) and empirical or conventional truth (*saṁvyavahārika satya*),
3. the doctrine of momentariness (*kṣaṇabhaṅgavāda*), and
4. the doctrine that all cognitions are self-revealing (*svasamvedya*).

Among these four, the first two are closely related to the Buddhist definition of *pramāṇa* as a cognition that leads to successful activity while the last two are intimately connected with the Buddhist theory of the identity between *pramāṇa* and *pramāṇaphala*. Let us now start with the Buddhist definition of valid cognition.

It may be noted in the beginning that according to the Buddhist thinkers, the importance of valid cognition lies in the fact that valid cognition holds the key to the success of activities. In the text *Pramāṇaviniścayaḥ* Dharmakīrti holds that "Perception and inference are valid cognitions because a person who acts having determined the object by means of these two cognitions is not deceived with regard to a purposeful action performed by the object."[8] In fact, the success of all human activities is preceded by valid cognition.[9] The word "precedes" is to be understood not merely in the sense of temporal succession but in the sense of causal connection. That is, valid cognition is the cause of successful activity.

If the word "precedes" (*pūrvikā*) is to be understood in the sense of causal precedence, the question obviously arises why did not Dharmakīrti use the word "cause" in place of "precedence"? The answer has been given by Dharmottara in his commentary. "Cause" is that which is antecedent to an effect, and so if the word "cause" had been used it would mean that valid cognition is the direct or immediate cause of the attainment of one's goal, which was not the Buddhists' intention. Hence, is the word "precedes" which signifies not only the direct or immediate cause but also the mediate causes, or to be specific, any valid cognition that precedes such attainment.[10] Let us explain the intention of the commentator in detail. There are two types of valid cognition — those revealing the causal efficiency character of objects (*arthakriyānirbhāsa*) and those inducing a man towards the object capable of causal efficiency (*arthakriyāsamarthe pravarttaka*). Example of the first variety is the direct awareness of the burning capacity of fire, while apprehending fire. In this case, the cause of the goal of burning is that knowledge which reveals the causally efficient character of knowledge. In the second type of knowledge the man does not have direct

8. Referred to by G. Dreyfus, *Dharmakīrti's Definition of Pramāṇa and its Interpreters*, p. 20.

9. *samyagjñānapūrvikā sarvapuruṣārthasiddhiḥ* I — *NB*, I.1.

10. *samyagjñānaṁ pūrvaṁ kāraṇaṁ yasyāḥ sā tathoktā* I *kāryāt pūrvaṁ bhavat kāraṇaṁ pūrvam uktaṁ* I *kāraṇaśabdopādāne tu puruṣārthasiddheḥ sākṣātkāraṇaṁ gamyeta* I *pūrvaśabde tu pūrvamātram* I

— *Nyāyabinduṭīkā*, 27.1-2.

acquaintance regarding the causal efficiency of the object. The person sees fire from a distance. Here he sees the visible appearance of fire and then if he has the need of fire, he will have an inclination (*pravṛtti*) to get that fire; and from that inclination he will be able to attain that fire and by that his goal will be achieved. In this case, the valid cognition is not the immediate cause of the attainment of his goal; rather it is a preceding event, a remote cause towards that attainment. So to emphasize this sort of valid cognition the word "precedes" has been used instead of "cause." In fact, the Buddhists are much more interested with the second variety of cognition, that is the cognition which reveals an object as capable of being causally efficient. The reason is that, in the first variety, there is no scope of inclination. Once there is the direct apprehension of the burning capacity of fire, the objective is satisfied. Accordingly, the individual has no more interest in the apprehension and so there is nothing left to examine. But there are lots of enquiries regarding that variety of cognition which shows the object as capable of performing causal function. Such knowledge is merely the antecedent of *puruṣārthasiddhi* and not the immediate antecedent event. Accordingly, Dharmakīrti is justified in using the word *pūrvikā* in his introductory statement.[11]

---

11. *dvividhaṁ ca samyagjñānam — arthakriyānirbhāsam, arthakriyāsamarthe ca pravarttakam* । *tayor madhye yat pravarttakaṁ tad iha parīkṣyate* । *tacca pūrvamātram* । *na tu sākṣātkāraṇam* । *samyagjñāne hi sati pūrvadṛṣṭasmaraṇam* । *smaraṇādabhilāṣaḥ* । *abhilāṣat pravṛttiḥ* । *pravṛtteś ca prāptiḥ* । *tato na sākṣād hetuḥ* । *arthakriyānirbhāsaṁ tu yadyapi sākṣāt prāptis tathāpi tanna parīkṣaṇīyam* । *yatra hi prekṣāvanto 'rthinaḥ sāśaṁkāḥ tat parīkṣyate* । *arthakriyānirbhāse ca jñāhte sati siddhaḥ puruṣārthaḥ* । *tena tatra na sāśaṁkā arthinaḥ* । *atas tanna parīkṣaṇīyam* । *tasmāt parīkṣārham asākṣāt kāraṇaṁ samyagjñānam ādarśayituṁ kāraṇaśabdaṁ parityajya pūrvagrahaṇaṁ kṛtam* ।

— *Nyāyabinduṭīkā*, 28.1–29.4.

II

Valid cognition is generally referred to as *pramā*; the prefix *pra* means superb or excellent and the root *mā* means cognition. Therefore, excellent knowledge alone is *pramā*. The excellent character of cognition consists in its expressing the proper nature of the object. When we mistake a snake for a rope, or mirage for the water, or silver for the shell, the cognition expresses a nature, which is other than the nature of the concerned object. Hence, none of these cognitions are regarded as valid or *pramā*. The Buddhist logician Dharmakīrti describes *pramā* as *samyag jñāna*. The question obviously arises as to, how to judge that the cognition is expressing the proper nature of the object? Each cognition expresses some object or other. So how can we determine that the object which is expressed by the cognition is not the proper object, but a mistaken one? In reply the Buddhists hold that the validity of cognition is determined by the success (*sāphalya*) of the voluntary action (*pravṛtti*). If the voluntary action, which results from the cognition to attain the object, actually leads to the attainment of the desired object, the cognition will be regarded as a valid one. That property of cognition which leads to the success in the attainment of the object is technically regarded as *avisaṁvādaka*. Accordingly, Dharmakīrti presents his first definition of valid cognition in terms of this feature of *avisaṁvādakatva*.

Def. 1: Valid Cognition or Pramāṇa is Non-contradictory or Non-discrepant in Character[12]

This definition indicates that *pramāṇa* or valid cognition has two features — (1) it is knowledge, and (2) it is non-contradictory or non-discrepant in character. Though the first

12. *pramāṇam avisaṁvādijñānam*, — *Pramāṇavārttika*, verse 3. cf. *avisaṁvādakaṁ jñānam samyagjñānam*, — *Nyāyabinduṭīkā*, 17.1.

feature seems to be a mere tautology like "A is A," it actually is not so. It is offered to indicate that according to the Buddhists anything other than knowledge, such as sense organs or the sense object contact cannot be regarded as means of valid cognition or *pramāṇa*. In fact, Dharmakīrti believed that the means of valid cognition is the most efficient cause (*sādhakatamam*) of knowledge. A moment of knowledge arises out of several causes belonging to the immediately preceding moment, e.g. sense organs, object, knowledge, etc. But none of them is regarded as more efficient than the other for all of them equally contribute to the production of knowledge. The most efficient among them, according to Dharmakīrti, is that which ultimately differentiates one knowledge from another.[13] For instance, knowledge of a cow is said to be distinguished from knowledge of the horse on the basis of the object concerned. But for Dharmakīrti the object cannot be the most efficient cause of knowledge, since when two persons A and B are looking at the object at the same time, the object is common to both of their knowledge and so we cannot distinguish A's knowledge of the object from that of B. What ultimately distinguishes one's knowledge from that of the other, is the objective image (*viṣayākāra*) projected on the knowledge by the external object.[14] So the means of valid cognition is nothing but the resultant cognition itself. To be specific, *pramāṇa* is that aspect of the cognition which consists in its possessing an objective image or resemblance with the object.[15]

---

13. *sarveṣāṁ upayoge 'pi kārakāṇāṁ kriyāṁ prati* ।
yadantyaṁ bhedakaṁ tasyās tat sādhakatamaṁ matam ॥
— *Pramāṇavārttikam* II.311.

14. *viṣayākārabhedāc ca dhiyo 'dhigamabhedataḥ* । — Ibid., I.6.

15. For a detailed discussion vide S. Katsura, Dharmakīrti's Theory of Truth, pp. 220-21.

Dharmakīrti tries to specify the nature of that cognition which is regarded as *pramāṇa* by saying that *pramāṇa* is non-contradictory or non-discrepant cognition. Prof. Eli Franco expresses this feature as "a cognition which does not belie [its promise]."[16] This non-contradictory or non-discrepant feature consists in the fulfilment of human end or purpose.[17] That is, attaining or obtaining the object which has been the subject of our volition, defines the non-discrepant character of cognition.[18] The term *avisaṁvādi* means "that which is free from *visaṁvāda*" (*visaṁvādanamuktam*). *Visaṁvāda* in the dictionary sense means false assertion or that which is disappointing. Accordingly, *avisaṁvādi* means non-contradictory or non-discrepant or simply true.[19] That is, that cognition which is consistent with our volition is regarded as *pramāṇa*. In our ordinary life, the individual who informs us about an object and following whose instructions we are able to attain the object, is regarded as *avisaṁvādaka* or simply *saṁvādaka*, i.e. a dependable guide. In a similar manner, being guided by *pramāṇa* we are able to attain our intended object.[20] As such *pramāṇa* is described as *avisaṁvādaka*.[21] Valid cognition is non-discrepant in the sense that it does not mislead the knower. The object

16. Eli Franco, "The Disjunction in *Pramāṇavārttika Pramāṇasiddhi* Chapter verse 5c."

17. *arthakriyāsthitiḥ avisaṁvādanam* । — *Pramāṇavārttikam*, I.3.

18. *avisaṁvādakaṁ pravṛttiviṣayavastuprāpakaṁ samyagjñānam iti* ।
— *DhP*, 17.13.

19. *yadavisaṁvādakaṁ tadabhrāntam* ।
— Vinītadeva's commentary 4.25.

20. *yathopadarśitārthasya kriyāyāḥ sthitiḥ pramāṇayogyatā = avisaṁvādanam*.
— *Pramāṇavārttikavṛtti*, 6.15-16.

21. *yathā loke satyavādiśabdapravṛttinimittasyopadarśitārthaprāpaṇasya puruṣe sambhavāt saṁvādakaśabdaḥ pravarttate, tathā jñāne 'pi tatsambhavād iti* । . . . *saṁvāda*[*ka*]*śabdaḥ pra*[*bdapra*]*vṛttinimittaṁ tu sarvatra samānam iti* । — *Dharmottarapradīpaḥ*, 17.17-23.

which is indicated by *pramāṇa* as belonging to a particular place in a particular time can be obtained by the agent in that particular place, thus leading to successful activity.[22] The property *avisaṁvādaka* is added to eliminate illusory knowledge like that of rope-snake or of silver-shell, etc. and doubts from the scope of *pramāṇa* for in none of the case the object indicated in the cognition can be obtained in that particular place at that particular time. This *avisaṁvādaka* feature, thus, points to the indubitable or certain character of valid cognition.

Obviously a question arises in this context. No cognition is such that it directly leads to the attainment of the object. So, how can knowledge be regarded as the *prāpaka* or indicator of the object? When a pot-maker produces a pot and hands it over to an individual, he is regarded as the *prāpaka*, since he makes the object available by producing the object. But knowledge does not produce any external object, so it cannot be regarded as a *prāpaka* like that of the pot-maker. Knowledge is regarded as *prāpaka* in the sense that it can induce us to activities leading to the attainment of the object.[23] In reply it has been said that when knowledge or cognition arises regarding a particular object, we have an inclination or volition (*pravṛtti*) for that object. Knowledge regarding an object leads our volition towards that object. By directing, leading our volition towards that object, we are able to attain it. Thus knowledge helps us to attain an object by directing our volition towards it and it is in this sense that knowledge becomes the *prāpaka*.[24] In short, to be *pramāṇa* is to be able to lead us to the

22. *tato 'rthakriyāsamarthavastupradarśakaṁ samyagjñānam* ।
— *NBT*, 23.3-4.

23. *na jñānaṁ janayad arthaṁ prāpyati, api tvarthe puruṣaṁ pravarttayat prāpayatyartham* । *pravarttakatvam api pravṛttiviṣayapradarśakatvam eva* ।
— *NBT*, 17.3–18.2.

24. *pradarśite cārthe pravartakatvam eva prāpakatvam, nānyat* ।
— *Nyāyabinduṭīkā*, 17.3.

satisfaction of our expectations.

But Dharmakīrti is not satisfied with this first definition alone. In *Pramāṇavārttika* he presents an alternative definition of *samyag jñāna* which may be regarded as his second definition.

Def. II: Pramāṇa or Valid Cognition is What Reveals an Object Previously Unknown.[25]

Durveka Miśra in his sub-commentary *Pradīpaḥ* makes the meaning of the expression "previously unknown" (*anadhigataviṣayam*) clear by saying that the object in the case of *pramāṇa* is such that it had not been earlier revealed through any other cognition.[26] It may be noted here that Diṅnāga in his *Pramāṇasamuccaya* has regarded this feature of apprehending the previously unapprehended, to be the general characteristic of *pramāṇa.*[27]

The Buddhist philosophers have highlighted this aspect of novelty in their analysis of valid cognition. Diṅnāga in his *Pramāṇasamuccayavṛtti* argues that "recollection, desire, aversion, etc. are not independent valid cognitions with respect to a previously cognized thing." That is, these cognitions are not valid since they apply to previously apprehended objects. Implicit in Diṅnāga's argument lies the assumption that a cognition must apprehend a new object in order to qualify as valid cognition. In Dharmakīrti also we hear the echo of the same idea that novelty is required for a cognition to be valid.

---

25. *ajñātārthaprakāśo vā . . .* — *Pramāṇavārttikam,* I.8,
cf. *anādhigataviṣayaṁ pramāṇam* । — *Nyāyabinduṭīkā* 19.2-3.
cf. *tatrāpūrvārthavijñānaṁ niścitaṁ bādhavarjitam, aduṣṭakāraṇārabdhaṁ pramāṇaṁ lokasammatam* । — *Pramānavārttikabhāṣya,* 21, 12.

26. *jñānāntareṇāparicchinno viṣayo 'rtho yasya tat pramāṇam bhavati* । — *Dharmottarapradīpaḥ,* 19.26.

27. *ajñātārthajñāpakaṁ pramāṇam iti pramāṇasāmānyalakṣaṇam* । — *PS*-Ṭīkā 11.15-16.

In *Pramāṇavārttika* chapter II he holds "since it apprehends what is already held conventional cognition is not accepted as a valid cognition." This statement implies that a cognition has to apprehend an object not yet apprehended if it is to be regarded as valid. The novelty aspect of valid cognition has also been emphasized by Dharmakīrti in the text *Hetubindu* where he speaks of valid cognition thus: "With respect to this, valid cognition is only that which first sees an uncommon object." A valid cognition sees an uncommon, i.e. individual, object which is such that has not yet been realized by the apprehender. It has further been stated in the same text —

> Because a recollective cognition apprehends an already completely apprehended object, it is not a valid cognition. [The reason for this is that], having seen the uncommon real thing one states "this is an uncommon thing," but such a judgment does not realize any previously unrealized object. Implicit in this passage is the idea that a cognition must realize a new object in order to be valid. A recollective cognition or a judgmental cognition is not valid because it does not bring any new information in the cognitive process. Therefore, it follows that in the framework of the epistemological systems of both Diṅnāga and Dharmakīrti, the requirement of novelty was highlighted. Later commentators also have described valid cognition in this direction. Thus, we find Devendrabuddhi and Prajñākaragupta thinking that it is on the basis of the condition of novelty that valid and non-valid cognitions can be differentiated.[28]

The above-mentioned two definitions of *pramāṇa* emphasize two aspects of valid cognition. The first definition is offered from the cognitive point of view while the second one is from the standpoint of the object. This second definition points out

28. For further discussion see G. Dreyfus, *Dharmakīrti's Definition of Pramāṇa and its Interpreters.*

two important aspects of the nature of knowledge:

(a) that *pramāṇa* is the revealer or knower of an object (*arthajñāpakam*), and

(b) that it always reveals something new (*ajñātārtha*), something that has not been expressed by any other previous cognition.

This idea is probably derived from a sort of common sense belief that knowledge does not have any meaning unless it expresses something new, gives us some new information. Through knowledge the knower comes to know an object and being guided by such information becomes desirous to get the object and performs action to get it. So for the attainment of the object the first cognition of the object is essential. Once the object is attained the agent does not feel any necessity to apprehend the same object again through any other cognition.[29]

As mentioned earlier the obvious corollary of this second definition is that knowledge of an already apprehended object is not valid.[30] Accordingly memory and recognition are not regarded as *pramāṇa* in the Buddhist epistemological system. In the case of memory the object is that which had been apprehended earlier. The object which had not been earlier apprehended by the agent cannot be remembered by him later on. Only that which had been known by him can be remembered later in appropriate circumstances. This means that memory is always knowledge of the known, it does not present the object as something new and hence cannot be regarded as *pramāṇa*. According to the Buddhists, existence

---

29. *yenaiva hi jñānena prathamam adhigato 'rthaḥ tenaiva pravartitaḥ puruṣaḥ, prāpitaś cārthaḥ* । *tatraiva cārthe kim anyena jñānena adhikaṁ kāryaṁ?* — *Nyāyabinduṭīkā*, 19.3-4.

30. *ato 'dhigataviṣayam apramāṇam* — Ibid., 19.4.

of an object consists in its causal efficiency. To know an object is to have knowledge of its causal efficiency. So when an object has already been apprehended the knower has the apprehension of its causal efficiency. Hence he does not feel any necessity to know the object again as something new.[31] Due to the same reason recognition or *pratyabhijñā* is not regarded as *pramāṇa*. Recognition arises in such cases as "This is the man whom I met earlier," where the object cognized has been identified with an object experienced earlier. Though in respect of the present object, there is no difference between knowledge and recognition as both are apprehending an object present, however, regarding the resultant cognition there is a difference between the two. Recognition, unlike perception, is concerned not merely with the present something but also takes into account what had earlier been experienced. That is, there is an element of memory involved in it. As such, recognition is not *pramāṇa,* while perception is so.[32]

If *pramāṇa* is defined as apprehension of something that had not been experienced, not only memory and recognition but also some cases of valid cognition will have to be eliminated from the scope of *pramāṇa*. For instance, it will not apply to the case of continuous perception where the same object is perceived for a longer period. In such cases though there are different perceptions occurring at consecutive moments, there is no difference in the object perceived. It remains one and the same. The perception of the second moment being

31. *smaraṇaṁ ca pūrvagṛhītārtha vikalparūpatvān nādhikagrāhi । gṛhīte ca prāktanam eva pramāṇam । idānīṁ tu smaraṇam apravartakam ।*
— *Pramāṇavārttikavṛtti,* 7.12-14.

32. *pratyabhijñātmakaṁ yadviśeṣadṛṣṭajñānaṁ tatpramāṇaṁ na bhavatītyarthaḥ । yadyapi jñānapratyabhijñānayor vastutaḥ bhedo nāsti tathāpi pramāṇaphalayor bhedakalpanajñānaṁ pratyabhijñeyārtham vijātīyam । gṛhītagrahaṇaṁ pratyabhijñānam ।*
— *Pramāṇavārttikavṛtti,* 10.

apprehension of the object perceived in the first moment, this perception cannot be regarded as valid according to the second definition of *pramāṇa.* But continuous perception is regarded as valid even by the Buddhists. Thus by excluding memory and recognition from the scope of *pramāṇa,* the Buddhists are at the same time excluding a valid case and thereby making the definition of *pramāṇa* overly restrictive. In reply the Buddhists will say that since the object is momentary the object of perception of each moment will be different. The cognition of an object, for example rose, which occurred in the first moment was destroyed along with the object in the second moment. In the second moment a completely different, causally effective rose occurred and that had been cognized in the second moment, and so on. In this way, the cognition and its object being different in each moment, we cannot regard the cognition of the later moments to be apprehension of what had been earlier apprehended. In other words, according to the doctrine of momentariness what appears to be a continuous perception is in fact a series of moments of perceptions which take in a new object with each ensuing moment. Hence, there is no difficulty to retain the validity of continuous perception by the second definition of *pramāṇa.*

It may be argued that by applying a similar kind of argument it is possible to prove the validity of memory. In the case of memory the object experienced along with the original experience no longer exists in the second moment. Later on when memory occurs that is a completely different cognition. So the object of that later cognition can be said to be totally different from that of the earlier moment. In such a case memory can also be regarded as a case of *agr̥hītagrāhī* like continuous perception and hence valid. But such an argument is not acceptable. Analysis of the nature of memory reveals that memory is always about a past object. We remember what we experienced earlier. So the object of memory and the object of past experience are not different rather one and the same. As such we cannot regard memory to be apprehension of the non-apprehended.[33] Moreover in the case of continuous perception we can have different and new cognitions of acceptance and rejection at each subsequent moments, but in the case of memory this cognition of acceptance and rejection regarding the object remains the same as it was in the case of the first apprehension of the object. As such memory cannot be regarded as a *pramāṇa.*

Thus we find that the Buddhists are accepting two different criteria of valid cognition — one is pragmatic presented in terms of non-contradiction with experience or existence of the fulfilment of human purpose, and the other purely epistemological, presented in terms of grasping something new. So combining these two features we can say that *pramāṇa* is non-contradictory knowledge which reveals an object as new, as not apprehended earlier. In other words, it is (a) knowledge, (b) non-contradictory, and (c) refers to a previously unknown object. In the text *Pramāṇavārttika,* Dharmakīrti seems to refer to the last two features as alternatives connected with the expression *vā.*[34]

The use of this disjunctive particle *vā* employed by Dharmakīrti in the *Pramāṇasiddhi* chapter of his *Pramāṇavārttika* has puzzled his interpreters and so far no satisfactory explanation of it has been arrived at in any of his commentaries and sub-commentaries or in the modern studies. The word *vā*

---

33. *smaraṇaṁ ca pūrvagr̥hītārtha-vikalparīpatvān nādhikagrāhi* ।
— *Pramāṇavārttikavr̥tti,* 7.12-13.

34. *pramāṇam avisaṁvādijñānam avisaṁvādanaśabdaniruktiḥ arthakriyāsthitiḥ* । *ajñātārthaprakāśo vā* . . . ॥ — *Pramāṇavārttika,* II.3.

translated in English as "or" may be interpreted in an inclusive sense or in an exclusive sense after the manuals of modern logic. The second alternative, namely, to take *vā* as an exclusive "or" can be immediately rejected for it is easy to see that the two definitions of *pramāṇa* were not meant to exclude each other. There is nothing to prevent a cognition from being both non-belying and illuminating an unapprehended object. Each of the two definitions independently is necessary but not sufficient for the validity of cognitions. Hence, it has been suggested by many scholars that the word *vā* in the definition must be understood in the sense of conjunction.

Let us take a brief note of the controversy that is found in the writings of the commentators of Dharmakīrti on the issue as to whether he has offered two separate definitions of *pramāṇa* or one single definition. Devendrabuddhi takes the two definitions Def. I and Def. II as independent of each other and holds that the verse five of the *Pramāṇasiddhi* chapter of the *Pramāṇavārttika* should be understood as a second definition of *pramāṇa*.[35] Prajñākaragupta as well agrees with Devendrabuddhi in admitting the second definition to be independent of the first one. It may be asked that if a cognition illuminating a non-apprehended object is regarded as *pramāṇa* without further qualification to guarantee its validity, then the illusion of a new object would have to be admitted as a *pramāṇa*. Devendrabuddhi explains that such a case is excluded from the scope of the definition by the use of the word *artha* which means a real object. The object of illusion such as a double moon is not real. This explanation is ingenious. Prajñākaragupta also supports Devendrabuddhi in this regard. He justifies the use of two separate definitions of *pramāṇa* by pointing out that

35. *ajñātārthaprakāśo vā, anyad dvitīyam lakṣaṇam* I
— quoted by Eli Franco [1991].

Def. II is given from the absolute (*pāramārthika*) point of view while Def. I is from the conventional (*sāmvyavahārika*) one.[36] By the word *artha* absolute reality is expressed. Thus illumination of an unapprehended object means illuminating absolute reality. And absolute reality consists in the cognition's having a non-dual nature. Hence, illumination of an unapprehended object is the definition of *pramāṇa* relating to absolute reality whereas the previous one, i.e. the cognition which is non-discrepant is a definition relating to the conventional one. Thus, we find that for Devendrabuddhi as also for Prajñākaragupta, these are two alternative definitions of *pramāṇa*, but while the former thinks that these two definitions are alternative ways of looking at the *same* thing, the latter thinks that they are given to emphasize two different aspects of reality. So both Devendrabuddhi and Prajñākaragupta take the word *vā* in the sense of alternation and have offered their own interpretations to show that they are separate definitions.

An altogether different approach in this regard can be found in Dharmottara. Dharmottara in his commentary on *Nyāyabindu* while speaking on *samyag jñāna* observes —

> A valid cognition is a cognition which does not belie. For among the people, the person who makes one obtain a previously indicated object is called "one who does not belie." In the same manner, a cognition too is said to be non-belying inasmuch as it enables one obtain the object indicated by the cognition itself. And to enable one obtain, means to induce one to action towards the indicated object, nothing else. For the cognition does not make one obtain the

---

36. *atha vārthaśabdena paramārtha ucyate । ajñātārthaprakāśa iti paramārthaprakāśa ityarthaḥ । paramārthaścādvaitarūpatā . . . tatra pāramārthikapramāṇalakṣaṇam etat । pūrvaṁ tu sāṁvyavahārikasya ।* — *Pramāṇavārttikabhāṣyā*, 30.19-22.

> object in the sense of producing it, but rather enables one to obtain the object by inducing one to act towards the object. To induce to action in its turn means only to indicate the object of action. For the cognition cannot induce a person to act by force. And precisely for this reason only the apprehension of the object is the result of knowledge (*pramāṇaphala*). For when the object is apprehended, the person is induced to act and the object is made to be obtained. And when this is the case, the activity of knowledge is completed with the apprehension of the object, and precisely for this, knowledge has an unapprehended object as its subject (*viṣaya*). Since, by whatever cognition the object is apprehended for the first time, by that very cognition the person is induced to act and the object is made to be attained. And in that respect, what else can be done by another cognition? Hence, inasmuch as the object is already apprehended, the second cognition cannot be a *pramāṇa*.[37]

This passage shows that Dharmottara is making a sort of equation among the concepts: valid cognition, non-belying cognition, indicator of the object of volition, inducer of action towards the indicated object, enabling to attain the indicated object: *samyag jñāna* = *avisaṁvādi jñāna* = *pravṛttiviṣayapradarśaka* = *pradarśitārthapravarttaka* = *pradarśitārthaprāpaka*.

This equation or more precisely the implication of each term by its succeeding one enables Dharmottara to deduce the second definition from the first. A cognition, which does not belie is a cognition which can make the cognizer obtain the apprehended object by indicating the object as an object of voluntary action to him. This is the reason why the result of *pramāṇa* is nothing but the apprehension of the object and not its actual attainment. Consequently, the subsequent cognition

37. NBT 17.1–19.4, translated by E. France in "The Disjunction in Pramāṇavārttika Pramāṇasiddhi, chapter, verse 5c."

of the same object cannot be a *pramāṇa* as the capacity to attain the object has already been produced by the former cognition and cannot be reproduced by the later cognition again.

This indicates that for the Buddhists, these two features, the pragmatic and the epistemological ones, are not completely distinct; rather they are linked with each other. If any cognition is non-contradictory in character it can reveal an unknown object. Because of this non-discrepant nature knowledge can lead the knower or the agent towards the object and enable him to get it. On the other hand, unless the object is something new the agent does not feel any urge to make any attempt to get it. That is, the unknown aspect of the object leads the agent to perform voluntary action which, if successful, makes the knowledge of that object *pramāṇa.* In the case of erroneous cognition like that of silver and shell, the agent feels an urge to get silver but as his action is not successful he cannot be said to know the silver.

III

In Indian philosophy generally a distinction is made between the means of valid cognition (*pramāṇa*) and the resultant cognition (*pramā*). For example in the Nyāya system *pramāṇa* is regarded as the means of valid cognition while *pramā* is the valid cognition itself. Although Vātsyāyana in his *Bhāṣya* has sometimes used the term *pramāṇa* in the sense of resultant cognition, he also admits a distinction between *pramāṇa* and *pramā.* It is a unique feature of the Buddhist logicians that they have identified the means of cognition with the resultant cognition itself, as is evident from their definition of *pramāṇa* as *avisaṁvādijñānam.*

Because of their adherence to the doctrine of momentariness the Buddhists believe that a moment of knowledge is the result of a sum total of certain causes like the sense organ, the object, knowledge, etc. None of them is considered to be more efficient than the other and all contribute equally to the production of the effect, viz. the resultant knowledge. We cannot distinguish one piece of cognition from the other on the basis of the object, for it is quite possible that when two persons are looking at one and the same object, they are having two different cognitions though the object is the same for both. What ultimately differentiates two pieces of knowledge is the objective image projected into knowledge by the external object. So *pramāṇa* or the means of valid cognition is nothing but the knowledge itself.

The Buddhists point out that only cognitions can be regarded as cases of *pramāṇa*. By so saying they exclude inert objects like the sense organ, etc. from the scope of being *pramāṇa*. Other schools of Indian philosophy like the Mīmāṁsakas or the Naiyāyikas have admitted sense organs or smoke as cases of *pramāṇa* which are not instances of cognitions. But the Buddhists do not admit such a view. Their view is that only cognition can be considered as cases of *pramāṇa*. According to them unless we restrict the notion of *pramāṇa* to cognition alone we would violate the rule that an instrument (*kāraṇa*) and its consequence (*phala*) must share the same locus. In the standard example of cutting the wood with an axe, the instrument is the axe and the bifurcating of the tree is said to be the result/consequence of this instrument. The axe and the bifurcation must always exist in the same locus, otherwise there would have been this absurd consequence that an axe put on a mango tree would bifurcate an oak tree. The Buddhists believe that such absurd situation will arise if entities other than cognition are regarded as *pramāṇa*. For instance, the sense organs like eye, etc. are regarded by Naiyāyikas and Bhāṭṭa Mīmāṁsakas as composite substances (*sāvayavadravya*) and composite substances are said to be located in their constituent parts (*avayavas*). The visual cognition produced by the eye is said by them to be a quality of the self which is also a substance. The qualities of a substance are located in that substance. Thus the visual cognition exists in the self. But the self is not the constituent part of any sense organ. Thus the sense organ and the cognition produced by it cannot have the same locus. The same argument holds in the case of smoke and inferential cognition. Accordingly the basic rule that an instrument and its result must have the same locus is violated if we treat entities like sense organ, smoke, etc. as instances of *pramāṇa*. But this problem does not arise if cognitions alone are said to be instances of *pramāṇa*. Since the result of a *pramāṇa* is certainly a cognition and if the *pramāṇa* is also a cognition, then they may very well share the same locus, viz. the knowing self. Hence we have to admit cognitions alone as *pramāṇa*.[38] In his chapter on perception, Dharmakīrti says that perceptual cognition is the result of *pramāṇa*[39] and as reason for that he states that this is because of the nature of the knowledge of the object,[40] i.e. from perceptual cognition we have knowledge of the object and being guided by that cognition it is possible for us to attain or obtain the object. So perceptual cognition becomes the agent or the *prāpaka* in respect of the attainment of the object. That which leads to the attainment of the object is regarded as the result of cognition. Perceptual cognition guiding/helping us in the attainment of the object becomes the result of *pramāṇa*. So the same perceptual cognition is

---

38. For a detailed discussion see The Buddhist Theory of Pramāṇa & Pramāṇaphala by Prof. Prabal Kr. Sen.
39. *tadeva ca pratyakṣaṁ jñānaṁ pramāṇaphalam* । — *Nyāyabindu*, I.18.
40. *arthapratītirūpatvāt* — Ibid., I.19.

pramāṇa and *pramāṇaphala* at the same time. In respect of its guiding character, cognition is *pramāṇa*, but in respect of the attainment of object the same cognition is *pramāṇaphala*. There is no distinction thus between a means of valid cognition and the resultant cognition.[41]

What Dharmakīrti has so far stated is only an elaboration of what his predecessor Diṅnāga had stated in *Pramāṇasamuccaya*. In this text Diṅnāga has said that we call the act of cognition *pramāṇa* or means of valid cognition, because it is usually conceived to include the act of cognizing, although primarily it is a result.[42] Because of that it is metaphorically regarded as *pramāṇa* but in reality or ultimately it is devoid of activity.[43] The effect/result of *pramāṇa* cannot be regarded as different from the act of cognition.[44] Diṅnāga observes that when a person cognizes something as blue this blue in the cognition is conceived to be the object. Here Diṅnāga appears to represent the Yogācāra position. As according to the Yogācāra position there is no object outside the cognition, the appearance of

---

41. *arthasya pratītir avagamaḥ, śaiva rūpaṁ yasya pratyakṣajñānasya tadarthapratītirūpam* । *tasya bhāvaḥ, tasmāt* । *etaduktaṁ bhavati – prāpakaṁ jñānaṁ pramāṇam* । *prāpaṇaśaktiś ca na kevalād arthāvinābhāvitvād bhavati* । *bījādyavinābhāvino 'pyaṁkurāder aprāpakatvāt* । *tasmāt prāpyād arthād utpattāv apyasyajñānasyāsti kaścid avaśyakartavyaḥ prāpakavyāpāro yena kṛtenārthaḥ prāpito bhavati* । *sa eva ca pramāṇaphalaṁ yad anuṣṭhānāt prāpakaṁ bhavati jñānam* । *uktañ ca purastāt pravṛttiviṣayapradarśanam eva prāpakasya prāpakavyāpāro nāma* । *tadeva ca pratyakṣam arthapratītirūpam arthapradarśanarūpam* । *atas tadeva pramāṇaphalam* । — *Nyāyabinduṭīkā*, 78.6-13.
42. *savyāpārapratītatvāt pramāṇam phalam eva sat* । — *Pramāṇasamuccaya* verse 8a.
43. *pramāṇatvopacārastu nirvyāpāre na vidyate* ॥ — Ibid., verse 8b.
44. *atrabāhyānāṁ yathā pramāṇātphalam arthāntaraṁ tathā nāsti* । *phalabhūtaṁ jñānam eva viṣayākāram utpadyamānaṁ savyāpāraṁ pratīyate ityupādānāt* ॥ — *PSV*, 23.4-6.

something as blue in the cognition does not have anything external corresponding to it. Accordingly the awareness or the cognition of something as blue (*svasaṁvitti*) is the result of the act of cognizing the object.[45] Even if we accept the Sautrāntika position and admit that the object of cognition exists in the external world, still we have to admit that a cognition is self-cognized. For even if there is an external object it is thought to exist only in conformity to the cognition and not by its own nature. When a man is aware of a pot in his cognition, it is the cognition of a pot that is cognized; the self-cognizing faculty functions as *pramāṇa* taking the pot-formed cognition as *prameya* and the *svasamvedana* as the result or *phala.* Though the Sautrāntikas admit the existence of the external object they cannot deny that there is no apprehension of the external object apart from the cognition of the cognition itself, because we have awareness of the external object only when its form appears in the cognition. The same point has been highlighted by Kamalaśīla in his *Pañjikā.* When the external object is the object of our cognition, the cognition of the object is the result of *pramāṇa* and similarity between the cognition of the object and the external object in respect of its form, is the *pramāṇa;* because in spite of the cognition of the object, this cognition of the object takes the form of the object.[46]

If the same piece of cognition is regarded both as *pramāṇa* and as *pramāṇaphala,* there will be the confusion of identifying the means with the end. It is in terms of the means that we arrive at the end. So how can the two be identified? In reply it has been said that while apprehending the object, one part or

45. *svasaṁvitti phalaṁ vātra tadrūpād arthaniścayaḥ* ।
viṣayākāra evāsya pramāṇaṁ tena mīyate ॥
— *Pramāṇasamuccaya,* verse 10.

46. *bāhye 'rthe prameye viṣayādhigamaḥ pramāṇaphalam, sārūpyaṁ tu pramāṇam* । *svasamvittāvapi satyaṁ yathākāram asya prathanāt* ।
— *Tattvasaṁgrahapañjikā,* 487.17-19.

aspect is regarded as the *pramāṇa* and the other as the *pramāṇaphala* and there is no contradiction in such apprehension. The cognition of an object is established by the identity of form (*arthasārūpya*). Since our cognition takes the form of blue we have apprehension of blue. From the mere contact of the visual sense organ and the blue object we cannot have the apprehension of blue unless this apprehension is compared with the other apprehensions of blue. So there is no relation of producer and produced (*janya-janaka*) between the *pramāṇa* and the *prameya*, there is only the relation of the determiner and the determined (*vyavasthāpya-vyavasthāpaka*). When we have a distinct cognition of something as blue, this cognition is recognized as being determined — the cognition of the thing as blue and not of anything else — and this determination is made on the basis of the appearance of something blue in the cognition itself.[47]

In asserting the identity of *pramāṇaphala* and *pramāṇa*, Diṅnāga actually is taking the stance of *sākārajñānavāda* the theory that cognition takes the form of the object within itself. The cognition as *pramāṇaphala* is the apprehension of an object (*viṣayādhigati*). If the doctrine of *nirākārajñānavādin* is accepted, then it would have to be said that knowledge is without any form (*nirākāra*). In such cases, although the object is believed to have forms (*sākāra*), the cognition itself would have to be regarded as the same in all cases irrespective of the fact which object is apprehended. In other words, knowledge of blue and knowledge of yellow would have to be regarded as one and the same, which is rather difficult to accept. Accordingly

47. *dhiyoṁ 'śayorākārādhigamalakṣaṇayoḥ sādhyasādhanasaṁsthitiḥ kriyākaraṇavyavasthā; tadvyavasthāśrayatvenākāravaśenādhigati-viśeṣavyavasthānāt । nāstyatra kāryakāraṇātmakaḥ kriyākāraṇabhāvaḥ, kintu vyavasthāpya-vyavasthāpakabhāvaḥ । sa ca tādātmye 'pya-viruddhaḥ ।* — *Pramāṇavārttikavṛtti*, 164.13-16.

knowledge of the object has to be regarded as *sākāra* — it assumes the form of the object (*viṣayākārāpanna*) which it cognizes. The *sākāra* cognition thus possesses the function of assuming the form of the object. It is because of this that the Buddhist logician Diṅnāga considers cognition or knowledge as *pramāṇa,* though it is primarily a *phala* in respect of being an apprehension (*adhigati*).[48]

While thinking that *svasaṁvedana* or *svasaṁvitti* is not differentiated as act and result, Diṅnāga and Dharmakīrti both are presupposing the doctrine of *vijñaptimātratā* of the Yogācāras. According to this theory the expressions *ātman, dharma,* etc. which stand for subject and object, are really metaphors applied to the transformation of the consciousness (*vijñānapariṇāma*). In reality there is neither subject nor object — they are simply constructions of imagination. When one attains the stage of Ultimate Reality one will avoid this imaginary distinction and will realize the state of pure consciousness (*vijñaptimātra*) which is free from all sorts of dichotomies. With such a theory of pure consciousness in mind the Buddhist logicians regard that for empirical purposes the undifferentiated fact of *svasaṁvedana* is presented in the form of the difference between *pramāṇa* and *prameya.*

Thus we see that in the epistemological context the Buddhists are attempting to provide a rational frame for human practice so that it becomes meaningful both in everyday life and in the pursuit of the ultimate goal indicated by Lord Buddha. In discussing epistemology the Buddhists are taking as their basis an ontology of Critical Realism tradition but ultimately ends up with a sort of idealism as they advocate the doctrine of *svasaṁvedana* or *vijñaptimātratā.*

---

48. For further discussion see M. Hattori, *Diṅnāga on Perception,* p. 98.

2

Knowledge
How it is Apprehended?

ANY standard epistemological theory is found to concentrate on two questions — one regarding the knowledge of external objects and the other regarding the knowledge of knowledge itself. Indian philosophers again view the second question from two perspectives — one from the perspective of origination (*utpatti*) and the other from the perspective of validity (*prāmāṇya*). That is, does knowledge that one knows originate at the time when one's knowledge of the object originates? From the perspective of validity the same question takes the following form — when one knows an object does one validly know that he knows the object? Indian philosophers are divided into rival schools regarding these two questions. We may formulate the rival theses as follows:

T_1 : If an awareness C_1 arises, it apprehends not only the object O_1 or the proposition *p*, but also C_1 itself by the same token.

T_2 : If C_1 arises, it apprehends only the object O_1 or the proposition P and we need another event C_2 to apprehend C_1.

The Prābhākara school of Mīmāṁsā along with the Buddhists of the Diṅnāga school accept T_1; while the rival thesis T_2 is accepted by the Nyāya-Vaiśeṣikas and the Bhāṭṭa school, although they understand and interpret it differently.

The Prābhākara school admits the existence of a soul-substance and hence an awareness is said to reveal the object to the self. Thus to say that the subject is aware of his own awareness means that the awareness reveals itself to the self. In fact, the Mīmāṁsakas hold that each awareness-event apprehends or reveals the "trio" — the object, the awareness itself and the cognizer self. In fact, all these three are perceived in each cognitive act; hence their theory is known as *tripuṭīpratyakṣatāvāda*. The Buddhists do not recognize the category of soul-substance, and hence "the subject is aware that he is aware" means for them simply that an awareness is aware of itself. Thus while the Prābhākaras regard T_1 as *svaprakāśavāda* or self-revelation theory of awareness, the Buddhists designate it as *svasaṁvedana* — the self-awareness character of awareness. For the Buddhists such *svasaṁvedana* is *perceptual* in character, since it has an inner mental perception of the cognitive event itself as its integral part. The Nyāya-Vaiśeṣikas, on the other hand, hold that each awareness event is usually followed by another episode of awareness, an inward perceptual recognition of the first event. This second episode is technically known as *anuvyavasāya*. The Bhāṭṭa school believes that an awareness event is by nature imperceptible and hence although we become mentally *aware* of an occurring awareness event, this second awareness is not perceptual in character. It is rather inferential. When an awareness apprehends an object, the object takes on a new character called "apprehendedness" (*jñātatā*). On the basis of this property of apprehendedness in the object, the subject infers that an awareness has arisen in him. This is, in a nutshell, the position of the rival theories regarding knowledge of knowledge or awareness of awareness.

In the background of all this let us try to go a bit deeper into the Buddhist account of such knowledge of knowledge, which is often expressed in their terminology as *svasaṁvedana* or *svasaṁvitti* or *ātmasaṁvedana*. The definition of *svasaṁvitti* has been given by Śāntarakṣita as:

> *svarūpavedanāyānyad vedakaṁ na vyapekṣate* ।
> *na cāviditam astūdam ityartho 'yaṁ svasaṁvidaḥ* ॥
> — *TS*, vs 2012

That is, knowledge does not wait or depend upon a different apprehender in order to apprehend itself. Nor does knowledge remain unapprehended. Accordingly, knowledge is regarded as self-apprehended or self-revealed. The term *svasaṁvedana* in general and the word *ātmasaṁvedana* in particular, literally may be translated as self-awareness. This translation may give rise to the confusion that it is consciousness aware of a Self, an *ātman*, a view which is unacceptable to the Buddhists. To avoid such confusion, the term *svasaṁvedana* is to be translated not literally as "self-awareness" but as "reflexive awareness" or "reflexive nature of awareness." Bhāvaviveka in his *Tarkajvāla* distinguishes between two aspects of consciousness and speaks of *svasaṁvedana* as the subjective aspect of consciousness apprehending the objective aspect. That which is spoken of as appearing to oneself is the subjective aspect and that which is spoken of as appearing as the object is the objective aspect. That very objective aspect which has taken on the aspect of the object is explained as the object of the subjective aspect. Therefore, the experience of the objective aspect by the subjective aspect is explained as the meaning of self-awareness. So what is called self-awareness is a different subjective aspect. However, it is not clear from the statement whether self-awareness is the result of the cognition by the subjective aspect, that is, experience of the objective aspect by the subjective aspect, or identical with the subjective aspect itself. Śāntarakṣita in his *Tattvasaṁgraha* points out that the coherent real sense of "self-awareness" cannot be "the subjective aspect experiencing the objective aspect" but is inherent self-knowing, that is, not being known by anything else. This sense of self-knowing is necessary in order to prevent the infinite regress — knowing that one knows that one knows that one knows . . ., etc. This certainly is a sense of "self-awareness" different from the one mentioned earlier, viz. the subjective aspect experiencing the objective aspect. Paul Griffiths in his book *The Reflexive Nature of Awareness* draws a distinction between two senses of self-awareness — self-awareness (1) stands for that which is the result of the subjective aspect taking the objective aspect as its object. Self-awareness (2) designated as the reflexive awareness or the reflexive nature of awareness stands for the sense of inherent self-knowing, that is, not requiring a further knower thus terminating any tendency towards infinite regress. Now self-awareness (1) requires self-awareness (2) but the latter is independent of the former. Any explanation of consciousness, even of those who regard consciousness as a conventional phenomenon, however requires self-awareness (2). In self-awareness (2) the term means reflexivity, where there is no sense of referring to an actual subject-object relationship and, therefore no stage of validation beyond the consciousness itself. Vinītadeva refers to this sense in his *Nyāyabinduṭikā* when he observes that consciousness reveals its own nature because it lies within the very nature of knowledge. Just as a lamp because of its illuminating character, is the revealer of itself and does not need any other lamp for its manifestation, similarly our knowledge/consciousness does not require the aid of any other knowledge or consciousness for apprehending its own character.[1] Kamalaśīla states that it would not be

1. *sarve hi citta-caittāḥ pratītisvabhāvatvāt svarūpajñāpakā bhavanti* । *yathā pradīpaḥ prakāśasvabhāvatvāt ātmanaḥ api prakāśako bhavati* →

appropriate to think of such self-awareness on the model of "*x* is aware of *y*" where *y* = *x*. In other words the epistemological model based on act and agent where an agent acts on itself is inappropriate, and therefore the common charge brought against the *svasaṁvedana* thesis, viz. the impossibility of an action being directed towards itself, simply does not apply in this case. Kamalaśīla makes the sense of *svasaṁvedana* very clear by his comments — "By self-cognition we do not mean the nature of a subject (the perceiver/*grāhaka*). Then what is it? It has as its nature illumination by itself intrinsically; it is just like the glow in the sky."[2] Thus self-awareness (2) is the essential characteristic of consciousness itself. This does not seem to be primarily a matter of argument, but is an articulated basic presupposition. There is something in consciousness, which distinguishes *sui generis* consciousness from everything else, viz. the insentience, and this is its reflexivity. Thus, wherever there is consciousness there is this characteristic of reflexivity. It is what makes consciousness. It has nothing to do with a particular epistemological situation or theory as such — it essentially does not involve in itself consciousness of anything, and therefore has nothing to do with consciousness of (it-)self. So consciousness is reflexive — because that is what it needs to be in order to be other than insentience. It may be noted here that according to some Buddhist commentators, for example Vinītadeva, even erroneous mental states like illusions, etc. are self-aware and

---

→ *svarūpaprakāśo ca pradīpāntaraṁ na apekṣate, tathā cittacaittā api svarūpāvabodhe jñānāntaraṁ na apekṣante* ।

— *Nyāyabinduṭīkā*, 10.31–11.1.

2. *na hi grāhakabhāvena ātmasaṁvedanam abhipretam* । *kiṁ tarhi* । *svayaṁ prakṛtyā prakāśātmatayā nabhastalabarttyālokavat* ।

— *Tattvasaṁgrahapañjikā* on verse 1999.

this has been hinted at by the word *sarva* in the definition.[3] Dharmottara, of course, does not share this view. His observation rather is that only states like pleasure, pain, etc. which are very intense, are self-revealing and not other conscious states.[4] The anonymous commentator of *Ṭippaṇī* on Dharmottara's commentary interestingly observes that Dharmottara's suggestion here is that during the stage of spiritual enlightenment known as *nirodhasamāpatti,* such states are not known through such perceptions.[5]

At the outset it must be borne in mind that the doctrine of *svasaṁvedana* is not admitted by all schools of Buddhism. For example, the Mādhyamika School of Buddhism does not regard knowledge to be *svasaṁvedya,* known by itself. Their conclusion is that just as it is useless to describe the playful activities of the daughter of a barren woman, similarly it is not worthwhile to discuss the question of knowledge of knowledge; for whether knowledge is illuminative or non-illuminative in character is a fact that is never known to anyone.[6] What we can at best say is as follows: just as a crystal has to depend on a blue object for its blue character while a blue object does

3. *sarvetyuktyī bhramajñānānyapi parigṛhyante* । *teṣāṁ ca yat svarūpa-prakāśanaṁ tadātmasaṁvedanam* — *NBVT,* of Vinītadeva.

4. *sukhādaya eva sphuṭānubhavatvāt svasaṁviditāḥ, nānyā cittāvasthā — ityetad āśaṅkā-nivṛttyarthaṁ sarvagrahaṇaṁ kṛtam* । *nāsti sā kācit cittāvasthā, yasyām ātmanaḥ saṁvedanaṁ na pratyakṣaṁ syāt* ।
— *NBT*. 65.4-6

5. *śuddhasya cittāvasthārūpasyasaṁveditasyābhāvamāheti bhāvaḥ* । *evaṁ bruvatā ṭīkākṛtānena nirodhasamāpattyāvasthāyāṁ śuddhacittābhāva evetyabhiprāyaḥ pradarśitaḥ* । *tasyām avasthāyāṁ na kācit cittāvasthāsaṁvedyate yataḥ* । — Ṭippaṇī on *NBT.*

   For details of the Buddhist argument vide the unpublished article "A Note on Svasaṁvedana" by Prabal Kr. Sen.

6. *prakāśā vāprakāśā vā yadā dṛṣṭā na kenacit* ।
   bandhyāduhitṛlīleva kathyamānāpi sā mudhā ॥
   — *Bodhicaryāvatāra,* ix.22

not, similarly there are some objects in the world which depend on something else for its knowledge while there are others which can be known independently of others. A lamp for example is of the second category — it can illuminate itself independent of other objects. Knowledge like lamp does not depend on anything else for its revelation.

Though the Mādhyamikas hold that knowledge does not depend on anything else for its expression they do not believe in the self-illuminating character of knowledge like the Yogācāra or Sautrāntika schools of Buddhism. The argument which the Mādhyamikas offer to disprove the self-illuminative character of knowledge is as follows. That a lamp illuminates can be said only when it is so apprehended. That is, it is through the medium of knowledge that the illuminative character of lamp is apprehended. But we cannot speak of any knowledge to which another piece of knowledge is revealed. In other words, we cannot speak of the self-illuminative character of knowledge because there is no "apprehender" cognition (KK1) which can apprehend the previous knowledge (K1). Further, if for the sake of argument it is accepted that knowledge reveals itself independently of anything else like a lamp, then we have to admit that knowledge is independent of the objects of knowledge (*prameya*) also. If the knowledge or *pramāṇa* is known independently of the objects of cognition, then the knowledge will be knowledge of nothing. Thus it would be of no use and hence will be defective. If, however, the knowledge is knowledge of something, then it is no longer *pramāṇa* independent of the objects to be cognized.[7] If to avoid

7. *yadi ca agnivat svataḥpramāṇasiddhiriti manyase, anapekṣyāpi prameyāṇi pramāṇānām siddhir bhaviṣyati iti | kiṁ kāraṇaṁ? nahi svataḥ [siddhiḥ] paramapekṣate | athāpekṣate, na svataḥprasiddhiḥ | atrāha–yadi nāpekṣyate prameyān arthān pramāṇāni, ko doṣo bhaviṣyati iti? atrocyate* →

this difficulty it is suggested that the *pramāṇa*s exist only in relation to the objects to be cognized, then there will be an interchange of *pramāṇa* and *prameya*. The *pramāṇa*s will become the *prameya*s as they are established by the *prameya*s and the *prameya*s will become the *pramāṇa* as they establish the *pramāṇa*s.[8] Hence we cannot speak of knowledge being known by itself, nor can knowledge be known by other piece of knowledge, nor are they established by the *prameya*s or accidentally.[9] In that case knowledge is to be regarded as *śūnya*.

The Mādhyamikas are aware of the fact that to say that knowledge is unknown may lead to the problem that nothing in the world can be claimed to be seen or heard or apprehended with the help of such knowledge. Accordingly they admit the possibility of self-illuminative knowledge in the empirical level only. It is only in the transcendental level that such self-revealing character is denied or discarded.[10] That is, from the ultimate point of view there is nothing that can be called *pramāṇa* or *prameya*. As such in that level the question of *svasaṁvedana* does not make any sense.

→ — *anapekṣya hi prameyān arthān yadi te pramāṇasiddhiḥ* । *bhavati na bhavati kasyacid evam imāni pramāṇāni* ॥

— *Vigrahavyāvarttanī*, verse 42, p. 288.6-10

8. *athāpi manyase apekṣaiva prameyānarthān pramāṇāni bhavanti, evaṁ hi sati mā bhūt pūrvoktadoṣa iti kṛtvā, evam te sati vyatyayaḥ pramāṇa-prameyāṇāṁ bhavati* । *pramāṇāni te prameyāṇi bhavanti, prameyaiḥ sādhitatvāt, pramāṇāni ca prameyāṇi bhavanti, pramāṇānāṁ sādhakatvāt* ।

— *Svopajñavṛtti* on *Vigrahavyāvarttanī* verse 46, p. 288.31-34.

9. *naiva svataḥ prasiddhir na parasparataḥ pramāṇair vā* ।
bhavati na ca prameyair na cāpyakasmāt pramāṇānām ॥

— Ibid., verse 52

10. *yathā dṛṣṭaṁ śrutaṁ jñātaṁ naiveha pratiṣidhyate* ।
satyataṁ kalpanā tvatra duḥkhahetur nirvāryyate ॥

— *Bodhicaryāvatāra*, ix.25

The master logician Diṅnāga in his *Pramāṇasamuccaya*, on the other hand, admits self-cognition or *svasaṁvedana* as valid. According to him every cognition is produced with a twofold appearance — namely that of itself as the subject (*svābhāsa*) and that of the object (*viṣayābhāsa*). The cognizing of itself as possessing these two aspects is regarded as *svasamvitti* and is considered to be the result of the cognitive act, since the determination of the object conforms to such self-cognition. When a cognition possessing the form of an object is itself the object to be cognized, then in accordance with the nature of such reflexive awareness, one conceives the object to be either desirable or undesirable — *svasaṁvittyānurūpa iṣṭo 'niṣṭo vārthaḥ pratīyate* । — *PST*.[11] In verse 10 of his text Diṅnāga points out that the word *svasaṁvitti* is expressive of the thought that a cognition is cognized by itself and does not need another cognition for its cognition — *svasaṁvittiḥ phalaṁ vātra tadrūpād arthaniścayaḥ*. When a man has the cognition of something blue (*nīla*), he has at the same time the awareness of the cognition of something blue (*nīladhī*). This awareness is caused by nothing other than the cognition itself. Thus the cognition, while cognizing an object, cognizes itself just as a lamp illuminates itself while illuminating other objects. This similie given by the Buddhists is different from the one given by the Naiyāyikas. According to the latter, knowledge is like a sense organ, e.g. an eye which can perceive an object but itself remains unperceived. In order to know the sense organ we have to take recourse to inference. Similarly knowledge can apprehend external objects but cannot know itself. It is known through a second level knowledge called *anuvyavasāya*. Accordingly the Nyāya school upholds the doctrine of *paraprakāśa* (revelation through others) while the Buddhist school advocates the doctrine of *svaprakāśa* (revelation by itself).

11. Quoted by Hattori, *Diṅnāga on Perception*, p. 104.

This self-revealing feature of knowledge is expressed through the doctrine of *svasaṁvedana* or *svasaṁvitti*.

The view of Diṅnāga that a cognition is produced with a twofold appearance is made from the Yogācāra standpoint. In his *Ālambanaparīkṣā,* Diṅnāga examines the theories concerning the object of cognition and proves that nothing existent in the external world, whether it be a single atom (*aṇu*) or the product of atoms (*sañcita*) or the collection of atoms (*saṁghāta*), can be considered as the object of knowledge. In conclusion he supports the Yogācāra doctrine that the object of cognition is nothing other than the appearance of an object in the cognition itself.[12] That form which is known internally but appears as external is called the object. What we call the sense organs (*indriya*) in relation to the object is not the physical organ but the ability to produce a cognition or the ability to cognize the appearance of the object. This ability of the cognition is referred to as *svābhāsa* or the cognition's appearance of itself as opposed to the appearance of the object in cognition (*viṣayābhāsa*). Thus when *svasaṁvitti* is regarded as the result of cognition (*pramāṇaphala*), the role of *pramāṇa* which takes the cognition as its *prameya* or object is that of the *svābhāsa* aspect of cognition. The Yogācāras do not admit the existence of any external object. In their view when a man is aware that something blue appears in his cognition, this theory of blue in the cognition is conceived as the object. As there is no object apart from the appearance of something blue in the cognition, it is established that the awareness of the cognition of something blue, i.e. *svasaṁvitti* is the result of the act of cognizing the object. So when Diṅnāga views *svasaṁvitti* as the *pramāṇaphala* he is upholding the Yogācāra position.

---

12. *yad antarjñeyarūpaṁ tu bahirvad avabhāṣāte so 'rthaḥ* ।
— *Ālambanaparīkṣā,* verse 6 cited in *TSP,* 582, 11–12.

From the statement of Diṅnāga it may appear that the doctrine of *svasaṁvedana* or *svasaṁvitti* holds for the Yogācāra philosophers only who do not admit any external object over and above the cognition itself and not for the Sautrāntikas who admit the reality of external objects. But the doctrine holds equally with the Sautrāntika school. The Sautrāntikas admit that when an external object (*bāhyārthaḥ*) is apprehended by cognition (*buddhyārūḍha*), the cognition possesses similarity (*sādṛśya*) to the form of the object (*viṣayākāra*); then there arises the awareness of this cognition, namely the *svasaṁvedana*. Inasmuch as this awareness is regarded as the *pramāṇaphala*, the *prameya* or the object is the cognition itself and not the external object. However Diṅnāga justifies the application of his theory from the Sautrāntika standpoint by regarding similarity (*sārūpya* or *viṣayākāratā*) as the *pramāṇa*, the means by which an external object is cognized.[13] For in this case we overlook the true nature of the cognition as that which is to be cognized by itself and regard its having the form of a thing as the means of knowing that thing. It may be said of the thing that it is known only through the cognition's having that form. Whatever form of a thing appears in the cognition, as for example something blue or non-blue, it is an object in that form which is cognized.[14] Thus the above line of Diṅnāga exhibits that according to him the *svasaṁvitti* thesis is true for the Sautrāntika position also. Jinendrabuddhi in his commentary presents the position of Diṅnāga in clear terms thus.

Even if there is an external object, it is thought to exist only in conformity to the cognition and not by its own nature.

---

13. *viṣayākāra evāsya pramāṇaṁ tena mīyate* — *PS*-Kārikā 10.

14. *yadā tu bāhya evārthaḥ prameyas tadā viṣayākārataivāsya pramāṇaṁ tadā hi jñānaṁ svasaṁvedyam api svarūpam anapekṣyārthābhāsataivāsyapramāṇam ǀ yasmāt so'rthaḥ tena mīyate yathā yathā hyarthasyākāraḥ śubhāditvena jñāne pratibhāti [niviśate]tad tadrūpaḥ sa viṣayaḥ pratīyate ǀ* — *PVBh*, 393.27-30.

It is not the fact that the cognition conforms to the object which exists by virtue of itself prior to the cognition, but rather the other way round. If the object existed by itself, there would have been the absurdity that a single object has various natures since it is cognized variously by different persons. When a man is aware of a pot in his cognition, it is the cognition of a pot that is cognized, and not the pot as something external. But in so far as there is such awareness a pot is said to exist in the external world. Thus determination of the object (*arthaniścaya*) is in accordance with the *svasaṁvitti* and it holds even when the object of cognition or *prameya* is considered to be something external. If it is the case that the cognition of a pot is cognized then there must be immanent in the cognition the self-cognizing faculty which functions as *pramāṇa* taking the pot-formed cognition for *prameya* and producing *svasaṁvedana* as its result (*phala*). Though this can be easily accounted for in the Yogācāra framework, there is a limitation in the Sautrāntika position, since unlike the *Yogācārins* they hold that the *prameya* is external. If the Sautrāntikas in agreement with the Yogācāras had admitted the self-cognizing faculty, that is, if *svābhāsa* = *grāhakākāra* were accepted as *pramāṇa*, their doctrine would have been violated, since *grāhakākāra* never takes external object as the *prameya.* Because of such limitations in the Sautrāntika doctrine, Diṅnāga considers the cognition's taking the form of the object (*viṣayākāratā*) as the *pramāṇa,* the external object is cognized by means of it and it is self-cognized. Diṅnāga repeats the same idea in a subsequent verse:

> *yadābhāṣām prameyam tatpramāṇam atha tatphalam* ।
> *grāhakākārasaṁvitti trayaṁ nātaḥ pṛthakkṛtam* ॥[15]

The form in which a cognition appears is regarded as the *prameya* or the object of cognition. The means of cognition

15. PS verse 11.

(*pramāṇa*) and the resultant cognition (*tatphalam*) are respectively the form of the subject apprehending the object (*grāhakākāra*) and the cognition cognizing itself. Therefore, these three factors, the object, the means of cognition and the resultant cognition, are not separate from each other.

The Mīmāṁsakas, the Naiyāyikas and the Vaibhāṣikas unanimously believe that a cognition simply represents the form (*ākāra*) of an external object but does not itself have any form. Cognition being thus formless (*nirākāra*) has only appearances (*svābhāsa*) regardless of the variety of objects to be cognized. Or it can be said that the cognition in which an object is represented has only *arthākāra* or the form of the object but has no form of its own. Thus those who maintain the view that knowledge does not have any form (*nirākārajñānavādins*) hold that cognition is of one form only (*ekarūpa*). Diṅnāga opposes this one-formedness feature of cognition and offers some argument to prove that cognition has two forms (*dvirūpa*) and so the theory of *svasaṁvedana* gets established. These two forms are the form of the cognition and the form of the cognition of cognition (*viṣayajñāna tajjñāna-viśeṣāt tu dvirūpatā*).[16]

The first argument presented by Diṅnāga is — that cognition has two forms follows from the difference between the cognition of the object and the cognition of that cognition.[17] The cognition which cognizes an object, such as a blue pot, has a twofold appearance — namely the appearance of the object and the appearance of itself as subject. And, the cognition which cognizes this cognition of the object, has also two forms — on the one hand the appearance of the cognition which is in conformity with the appearance of the object and the appearance of itself. If it were not so, that is, if the cognition

16. Vibhuti, quoted by Hattori, 108.

17. *viṣayajñāna-tajjñāna-bhedād buddher dvirūpatā* । — *PS*, verse 12.

of the object had only the form of the object or the form of itself, then the cognition of cognition would be indistinguishable from the cognition of the object. Let us try to elaborate this point with some symbols:

Cognition of the object = C_1

Cognition of cognition of the object = C_2

The appearance of object in cognition$_1$ = O_1

The appearance of object in cognition$_2$ = O_2

The appearance of itself in cognition$_1$ = S_1

The appearance of itself in cognition$_2$ = S_2

According to Diṅnāga, $C_1 = (S_1 \rightarrow O_1)$
[$\rightarrow$ signifies "in relation to"]

$$C_2 = (S_2 \rightarrow O_2)$$

Since C_2 takes C_1 as its object,

$$O_2 = (S_1 \rightarrow O_1)$$

Therefore, $C_2 = [S_2 \rightarrow (S_1 \rightarrow O_1)]$

Therefore, $C_2 \# C_1$[18]

In case cognition had only the appearance of the object (*arthākāra*) then $C_1 = O_1$, and $C_2 = O_2$. Since C_2 takes C_1 for its object, $O_2 = O_1$. Hence, $C_2 = C_1$. That is, the cognition of the cognition of an object would be identical with the cognition of the object. Again, if the cognition was regarded to have its own appearance only (*svābhāsa*), then $C_1 = S_1$ and $C_2 = S_2$; and as cognition which does not possess the form of the object always remains the same, $S_2 = S_1$, therefore, $C_2 = C_1$. Thus if the "one-formedness" thesis of cognition is admitted, we have to admit

18. For details, vide Hattori, p. 108.

that the cognition of an object is the same as the cognition of the cognition of the object, which is not an acceptable position. Hence, to distinguish between the two cognitions we have to admit that cognition has two forms.

The second argument offered by Diṅnāga in support of the cognition of cognition thesis is based on the doctrine of momentariness. Since according to the Buddhists everything is momentary, nothing has stability or duration, the object apprehended by a particular cognition ceases to exist before the succeeding cognition arises. So if it is assumed that an external object is represented in the formless (*nirākāra*) cognition, the form of the object in the preceding cognition would never appear in the succeeding cognition. But this is contrary to our experience; since, we can recollect past objects in our subsequent cognition. Hence it follows that the cognition has the form of the object (*viṣayākāra* or *arthākāra*) within itself. Thus by the fact of the recollection of past cognition, Diṅnāga proves that the cognition has *svākāra,* its own form, along with the form of the past object. The recollection is caused by the impression (*saṁskāra*) of past experience. Those who believe that cognition does not have a form of its own and hold that an external object is experienced by the cognition which is in itself unconscious, find it difficult to explain the fact of recollection as expressed in the statement "I remember that I cognized this object." As the cognition, according to them, has not been experienced before, it cannot have left an impression capable of giving rise to recollection. The recollection of past cognition can be accounted for only by admitting that the cognition is cognized by itself. Thus from the fact of recollection it follows that a cognition has its own form; and the fact that a cognition has its own form as well as the form of an object implies that a cognition is cognized by itself. In other words the fact of recollection of previous cognition is the proof of self-cognition also.[19] It may be argued that the fact of recollection does not prove the fact that a cognition is cognized by itself. For example, the Naiyāyikas argue that a cognition is apprehended by a second piece of cognition called *anuvyavasāya*. In reply the Buddhists hold that to admit that a cognition is apprehended by a second piece of cognition would lead to the fallacy of infinite regress. Inasmuch as there is a later recollection of C_1, it must be admitted that C_1 is cognized in some way. If it is held that C_1 is cognized by C_2, then it necessarily follows that C_2 is cognized by C_3, C_3 by C_4 and so on, since C_2, C_3, C_4, . . . are also recollected later. Thus the Naiyāyikas are inevitably led to the absurd conclusion that an endless series of cognition follows from a single cognition of an object. To avoid this fallacy of infinite regress we have to admit that cognitions are self-cognized.

The Bhāṭṭa Mīmāṁsakas do not feel the necessity to admit the self-cognizing character of cognition. They think that it is contrary to the experience of an ordinary man to argue that an endless series of cognitions C_1, C_2, C_3, . . . is recollected. They explain the recollection of cognition by their theory that a cognition is inferred from its result, i.e. cognizedness (*jñātatā*). Immediately after an object is cognized, the cognition is inferred from cognizedness, by means of hypothetical proof (*arthāpatti*) — had there been no cognition, there can be no cognizedness. C_1 is thus cognized by C_2, that is *jñātatā* is produced on C_1; from this cognizedness, C_2 is inferred by means of hypothetical proof. In this way there arises a number

19. *atha rūpādivat jñānam api jñānāntareṇa anubhūyate cet* । *tadapi na yujyate* । *kutaḥ* । *jñānantareṇetyādi* । *anavastheti* । *jñānaṁ jñānānantareṇānubhūyate* । *kathaṁ cet* । *tatra cetyādi* । *tatra vijñānāntare paścāt smṛtir dṛśyate* । *atas tasyāpi jñānāntareṇānubhave 'navasthā* । *tasmād avaśyaṁ jñānaṁ svasaṁvedanam abhyupagantavyam* ।
— *Pramāṇasamuccayavṛtti*, 30-31.

of cognitions each cognizing the preceding one and this process continues so long as the cognizer attempts to apprehend the cognition. As many cognitions as are cognized in this way, they can be recollected. So there may be a series of recollection of cognitions, but that series is not an endless one. The process of recollection can be terminated according to the wish of the individual. Dharmakīrti counters the attack of the Bhāṭṭa Mīmāṁsakas and argues in favour of the self-cognition thesis. His point is that inasmuch as we admit the movement of the cognition of one object to another, the series of cognition must be stopped at a certain point. If this is the case, the last in the series of cognitions is not cognized by any other cognition. But this conclusion is untenable. Since all cognitions are of the same nature, the last one must be cognized so that it may be recollected. If the opponents insist that the last one is not cognized, they have to admit that no cognition is ever cognized by another cognition, and subsequently recollection of cognition would be impossible, which is quite contrary to what has been experienced. If to avoid this, they admit that the last cognition is cognized by itself, then they have to admit that all cognitions are cognized by themselves. In other words, the theory of self-cognition gets established. Later on Śāntarakṣita in his *Tattvasaṁgraha* expresses the same point that if one does not know that one knows then the consciousness itself is unknown. If the consciousness itself is unknown then it could not know other objects. Hence we have to admit that cognition apprehends itself.

Dharmakīrti in his *Pramāṇavārttika* points out that from the fact of the two-formedness of cognitions, the fact of self-cognition gets established — the form of its own apprehension gets apprehended at the moment of apprehending the form of the object —

> *dvairūpyasādhanenāpi prāyaḥ siddhaṁ svavedanam* ।
> *svarūpabhūtābhāṣasya tadā saṁvedanekṣaṇāt* ॥[20]

If the fact of self-apprehension is not admitted, that is, if it is regarded that a piece of cognition while apprehending the form of the object, does not apprehend its own form but requires another piece of cognition to get apprehended, then we have to admit the absurd view that there is no apprehension at all.[21] It may be argued that knowledge is apprehended by a second knowledge just as an object is apprehended by a piece of cognition. That is, the former knowledge is viewed as an object. In such a situation we need not admit knowledge of knowledge at the same time when knowledge of object occurs. The difficulty, however, would be that the first knowledge will become an object apprehended (*grāhya*) and not the apprehender (*grāhaka*). But at the moment when knowledge apprehends an object, the knowledge is not apprehended; it is the apprehender only. In the second moment when there is the apprehender (*grāhakajñāna*) cognition to apprehend the apprehended cognition, there is no apprehended cognition. So we have to say that knowledge is not possible at all. To avoid this, we have to admit that cognition is self-cognized. When an object is apprehended, at that very moment that apprehension is apprehended. There is no difference between the cognition of the object and the cognition of cognition in respect of time.[22] The difference between the two lies in the fact that in the case

20. *Pramāṇavārttikam*, II.426.

21. *svaṁ ca rūpaṁ na sā vettītyutsanno 'nubhavo 'khilaḥ* । — Ibid., II.427.

22. *jñānaprakāśo hi arthaprakāśaḥ, sa ca svaparakālayor nāstīti prakāśo na syāt sarvasya* । — PVV, 189.18-20.

of external object, the cognition expresses itself as something external like the knowledge of blue; while in the case of cognition the same apprehender cognition takes on the appearance of the knower. So when an object is cognized, its knowledge is also cognized.[23] Dharmakīrti, therefore, strongly supports the doctrine that knowledge is self-cognized and such cognition is perceptual in character. He believes that there can be no conflict among people regarding the direct apprehensibility character of cognition — *saṁvedanasya tādātmye na vivādo 'sti kasyacit.*[24]

In support of the self-cognition thesis, Dharmakīrti offers an argument concerning the nature of suffering and happiness as they reveal the deeper nature of mental states. For Dharmakīrti suffering and happiness are not external to consciousness but integral to our awareness of external objects. Suffering and happiness are feelings experienced through the same mental states that apprehend external objects. They are not experienced separately from the objects we see, although they are different from them. A single mental state is able to apprehend an external object and experience a sensation at the same time, because it has a dual aspect. The first aspect is that of the external object or better its representation and the second one is the apprehension of that representation. The first one is regarded as *grāhyākāra* and the second one *grāhakākāra* which Dharmakīrti designates as *svasaṁvedana.* Accordingly Dharmakīrti observes, "Therefore, happiness, etc. is commonly understood as [an experience of objects] because it has the appearance of objects being transferred onto itself

23. *bahirmukhaṁ ca tajjñānaṁ bhātyārthapratibhāsavat* ।
buddheśca grāhikā vittir nityam antarmukhātmani ॥
— *PV*, II.428

24. Ibid., II.423.

and is experienced. Happiness does not, however, directly cognize the external object but cognizes itself through being merely produced from an external object."[25] The term "apprehension of external objects" refers to this causal process in which an external object induces a mental state to experience itself under a certain aspect. Hence, when we are aware of something we are at the same time cognizant of this awareness.

25. *na hi satyantaraṅge 'rthe śakte dhīr bāhyadarśanī* ।
arthagrahe sukhādīnāṁ tajjānāṁ syād avedanam ॥
dhiyor yugapadutpattau tattadviṣayasambhavāt ।
sukhaduḥkhavidau syātāṁ sakṛd arthasya sambhave ॥
— PV, II.231–32.4.

3

Validity

How it is Ascertained?

Related to the problem of knowledge is another issue, known as *prāmāṇyavāda* or the theory of truth or justification. Under this head is discussed the question whether such properties of cognition as validity and invalidity are intrinsic (*svataḥ*) or extrinsic (*parataḥ*). Though the topic of *prāmāṇayavāda* had been systematically discussed for the first time by Kumārila Bhaṭṭa in his *Ślokavārttika* this had occurred in the course of discussion of other schools of Indian philosophy also like those of the Nyāya, the Buddhists, etc. In fact, Kumārila became the main opponent of the Buddhist epistemologists from Dharmakīrti onwards. The intrinsic and extrinsic character of the properties, validity and invalidity have been analysed from several perspectives. Of them two are main which are as follows: (1) *utpatti* or the origination of validity and invalidity, (2) *jñapti* or the way how to justify cognition. That is, with regard to a piece of cognition, C, we have a set of four questions — (1) Do the factors that give rise to C also give rise to the validity of C? If it does then truth or validity is intrinsic and if not truth is extrinsic. (2) Do the factors that give rise to C, give rise to the falsity of C (assuming that C is false)? (3) When C is cognized, is the validity of C also cognized? (4) Or, is the validity or invalidity of C cognized later, because of something else? If the answer to (3) is positive, truth with regard to apprehension is regarded as intrinsic; whereas if the answer to (4) is affirmative, truth (or falsity) with regard to apprehension is regarded as extrinsic.

In Indian philosophy, the Nyāya school of philosophers are well known for their support of "extrinsic validity theory" (*parataḥprāmāṇyavāda*) both with regard to the origin as also apprehension of validity. They believe that the validity as well as the invalidity of a piece of cognition do not occur by the conditions that give rise to cognition itself, something else is required. For instance the validity originates by *guṇa* or special excellence while the invalidity occurs because of some *doṣa* or special deficiency. This school of thinkers also believe that the process which apprehends the occurrence of a piece of cognition does not apprehend the validity or invalidity of that piece of cognition. The validity of the cognition is apprehended later by the success or failure of the practical response to *C* whereas the occurrence of a piece of cognition of *C* is apprehended by a subsequent cognition which is of the nature of inner perception and which they call *anuvyavasāya.* The Prābhākara Mīmāṁsakas, on the other hand, believe in the doctrine of intrinsic validity with regard to the occurrence and apprehension of cognition. That is, they believe (1) that the veridicality of a veridical cognition is brought about by precisely those factors that are responsible for producing the cognition, and (2) that cognizers should initially accept their cognitions as veridical; rejection of a cognition as non-veridical occurs only upon the presentation of falsifying evidence which necessarily occurs subsequent to the occurrence of the cognition in question. The idea behind such theory is that in the normal situation, that is, in the absence of any additional distorting causes, the factors that give rise to a cognition are also responsible for ensuring its truth or object-representing character. Accordingly, the doxastic attitude of credence towards the contents of our cognitive states is justified in the absence of any countervailing evidence. The Prābhākaras believe that when a cognition is apprehended its validity is also apprehended, but the invalidity of the cognition is determined later on the basis of unsuccessful practice (as for instance not getting one's thirst quenched by the mirage water).

Though the Buddhists are not supporters of the *svataḥpramāṇyavāda* thesis, their view is not completely similar to the Nyāya view either. Śāntarakṣita in a long section entitled *Svataḥprāmāṇyaparīkṣā* of his text *Tattvasaṁgraha* points out the distinctiveness of the Buddhist view regarding validity from the Mīmāṁsā view through the following remark — ". . . some strongly pronounce the restriction that (a cognition) is valid only by itself, others hold no such restriction, when they say that some cognitions are valid by themselves, and some by something else."[1] The first opinion is upheld by the Mīmāṁsakas who believe in the intrinsic validity thesis regarding knowledge. But for the Buddhists, some cognitions are intrinsically valid, while others are valid by some other factors.

Dharmakīrti in his *Pramāṇavārttika* formulates the Buddhist's view as — *svarūpasya svato gatiḥ* I *prāmāṇyam vyavahāreṇa* . . . II[2] That is, the occurrence of a particular piece of cognition can be known by itself, but its validity is to be known from its use. When a piece of cognition occurs it itself becomes known. In this respect cognition is comparable to a lamp. Just as a lamp does not need any other lamp to reveal itself, similarly cognition is self-illuminatory. But its validity,

1. *yenaikaiḥ svata eveti proccaiḥ niyama ucyate* I
kiñcit svato 'nyataḥ kiñcit paraiś cāniyamo mataḥ II — *TS*, verse 2944.

2. *PV*, verse 1.3.

i.e. whether the piece of cognition is valid or not cannot be judged by itself, it is to be determined extrinsically. This is the view of Dharmakīrti. He appears to support the theory of extrinsic ascertainment of truth, since he believes that being guided by knowledge we make an attempt to get the desired object or avoid the unwanted one; and if we are successful in our attempt in getting the object or getting rid of the object in that particular place as indicated by knowledge, our knowledge is regarded as valid, otherwise invalid. This indicates that the validity of cognition is established through something other than the knowledge itself, viz. the success or failure of voluntary action. Apparently there seems to be a difference between this view of Dharmakīrti and what Śāntarakṣita had later said. Dharmakīrti seems to be advocating a sort of extrinsicalism in respect of the ascertainment of validity of all cognitions, whereas Śāntarakṣita reports that in some cases validity is intrinsically determined while in other cases it is extrinsically ascertained. Hence, the difference. But the difference is only apparent. For Dharmakīrti also intends to say that in respect of empirical cognition only, validity is to be determined extrinsically (*sāṁvyavahārikasyedam pramāṇasya lakṣaṇam*).[3] Since in the case of empirical knowledge the agent does not have any certain knowledge but is doubtful about the validity of cognition, he takes the help of success of voluntary cognition to apprehend the truth.[4] However for indeterminate cognition (*nirvikalpaka pratyakṣa*), the knowledge of a *yogī* (*yogījñāna*) and self-consciousness (*svasaṁvedana*)

---

3. *PVV*, 6.20-21.

4. *prāmāṇyam vyavahāreṇa arthakriyājñānena* । *yasya sādhanajñānasya tādātmyād anubhūte 'pi prāmāṇye sāśaṁkā vyavaharttāro 'nabhyāsavaśād anutpannānurūpaniścayāḥ, tatrārthakriyājñānena prāmāṇyaniścayaḥ* । *anyatra tu vibhramaśaṁkāsaṁkocād utpattāv eva svarūpasya prāmāṇyasya svato gatir ityuktam* । — *PVV*, 6.5-8.

validity is determined intrinsically, by itself, because such cognitions are free from all sorts of doubt and uncertainty.[5] Though Śāntarakṣita has not elaborately discussed which types of cognitions are intrinsically ascertained and in which cases the validity is externally determined, his commentator, Kamalaśīla has provided us with a neat list of the two cases of valid cognition according to Buddhist epistemological tradition. There he distinguishes seven kinds of valid cognition and says that —

1. the self-awareness perception (*svasaṁvedanapratyakṣa*),
2. yogic cognition (*yogījñāna*),
3. cognition of the fulfilment of purposes (*arthakriyājñāna*),
4. inference (*anumāna*),
5. trained perception (*abhyāsavat pratyakṣam*) as intrinsically valid,
6. cognition produced by prescription (*codanājanitam jñānam*), and
7. perception that is not free from causes of error (*pratyakṣamanapagatabhrāntinimittam*)

are extrinsically (*anyataḥ*) valid. A comparable but different list can be gathered from Dharmottara's commentary on the *Pramāṇaviniścaya*, Devendrabuddhi, and Śākyabuddhi's discussion also. In short, the Buddhists' view is a complicated one combining intrinsic validity in respect of origination, with extrinsic validity in respect of determination. Since they advocate the doctrine that all knowledge is self-cognizing, it suggests that truth, being the property of knowledge has occurred at the time of the occurrence of knowledge, though

5. *ataeva pratyakṣasya svataḥ prāmāṇyam । kasyacit tu parataḥ । yogijñānasya svasaṁvedyajñānasya ca svata eva prāmāṇyam । anumānasya tu niścayātmakatvāt svata eva prāmāṇyam ।*
— *TBh*, 3.6-9.

it has not been apprehended. The self-cognized truth comes to be realized or recognized later by a pragmatic criterion, viz. the ability to lead to the satisfaction of our expectation.

At this point a problem arises. Since the Buddhists are strong believers in the doctrine of momentariness, they have to admit that the object of knowledge is different from the object of the particular activity induced by that knowledge; and as a consequence of that we have to say that the truth/validity of knowledge can never be determined by us. This is quite true and in the strict sense, perhaps, the truth/validity of cognition cannot be ascertained in any way, for if we deal with the problem in the realm of moments and at the level of sensation, neither an action in general nor any particular human activity will come under consideration. Nevertheless, it is to be noted that in discussing *samyag jñāna,* Dharmakīrti has often referred to the fulfilment of human activity (*arthakriyāsthitiḥ*) (for instance *pramāṇam avisaṁvādijñānam arthakriyāsthitiḥ*), "human activity" (*pravṛtti* as — *pravṛttes tal pradhānatvāt heyopādeyavastūni*) and experience (*vyavahāraḥ* as — *prāmāṇyam vyavahāreṇa*). If we have a look at Dharmakīrti's ontology along with his epistemology, we find that according to him a moment of the object has causal power to produce a sensation in the next moment and this may be regarded as the particular causal power of the object. By sensation the object, for example a seed, is grasped along with all its specific properties, viz. roundness, momentariness, seedness, brown colour, etc. Each of its specific properties is grasped by our conceptual cognition which follows the sensation. Hence, it can be said that in addition to the particular causal power the object possesses a general causal power which can give rise to the judgement regarding the specific properties of the object, e.g. this is a seed, this is round, etc. At the level of such judgement we are not considering the momentary object but the object as a continuum of moments; and only such continuum of moments can give rise to the expectation regarding such object, as "this will give rise to a tree" or "this quenches my thirst," "this can contain milk," etc. In other words we are superimposing some practicality, the power to satisfy some human purpose upon a continuum of objects. Thus we are thinking of two kinds of causal powers — one particular and the other universal. But actually in reality, at the level of the momentary object, there is only one and the same causal power which can produce the result in the natural flow. This causal power is regarded as particular at the level of sensation, while the same causal power is regarded as universal satisfying human purpose at the level of judgement. Thus one and the same momentary object produces both sensation and judgement; and it is only when the judgement about an object is made, can activity towards the object be possible. This indicates that when we are considering the *arthakriyāsthitiḥ, pravṛttiḥ* or *vyavahāraḥ* we are taking into consideration not the particular causal power, but the universal causal power. Therefore, the object of knowledge under consideration is not to be understood in its momentary nature, but should be grasped as a continuum of moments.[6] Continuity and identity being preserved, it can be said that the validity of knowledge is ascertained later by the success of our activity, in spite of the temporal difference of the actual object. Such an account of the ascertainment of truth points to the pragmatic and conventional nature of the Buddhist definition of valid cognition.

That we cannot attain the same object which we have seen may be pointed out in another way. That which we see and that which we attain are different, since what we perceive

---

6. For detailed discussion vide S. Katsura "Dharmakīrti's Theory of Truth," *Journal of Indian Philosophy*, vol. 12, year 1984, pp. 215–35.

through our visual sense organ is the colour form of the object while what we attain is the tangibility of the object. Thus one thing is seen and another is attained. So, how can we account for the validity of cognition in terms of the success of attainment of the desired object?[7] In reply it is said by the Buddhists that even if what we see is different from what we attain, we have the identity of the two in our judgemental awareness which takes the form "I have attained what I have seen." This sort of determination (*adhyavasāya*) is regarded as the attainment of the object.[8] Thus, the point is that although in the actual world, the object seen and the object reached are different, still the ordinary user because of his ignorance, is not able to grasp the difference between the objects of two consecutive moments, rather thinks them to be the same. That is why, he can believe that he is attaining the same object which he has seen. But in the case of illusion, as for instance in the case of mirage water, we do not have this sort of determination.[9] Hence it is regarded as invalid.

Still, there remains a problem. Whether an object is attainable or not cannot be determined without the attainment of the causal efficiency. In such a situation, it is not possible to determine whether a piece of cognition is valid or not from its simple occurrence. Therefore, how can the knowledge determining the essential quality of an object be regarded as valid? In the case of empirical objects, appropriate action does not require determination of truth, it requires only

7. *rūpam tu dṛśyate sparśaḥ prāpyate* ၊ *tasmād anyaṛṣṭatvā 'nyasmin prāpyamāṇe nirdhāraṇam nāsti* ၊ *prāpaṇāt kathaṁ prāmāṇyam bhavatīti cet* ၊
— *TBh*, 2.3-5.

8. *vastuto 'nyaprāptir gṛhyate* ၊ *nanu paśyata evāhaṁ prāpnomīti cintāyām ekam atiriktam iti cet* ၊ *asmābhir nirdhāraṇam prāptir ucyate* ၊
— *TBh*, p. 2.5-7.

9. *yat tu marīcikādāvudakādivijñānaṁ tasyārthaprāpaṇāyogyatvād aprāmāṇyam eva* ၊
— *TBh*, 2.7-8.

apprehension of the object. But how can one have certainty about the object unless one has also ascertainment that the knowledge one has of the object is true? In reply, it can be said that knowledge gives a certainty about its object which gives rise to appropriate practical response. If that leads to successful result, one is led to infer that the knowledge was true. Ordinarily if the knowledge is of a familiar sort, one can immediately infer its truth, although the action is caused by the knowledge, not by such inference of its truth. In this account of the role of truth determination and of appropriate practice in ordinary experience a crucial question concerns the nature of the knowledge of the result. If the truth of a cognition, whose object is not quite familiar, is determined inferentially upon satisfaction of the action that follows from that cognition, then how is the truth of the experience or cognition of the final result (in the case of perception of water, the quenching of thirst) to be ascertained. It seems as though there are only two alternatives — to say that the cognition of the result is intrinsically true, having no need for any sort of confirmatory cognition, or to say that there is need of confirmation of this cognition which itself is in need of further cognition and thus giving rise to a series of infinite regress. The Buddhists here point to some kind of confirmatory cognition of result, but believe that this confirmatory cognition does not involve any fallacy. As Dharmottara, the famous commentator of Dharmakīrti points out — if there is immediate reaching of the object in the case of the appearance of causal efficacy that does not yet need to be examined;[10] for with this cognition the agent's goal is achieved and there is no occasion for any doubt which could justify further examination of its truth. The question of confirmatory cognition arises where the

---

10. *arthakriyānirbhāse tu yadyapi sākṣāt prāptiḥ tathāpi tan na parīkṣaṇīyam* I —*NBT*, 29.1.

observer has a doubt as to whether what is appearing is the real nature of the object. But when there is the appearance of causal efficacy and at the same time there is the knowledge of the object, his goal is achieved. Hence he does not have any doubt as to whether the object can be achieved or not. Hence there is no need of further confirmation.[11] Actually confirmatory cognition becomes essential when there is doubt or when there is possibility of error. So even if on the basis of primary cognition, the individual starts with an activity, because of the chance of error, he has to verify or examine whether the cognition is valid or not. But where the individual becomes successful in his activity through the attainment of his desired result, he is satisfied. As such he does not feel any urge for verifying whether that cognition was valid or not. The success of his activity is the sufficient proof of the validity of his cognition.[12] However the individual who is going to determine the nature of the object for the first time wishing for effective operation, is guided by the doubt as to whether the object is fire or something else. Even if he is guided to action without any clear consciousness regarding such doubt, the situation is not different, since the uncertainty that is associated with his undertaking, can by no means be removed, and so he cannot be said to have valid cognition. Thus to the main question regarding whether the validity of cognition can be apprehended intrinsically or extrinsically, the Buddhists

11. *yatraiva hi prekṣāvanto 'rthinaḥ sāśaṁkāḥ, tat parīkṣyate* | *arthakriyānirbhāsve ca jñāte sati siddhaḥ puruṣārthaḥ* | *tena tatra na sāśaṁkā arthinaḥ* | *atas tanna parīkṣaṇīyam* | — *NBT*, 29.1-3.

12. *saṁśayaviparyāsāpasāraṇām ca vyutpādyajanaprayojanam* | *tato yatraiva te tathāpravr̥ttayas tadeva parīkṣyata iti* | *arthakriyānirbhāse 'pi te tathāvr̥ttaya ityāha — arthakriyeti* | *ca śabdastuśabdasyārthe* | *kuto na tathāvr̥ttayaḥ? yena sākṣātkāraṇe 'smin sati siddhaḥ puruṣārthaḥ tenānantaram eva phalasyānubhūyamānatvāt* | *tadaiva santoṣādigamanād vā* | — *DhP*, 29.14-18.

do not have a straightforward answer. Rather they would say that in some cases the validity is determined intrinsically and in some cases extrinsically.

Kamalaśīla in his *Pañjikā* enumerates four possible alternatives regarding the issue of determining the validity of cognition. These are — (1) both validity and non-validity are determined intrinsically, (2) both are proved extrinsically; (3) validity is proved intrinsically and invalidity extrinsically, and (4) validity is proved by external cognition and invalidity intrinsically. After an elaborate examination of all these four alternatives he observes that the Buddhists do not accept any of these positions, rather they hold that the validity of cognition is proved sometimes intrinsically and sometimes extrinsically since there is no definite principle.[13] In fact, regarding the cases where validity of cognition can be determined intrinsically and where the validity is determined extrinsically, we do not find any unanimity among the commentators of Dharmakīrti and also among the later writers. Though we do not find any detailed discussion of the issue in the works of Diṅnāga and Dharmakīrti, later writers like Dharmottara, Devendrabuddhi, Śākyabuddhi, Kamalaśīla and others have taken up this issue and tried to provide answers from their respective standpoints.[14] Let us try to have a look at those different answers:

Devendrabuddhi

A. *intrinsic validity* — 1. valid cognition, i.e. perception

---

13. *na hi buddhair eṣāṁ caturṇām ekamato 'pi pakṣo 'bhīṣṭo 'niyama pakṣasyeṣṭatvāt* । — *TSP*, 811.

14. For a detailed discussion vide Krasser, Helmut — "On the ascertainment of Validity in the Buddhist Epistemological Tradition," *Journal of Indian Philosophy*, vol. 31, no. 1-3, yr. 2003, pp. 161-84.

related to the actual fulfilment of a purpose (*arthakriyāviṣayam pramāṇam*)

2. inference (*anumāna*)

B. *Extrinsic validity* — 1. perception with variegated causes for error

C. ascertaining cognition of B.1 is A.1.

Śākyabuddhi

A. *intrinsic validity* — 1. trained perception (*abhyāsavat*) — perception related to an object that is capable of fulfilling a purpose when there are no causes for error (*bhrāntinimitta*)

2. inference

3. perception of the fulfilment of a purpose.

B. *extrinsic validity* — 1. first occurrence of perception with causes for error (*bhrāntinimitta*) or where the causes cannot be ascertained.

C. ascertaining cognition: no explicit statement.

Dharmottara[15]

A. *intrinsic validity* — 1. perception in which the actual fulfilment of a purpose appears (*arthakriyānirbhāsam pratyakṣam*)

2. inference

3. trained perception.

B. *extrinsic validity* — 1. perception in which the necessary connection with the object is uncertain (*arthāvinābhāva-saṁśayaḥ*)

---

15. In his *NBT* Dharmottara does not make any detailed discussion, but in his *Prāmāṇyaparīkṣā* and at the beginning of his commentary on the *Pramāṇaviniścayaḥ* he makes a detailed discussion of the topic.

2. perception with doubt as to whether the apparent (*pratibhāsamān*) object, e.g. fire is real (*satya*) or not: in this case the validity with regard to all aspects (*sarvātmani*) has to be ascertained by a subsequent cognition.

3. perception of the general aspect of something with branches in which the specific aspect (*viśeṣa*), e.g. that it is a mango tree or not is uncertain: in this case the validity with regard to the general aspect is considered to be intrinsic but with regard to the specific aspect validity is extrinsic.

4. perception uncertain with regard to the appearance itself.

C. *ascertaining cognition*: no explicit statement.

Kamalasīla

A. *intrinsic validity* — 1. the self-awareness-perception (*svasaṁvedanapratyakṣa*)

2. yogic cognition

3. cognition of the fulfilment of a purpose (*arthakriyājñānam*)

4. inference (*anumānam*)

5. trained perception (*abhyāsavat pratyakṣam*)

B. *extrinsic validity* — 1. cognition produced by prescription (*codanājanitamjñānam*)

2. perception that is not free from causes of error (*pratyakṣam anapagata-bhrānti-nimittam*)

C. *ascertaining cognition*: no explicit statement.

Manorathanandi

A. *intrinsic validity* — 1. trained perception of an object that realizes a purpose (*asakṛvyavahārābhāsād darśana-*

mātreṇopalakṣita-bhrama-vivikta-svarūpaviśeṣam sādhanādhyakṣam)

2. inference

3. perception in which the fulfilment of a purpose appears

B. *extrinsic validity* — 1. untrained perception in which the validity is doubtful (*sandigdhaprāmāṇyam*)

C. ascertaining cognitions of B.1 are A.2 and A.3.

Karṇakagomin mentions that the validity in the case of perception with causes for error is ascertained by inference, in other cases due to perception itself and refers to the second chapter of his commentary where he intends to deal elaborately with this topic. But as this chapter is not available to us yet we cannot get the detailed opinion on this issue.

The Buddhist logicians divide sense-perception into two types — (1) perception of which the object has repeatedly been cognized by us and in which the particular nature, viz. the efficiency is discerned as soon as we get it. The validity of such perception is proved by itself. (2) But there is another variety of perception where we are not accustomed with the object. In such perception validity cannot be proved by itself. There we have to take the help of some other perception representing the effective action of the object or inference in order to determine the validity of the first perception. Thus validity of such perception is proved extrinsically. In the case of *mānasa pratyakṣa, yogījñāna, svasaṁvedana* or inference, knowledge does not depend on any external object and so to establish their validity we do not need to apply any extrinsic means — their validity is intrinsically determined.[16]

---

16. For further discussion, vide Kajiyama — *An Introduction to Buddhist Philosophy*, ch. 1.

From the fact that Diṅnāga did not make any detailed study on the theme of the ascertainment of validity, and Dharmakīrti only made a few cryptic remarks on this vital issue, it has been remarked by many that in the Indian Buddhist epistemological school the problem was — with the exception of Dharmottara — of only marginal interest. The Tibetan Buddhist scholars also observed that neither Diṅnāga's works nor Dharmakīrti's works are very clear about the intrinsic or extrinsic ascertainment of validity. To quote the words of gSer mdog paṇ chen Shakya mchog Idan (1428–1507) — "With respect to the twofold divisions of intrinsic ascertainment and extrinsic ascertainment in the case of a valid cognition, the sources (consisting) of the *Pramāṇasamuccaya* and the Seven Treatises are not clear (gsal po med). The commentators, too, did not clearly distinguish that this was the way these two have been taught by the sources and (this was) the definition of each (definiendum) and (this was) the exemplificate. Particularly the opinion that intrinsic ascertainment and extrinsic ascertainment are respectively explained by the two (!) feet "PVII4d" [and "PV II5c"] is not held by anybody competent (*tshad Idan*) and is also in general impossible."[17]

This passage clearly indicates that the Buddhist epistemologists did not feel the urge at the early stage of their philosophy to concentrate much on the issue of the ascertainment of validity, though in the later stage we find elaborate discussion. But in Tibetan Buddhism, from the very beginning much importance had been given to such a study. There this theme forms a corollary to the definition of valid

---

17. Quoted by E. Steinkellner — "Early Tibetan Ideas on the Ascertainment of Validity," *Tibetan Studies*, vol. 1 (Buddhist Philosophy and Literature), ed. I. Shoren and Y. Zuiho, Naritasan Shinshoji, 1992, pp. 260.

cognition and has been dealt with, more or less extensively, in all relevant treatises. Since our major concern here is with Indian Buddhism, we have refrained ourselves from discussion of the approaches found in Tibetan epistemological literature in this regard.

Regarding the discussion found in Indian Buddhist epistemological literature, it can be said that while upholding the view that some cognitions are intrinsically valid while others are extrinsically so, the Buddhists, strictly speaking those belonging to the Yogācāra-Sautrāntika tradition, are admitting a view which has some speciality of its own. First of all, it cannot be described as "inherentism" the view that veridicality or validity is intrinsic to valid cognitions. What the Buddhist philosopher Śāntarakṣita explicitly asserts is that it is wise to withhold judgement until further evidence occurs, as to whether the cognition itself is either veridical or non-veridical from the outset. It is only our doxastic attitude that is dependent on further factors and not the validity of valid cognitions. To quote from *Tattvasaṁgraha:* "In case of a cognition where doubt is possible even though validity (*māṇatva*) is present, it is not possible to be certain; that [validity] is cognized only from a second cognition of the efficacy resulting from the cognition's object."[18] "Kamalaśīla in his *Pañjikā* explains that where validity (*prāmāṇyatva*) has been apprehended but certainty is not possible due to the presence of causes of error, there one becomes certain from a distinct cognition of the efficacy of the object.[19] From the

18. *ataś ca prathamam jñānam tatsaṁvādam apekṣate* ı
saṁvādenāpi saṁvādaḥ punar mṛgyas tathaiva na ıı — *TS*, vs 2971.

19. *yatra hyānubhūtam api prāmāṇyam bhrāntikāraṇasadbhāvād viniścetum na śakyate, tatra parato 'rthakriyājñānan niścīyate, tāvanmātrenaiva ca puruṣasyābhīstārthasaṁsiddher ākāṁkṣā vinivṛtteti na punaḥ samvādenāpyaparaḥ saṁvādas tathaiva = ādyajñānavadapekṣanīyaḥ* ı
— *TSP*, 945, 25–946.9.

context it is clear that by the apprehension of validity, Kamalaśīla means not that one is aware of the validity of the cognition in question, but rather just that one is aware of a cognition that is in fact veridical. From these observations it would be misleading to regard the Buddhist doctrine as straightforward extrinsicalism, the view that the validity of valid cognition is externally produced. Mark Siderits prefers to describe the Buddhist position as "extrinsic credulism" — credulism, according to him being the view that "we should adopt a doxastic stance of initial credence toward all our cognitions." The Buddhist credulism is extrinsic, since one's doxastic stance towards a given cognition is to be determined by contextual factors. Thus what strikes interesting in the Buddhist theory of ascertainment of validity is their pragmatic and context-sensitive approach. Where there is no reason to entertain doubts about the veridicality of a cognition, the attitude of initial credence is the reasonable stance to take, but where the object of a novel perception is something distant, there is no other way but to adopt the cognition of efficacy to dispel doubt. It is this context-sensitive attitude of the Buddhist philosophers that seems to make their theory more modern than as compared to their age.

4

Knowledge
Its Different Varieties

REGARDING the number of *pramāṇas* there is a controversy among the different schools of Indian philosophy. The Buddhists admit only two varieties of valid cognition (*pramāṇa*), viz. perception (*pratyakṣa*) and inference (*anumāna*), because there are, in their opinion, only two varieties of objects of cognition[1] (*prameya*) — the *svalakṣaṇa* or the basic particular and the *sāmānya lakṣaṇa* or the universal/class character. Of these two, the *svalakṣaṇa* or the bare particulars are alone real entities while the *sāmānya lakṣaṇas* are the constructions of our conceptual thinking. Unlike the Nyāya school, the Buddhists do not believe that the same object can possess both the particular (*viśeṣa*) and the universal (*sāmānya/jāti*) characters at the same time. According to the Nyāya school, every existing thing with the exception of the extreme universal (*parā-sāmānya*) and the extreme individual (*antya-viśeṣa*), possesses both the universality (*jāti*) and the particularity (*viśeṣa*). In perceiving a thing, one perceives it at the first moment vaguely without making any distinction between the universality and the particularity and this stage they describe as indeterminate perception (*nirvikalpaka pratyakṣa*); but later on we can have knowledge determinately, where we are able to combine the

1. *māṇaṁ dvividhaṁ viṣayadvaividhyatvāt* . . . — *PV*, II.1.

universal character and the particular character both. But this view is not admitted by the Buddhists.

Diṅnāga first, and later on his followers like Dharmakīrti and others draw a very clear line of discrimination between the *svalakṣaṇa* and the *sāmānya lakṣaṇa.* The former is real since it alone is causally efficient while the latter is not real. It can at best be regarded to be empirically real while the former one is real from the ultimate point of view.[2] Dharmakīrti in the second chapter of his *Pramāṇavārttika* lists some fundamental points of distinction between the *svalakṣaṇa* and the *sāmānya lakṣaṇa.* (1) *Svalakṣaṇa* has a power to produce effect while the *sāmānya lakṣaṇa* conceived only for the purpose of discrimination, does not have any such power.[3] (2) *Svalakṣaṇa*s are specific in character since they are distinguished from everything other than itself, *sāmānya lakṣaṇa*s have general character, since they can be common among many things.[4] (3) *Svalakṣaṇa* is not expressible through words while the *sāmānya lakṣaṇa* is/can be expressed through words.[5] (4) *Svalakṣaṇa* is apprehensible without depending on other factors like verbal conventions whereas *sāmānya lakṣaṇa*s cannot be apprehended without depending on such other factors.[6] Thus according to Dharmakīrti there are fundamental differences between *svalakṣaṇa* and *sāmānya lakṣaṇa* in respect of causal efficiency,

2. *arthakriyāsamarthaṁ yat tad atra paramārthasat* ǀ
anyat saṁvṛtisat proktam; te svasāmānyalakṣaṇe ǁ — *PV*, II.3.

3. *svalakṣaṇasyārthakriyāśaktatvāt, vijātīyavyāṛttiyupakalpitasya ca sāmānyasyāśaktatvād viṣayadvaividhyam* ǀ — *PVV*, 84.6-7.

4. *sadṛśaṁ sāmānyam; sarvayaktisādhāraṇatvāt* ǀ *asadṛśaṁ svalakṣaṇam; sarvato vyāvṛttatvāt* ǀ — Ibid., 84.12-13.

5. *śabdasya viṣayaḥ sāmānyam aviṣayaḥ svalakṣaṇam* ǀ
— Ibid., p. 84.16-17.

6. *tathā viṣayādanyeṣāṁ nimittānāṁ manaskāravat sādguṇyasaṁketagrahaṇānāṁ bhāve grāhikāyā dhiyaḥ sāmānye sattvāt svalakṣaṇe cābhāvāt viṣayadvaividhyam* ǀ — Ibid., 84. 19-21.

similarity, expressibility through words and apprehensibility through other factors.[7] Because of such fundamental differences in the nature of the two objects, two different means of cognition are required to apprehend the two different types of objects. Perception is fit to apprehend the *svalakṣaṇa* while inference is for *sāmānya lakṣaṇa*. If we compare Dharmakīrti's analysis with that of Diṅnāga regarding the distinction between these two types of objects, we find that the concept of causal efficiency (*arthakriyā*) was unfamiliar to Diṅnāga. It is a new addition by Dharmakīrti. Dharmakīrti adds this further concept to the unreality of universal or *sāmānya*. Later on in the same chapter of *Pramāṇavārttika* he states that the bare particular alone is the object of valid cognition[8] and shows that this is not at all inconsistent with his previous statement that there are two means of valid cognition since there are two different types of objects. *Prameya* is said to be twofold because the *svalakṣaṇa* or the bare particular can be apprehended in two ways, as it is (*svarūpeṇa*) and as something other than itself (*pararūpeṇa*). So it is not the case that there is real *sāmānya* apart from the *svalakṣaṇas*. It is simply on the basis of apprehending the bare particulars (*svalakṣaṇa*) in two different ways that we have two different objects of valid cognition.[9] Let us now have a look at these different *pramāṇas* independently.

---

7. . . . *śaktyaśaktitaḥ* ।
arthakriyāyām; keśādirnārtho 'narthādhimokṣataḥ ।
sadṛśāsadṛśatvāc ca viṣayāviṣayatvataḥ ।
śabdasyānyanimittānāṁ bhāve dhīsadasattvataḥ ॥ — *PV*, II.1-2.

8. *meyaṁ tvekaṁ svalakṣaṇam* ॥ — *PV*, II.53.

9. *tasya sva-para-rūpābhyāṁ gater meyadvayaṁ matam* ॥ — *PV*, II.54.

   tasya svalakṣaṇasya pratyakṣataḥ svarūpeṇānumānataḥ pararūpeṇa sāmānyākāreṇa gater meyadvayaṁ matam, na tu bhūtasāmānyasya sattvāt ॥ — *PVV*, 100.10-12.

5

Perception

Its Nature

Of the different means of cognition (*pramāṇa*), the one which is universally accepted by all, irrespective of being a philosopher or not, is perception. In India, all the schools including even the Cārvākas who raise questions regarding all other varieties of knowledge, admit the validity of perception. Even though the skeptics cite the cases of illusion and hallucination to raise doubt as to whether we can rely on our sense organs or not, it is a fact in our ordinary day-to-day life that we trust our sense organs more than anything else. Accordingly, what comes to us through such sense organs is considered to be authentic; hence, the validity of perception is admitted by all. Some schools of Indian philosophy, for example the Nyāya school, regard perception to be the highest (*jyeṣṭha pramāṇa*), for all other means of cognition are dependent on this. Inference of fire in a particular place can be done only when we perceive smoke there. We can recognize something to be a *gavaya* through comparison only when its similarity with a cow is perceived. Again for knowing something through verbal expressions, we need to have auditory perception of the word. Thus it can be seen that the efficacy of other means of cognition becomes possible only when there is perception, and hence the superiority of perception. However, the Buddhists do not make any distinction between the two *pramāṇas* in respect of superiority and rather consider both of them to be of equal status.[1] Just as perception has invariable relationship with the object, inference has invariable relationships with its object. The objects of these two *pramāṇa*-s are different but relationships with their respective objects are the same. As such we cannot say that one is superior to the other.[2]

Though all schools of Indian philosophy admit the validity of perception, they are not unanimous in explaining its nature or its varieties. Our objective here is to concentrate on how the Buddhists explain perception. Diṅnāga in his *Nyāyamukha* has provided an etymological analysis of the term *pratyakṣa* as it is so named because it occurs in close relation with the sense organs.[3] In this analysis Diṅnāga is showing his affinity to the doctrines of the Abhidharma school where it has been said that since sense organs are the specific causes of this variety of cognition it is to be named after the sense organs and not after the objects which are also needed for its occurrence. Vasubandhu in his *Abhidharmakośa* points to one more reason as to why perception is to be named after the sense organs. That is, in addition to being the specific causes of perception sense organs are also the locus/basis of such variety of cognition.[4] This second analysis has been accepted by later Buddhists like Dharmottara. In their analysis, the term *pratyakṣa* is to be interpreted as *pratigatam akṣam* meaning "depending on the sense organs," i.e. this variety of cognition

1. *cakāraḥ pratyakṣānumānay stulyabalatvam samuccinoti* I — *NBT*, 40.3.
2. *pratyakṣasyāpi yad arthāvinābhāvitvam tat tadutpattinimittakam eva* I *taccānumānasyāpi samānam iti arthāvyabhicāreṇāpi nimittinā samānena bhāvyam iti* II — *Pradīpa*, 40.28-29.
3. *asādhāraṇakāraṇatvāt akṣam akṣam prati varttata iti pratyakṣam* I
4. *tadvikāra-vikāritvād-āśrayāś cakṣurādayaḥ* I
ato 'sādhāraṇatvāc ca vijñānam tair nirucyate II — *AbhK*, I.45.

occurs from the sense organs. Though the word "sense organ" (*akṣa*) has been used in a very extended sense in the Abhidharma literature, in the particular context, viz. in the occurrence of perception, the term "sense organ" stands for those which are ordinarily or in the common-sense level, regarded as sense organs, namely eye, ear, nose, tongue and the skin.[5] Knowledge arising out of them is regarded as perception.

However, if perception is defined as knowledge arising out of the sense organs alone, the definition will be overly restrictive as it would exclude mental perception, self-consciousness, knowledge of the seers or the *yogīs* from the scope of perception, for none of them arises from the sense organs.[6] In reply, it has been said that when we analyse the term *pratyakṣa* as *pratigatam akṣam* that is completely an etymological analysis (*vyutpattinimitta*), and not its actual applicational criterion (*pravṛttinimitta*). The applicational analysis of the term *pratyakṣa* is to be understood as direct apprehension *sākṣātkārījñāna* which is quite in accordance with its conventional sense.[7] That sometimes the applicational meaning of a term as different from the etymological meaning has to be accepted, is very much evident in our linguistic practice. We may cite for example the analysis of the Sanskrit terms *paṅkaja* (meaning lotus) and also *go* (meaning cow). The

5. *akṣam tvindriyam cakṣuḥśrotraghrāṇajihvākāyākhyam* ।
— *TBh*, 3.18-19.

6. *atha pratigatam āśritam akṣam ityasyām api vyutpattau mānasa-svasaṁvedana-yogipratyakṣāṇām na syāt pratyakṣaśabdavācyatā* . . .
— *Pradīpa* 39.7-8.

7. *pratigatam āśritam akṣam* ॥ . . . *akṣāśritatvam ca vyutpattinimittam śabdasya* । *na tu pravṛttinimittam* । *anena tvakṣāśritatvenaikārthasamavetam arthasākṣātkāritvaṁ lakṣyate* । *tadeva śabdasya pravṛttinimittam* । *tataś ca yatkiñcid arthasya sākṣātkārijñānam tat pratyakṣam ucyate* ।
— *NBT*, 38.1-6.

term *paṅkaja* etymologically signifies anything which is born in mud (*paṅke jāyate yaḥ*), but in its actual application it signifies only one specific variety of thing born out of the mud, viz. the lotus. Similar is the case with the term *go* meaning cow. The word *go* being derived from the root *gam* signifying "going" etymologically can denote the going cow only, which however makes the meaning of the term restrictive. As such, to account for its proper meaning we have to take into consideration the applicational analysis by which the term *go* applies to all cows, irrespective of whether it is going or not.[8] Such a practice is to be followed in the case of *pratyakṣa* also. If we give up the etymological analysis and take into consideration the applicational analysis of the term *pratyakṣa* as direct or immediate apprehension, we can see that self-consciousness, mental perception as well as the perception of the seers can be included within the scope of *pratyakṣa* since all of them are cases of direct awareness. Durveka Miśra, however, points to another way of reconciling these two interpretations of the term *pratyakṣa*. According to him, since in the occurrence of perception the presence of the sense organs is essential and without the sense organs that particular variety of perception cannot arise, therefore the term *pratyakṣa* is primarily taken to mean knowledge arising out of the sense organs; but since there are many cases which are similar to such apprehensions, though are not due to any sense organ, the term *pratyakṣa* secondarily means the cases of direct or immediate apprehension[9] or simply direct awareness of objects.

8. *yadi tvakṣāśitatvam eva pravṛttinimittaṁ syād indriyavijñānam eva pratyakṣam ucyeta, na mānasādi* । *yathā gacchatīti gauḥ iti gamanakriyāyāṁ vyutpādito 'pi gośabdo gamanakriyopalakṣitam ekārthasamavetaṁ gotvaṁ pravṛttinimittīkaroti* । *tathā ca gacchatyagacchati ca gavi gośabdaḥ siddho bhavati* । — NBT, 39.1-4.

9. *tathā hi prathamam yat tad indriyānvayavyatirekānuvidhāyitayā pratyakṣam prasiddham iti pratipādyate* । *tadanu yadīdamindriyāśritaṁ* →

It may be said by the opponents that the expression "direct awareness of objects" also contains within it the sense of "dependence on sense organs"; in such a case the charge of being overly restrictive still remains — the term even in its applicational analysis would not be able to include mental perception and others.[10] In reply it has been said that this sort of objection does not arise at all if we look into ordinary linguistic practice. When we say "keep the food away from crows" though we are using the term "crows" we do not mean simply the crows but anything of that variety like sparrows, and even other animals. That is, though we are mentioning a particular entity, its scope is not limited to that. This practice is to be followed in the case of *pratyakṣa* also. Though the term *artha-sākṣātkāritva* generally implies apprehension through the sense organs, it equally applies to other cases of direct or immediate apprehension.[11] So the charge of being overly restrictive no longer holds with the applicational analysis of the term *pratyakṣa.*

Thus, accepting immediate/direct apprehension of the objects as the meaning of the term *pratyakṣa* the Buddhists proceed towards the definitions for such cognition. We may

---

→ *jñānaṁ bhavatāṁ pratyakṣaṁ prasiddhaṁ tatrāpi pratyakṣaśabda-pravṛttāvartha-sākṣātkāritvam eva nimittaṁ jānīte iti pratipādyate* ।
— *Pradīpaḥ*, 41.24-26.

10. *yadarthasākṣātkaraṇam āśritatvena samavetaṁ tad evānenopalakṣaṇīyam iti tadāvasthe mānasāder asaṁgraha* ।
— Ibid., 39.22-23.

11. *akṣajatvasyo palakṣaṇatvenāprādhānyād arthasākṣātkāritvam upalakṣyamāṇam pradhānam upalakṣaiva nivṛtter adoṣa eva* । *yathā kākebhyo dadhi rakṣyatām ityatra* । *anyathā 'trāpi kākatvenaikārtha-samavetasyopaghātakatvasyopalakṣaṇāt śvādibhyo dadhirakṣā na syāt* । *atha yadevopaghātakaṁ kākeṣu samavetaṁ tad evānyatrāpi* । *taccopalakṣitam iti tadanyato 'pi dadhirakṣo 'cyate* । *arthasākṣātkāritve 'pi samānaṁ idam iti kathaṁ na mānasādeḥ pratyakṣaśabdābhilāpyatvam iti* ।
— Ibid., 39.23-28.

start with the definition offered by the master logician Diṅnāga. In his *Pramāṇasamuccaya* Diṅnāga presents the definition of perception in this way —

> D1. Perception is that which is free from conceptual construction that is from the association of name, class, character, etc.[12]

Dharmakīrti also accepts this definition but adds another epithet "non-erroneous" to it. So his definition becomes:

> D2. Perception is that which is free from conceptual construction and which is non-erroneous.[13]

If we look into these two definitions D1 and D2, it can be seen that both of them unambiguously highlight the indeterminate character of perception — perception is "free from conceptual construction" (*kalpanāpoḍha*). So the question immediately arises: What is meant by *kalpanā*? Before answering this question, let us concentrate on the *kalpanāpoḍha* character of perception. It may be noted at the outset that Diṅnāga was not the only person to define perception in this way. Vindhyavāsin, an elder contemporary of Vasubandhu defined perception as not characterized by anything which is existent in the auditory organ.[14] Jayanta Bhaṭṭa in his *Nyāyamañjarī* considers this definition to be identical with the Buddhist definition. However, the contribution of Diṅnāga was to provide a logical base for such definition by pointing out that *svalakṣaṇa* is the variety of object with which perception deals and since this object is the bare particular without any property

12. *pratyakṣam kalpanā 'poḍham nāmajātyādyasaṁyutam* ।
— *PS*, verse 3

13. *tatra pratyakṣam kalpanā 'poḍham abhrāntam* ॥ — *NB*, I.4.

14. *śrotrādi-vṛttir avikalpikā* referred to by Hattori in *Diṅnāga on Perception*, p. 82.

or character whatsoever, perception is free from conceptual constructs. This definition of Diṅnāga was severely criticized by the opponents, specially the Nyāya school of philosophers. Uddyotakara objected that if perception is really devoid of any conceptual construction, it could not be expressed by the property *kalpanāpoḍhatva*; nor by the word *pratyakṣa* itself, nor by the sentence *pratyakṣam kalpanāpoḍham* itself. Moreover, if the word *kalpanāpoḍha* were taken to mean "inexpressible in its specific aspect" then anything in the world would be regarded as *pratyakṣa* since a word can express only the generic character of a thing and not its specific character. It would further not be wise to regard a thing as inexpressible on the ground that its specific character is inexpressible. A brāhmaṇa may be described as a man though the word "man" does not express his specific character. Alternatively if the specific character of *pratyakṣa* is described as *kalpanāpoḍha*, it will be self-contradictory, for the expression *kalpanāpoḍha* means "indescribable." Lastly, if the word *kalpanāpoḍha* were understood to express nothing, the definition would have to be regarded as completely useless. Later Buddhist scholars like Śāntarakṣita and Kamalaśīla have replied to these objections of the Nyāya school by pointing out that the expression *kalpanāpoḍhatva* does not signify that perception is ineffable (*anabhidheya*); it signifies that perception is devoid of conceptual constructions (*avikalpikā*). Hence the charges do not hold.

Let us now have a look into the meaning of the term *kalpanā*. In Diṅnāga's philosophy, a thing which is in itself inexpressible, can be expressed with words only when it is presented in association with names and other factors. *Kalpanā* or conceptual construction is the name of this process of associating a name, etc. with a particular individual. Diṅnāga distinguishes these factors under five heads — *nāma, jāti, guṇa, kriyā* and *dravya* which function respectively in relating a proper name (*yadṛcchāśabda*), common noun (*jātiśabda*), attribute (*guṇa*), activity (*kriyā*) and a substance word (*dravya*) to the object. Making such distinction among linguistic expressions, Diṅnāga is showing his affinity to the grammatical tradition. In the grammatical tradition, for instance in the *Mahābhāṣya*, Patañjali classifies a linguistic expression into four categories — *jātiśabda, guṇaśabda, kriyāśabda,* and *yadṛcchāśabda.* Śāntarakṣita in his *Tattvasaṁgraha* has pointed out that since from the Buddhist standpoint there is no such thing as "substance" (*dravya*), all words are to be regarded either as arbitrary words (*yadṛcchāśabda*) or as genus words inasmuch as they stand for what is common to many individual moments or entities. So according to Śāntarakṣita and his commentator Kamalaśīla, the word *kalpanā* as used by Diṅnāga, stands not for class-terms, action-terms, etc. but as being inseparably related to words. According to their interpretation, the term *nāma* in Diṅnāga's definition of *kalpanā,* is to be separated from *jātyādi.* This expression *jātyādi-yojanā* according to them is a heretical theory which has to be discarded, since Diṅnāga does not admit any such entity as *jāti,* etc. Thus, they think that Diṅnāga's own interpretation of *kalpanā* is *nāmayojanā*. They, further point out that even on the assumption that *jāti,* etc. can be admitted as provisional entities, it has to be noted that they (*jāti,* etc.) can be related to particular things only through names. Hence, their conclusion is that association with word is the distinctive feature of Diṅnāga's notion of *kalpanā.* Accordingly, they defined *kalpanā* as "cognition associated with words" (*abhilāpinī pratīti*). Though the arguments of Śāntarakṣita and Kamalaśīla cannot be refuted as false, it cannot be shown to be in complete agreement with what Diṅnāga himself has said about *kalpanā.* So, following what

Diṅnāga himself has said in his *Pramāṇasamuccayavṛtti* we accept that according to him *kalpanā* is associated with proper nouns, common nouns, adjectives, verbs and words denoting substances.

In his formulation of *kalpanā,* Dharmakīrti is more cautious than his predecessor Diṅnāga. He does not specify the type of words which when associated with words will constitute *kalpanā.* He simply presents the definition as a cognition of representation which is capable of being associated with a verbal designation.[15] For instance, the expression "pot" is a *kalpanā* as it presents before us the object pot as designated by the term "pot".[16] Dharmottara elaborates this idea by pointing out that conceptual construction is the presentation of the designator and the designated as associated in a piece of cognition.[17] What is meant by this "designator-designated relationship"? It is nothing but the presentation of the substance-attribute form in a piece of cognition.[18] It may be that this representation, at present, is not actually expressed with linguistic sign; but it has the ability to be expressed by such verbal expressions. As such Dharmakīrti uses the expression "capable" (*yogya*) in his definition and in that sense the infant can be said to possess *kalpanā.*[19]

---

15. *abhilāpa-saṁsarga-yogya-pratibhāsā pratītiḥ kalpanā* । — *NB,* I.5.

16. *yathā vyutpanna-saṁketasya ghaṭātha-kalpanā ghaṭaśabdasaṁsṛṣṭā-rthāvabhāsā bhavati* । — *NBT,* 48.4-5.

17. *abhilapyate 'neneti abhilāpaḥ vācakaḥ śabdaḥ* । *abhilāpena saṁsargaḥ — abhilāpasaṁsargaḥ — ekasmin jñāne 'bhidheyākārasyā-bhidhānākareṇa saha grāhyākāratayā milanam* । — *NBT,* 47.9–48.1.

18. *ekasmin jñāne viśeṣya-viśeṣaṇatvenā-kārapratibhāsa evānayor vācya-vācakatva-grahaṇam iti bhāvaḥ* । — *Pradīpaḥ,* 48.20-21.

19. *kācit tvabhilāpenāsaṁsṛṣṭāpi abhilāpasaṁsargayogyābhāsā bhavati* । *yathā bālakasyāvyutpannasaṁketasya kalpanā* । — *NBT,* 48.5-6.

However, this is not able to solve all problems. If *kalpanā* is defined as association with verbal designation it follows that those who are not able to communicate through verbal expressions, do not possess any such conceptual construction. The reason is that, in that case the dumb, who may never be able to use verbal expressions, would be denied to have *kalpanā*. To include their cases, *kalpanā* has been said to be such cognition of an object that is associated with a word or with an inarticulate representation (*antarjalpa*), made possible through linking together the preceding and succeeding moments of momentary objects.[20] Thus when an intelligent person uses the word "pot" to designate the object of that particular shape, he will be said to possess *kalpanā*. Just in the same way when a child or a dumb person expresses the object by finger pointing or by other means we cannot but admit that they also have *kalpanā*, though they are not able to use any verbal means. The term "inarticulate expression" (*antarjalpa*) has been added to include such cases.

Here a problem arises. In the case of verbal expressions we can speak of the existence of *kalpanā* from the spoken words. For instance when a person uses the word "pen" to express something we can tell that he has the conception from his use of the term "pen." But in the case of inarticulate representation how can we be sure of such *kalpanā*? In reply it has been said that this is done through inference. That is, we infer determinations in their cases from the occurrence of the effects of determining factors, namely the acceptance of the desired consequence or the rejection of the undesired one. Such effects are also observed in the case of children and dumb people. They also accept their desired object and refuse to

---

20. *pūrvāparam anusandhāya śabdasamyuktākārā pratītir antarjalpākārā vā kalpanā* ।
— *TBh*, 7.18-19.

accept what they do not like. So, from such activities it is possible to infer the presence of such determinations in them. By admitting the possibility that children and dumb are also capable of having determinants/constructions, Mokṣakaragupta is actually refuting the view of the Mīmāṁsakas, specially of Kumārila Bhaṭṭa that there is a primary intuitive apprehension, an unqualified perception arising from the mere real like the apprehension of the infants and the dumb which arise simply out of awe or satisfaction.[21]

Once the meaning of the term *kalpanā* is made clear, the question immediately arises, why is it that determinate cognitions or knowledge associated with determinations are considered to be confused cognitions and not unerring? In other words why is determinate cognition regarded as invalid? In reply, it has been said that it is a well-accepted fact that perception is such knowledge which directly reveals the nature of the object. If there is any confusion with regard to the determination it is not able to reveal the proper nature of the object.[22] There is no chance of such possibility of error in the level of indeterminate cognition. For knowledge grasping an object is the effect of the object, and object is the direct cause of such knowledge. In other words the essence of a sense-object consists in its being a cause capable of leaving its image in the cognition. Naturally when the object is there, there is no chance of making any mistake in respect of its cognition. But the question arises, how can an object, which exists at a particular moment different from that of the indeterminate

21. *asti hy ālocanājñānaṁ prathamaṁ nirvikalpakam |*
bālamūkādivijñānasadr̥śaṁ mugdhavastujam || — *SV*, v 112.

22. *kiṁ punaḥ kāraṇam kalpanāvibhramātmakaṁ jñānaṁ na pramāṇam iti cet | arthasvarūpa-sākṣātkāri hi jñānaṁ pratyakṣaṁ sarveṣāṁ sammatam | na ca kalpanāvibhramāvarthaṁ sākṣātkartuṁ samarthau |* — *TBh*, 7.24-26.

cognition grasping it to be the object of that indeterminate cognition?[23] Since in the case of determinate cognition, there is a role to be played by past impressions, it is quite possible for such cognition to occur even when there is no corresponding object. No concomitant relationship can be found between an object and determinate cognition; in such a case it would be too much to claim that such cognition is the effect of such an object. If *x* can occur without there being *y*, *x* cannot be said to be the effect of *y*. On the other hand, if the existence of an object implies that there is a determinate cognition of the object, then when a pot is there would imply that there is a determinate cognition of the pot. In that case even a blind could have the determinate cognition of the pot. But such is not the case.[24] Hence it is said that determinate cognition has no role to play in the immediate apprehension of the object, since the object is not manifested in verbal cognition as it is in indeterminate cognition.[25] With the help of this argument the Buddhists are able to refute the oft-quoted view of Bhartṛhari that "There is in this world no cognition which is not accompanied by a verbal expression. All cognition appears as if penetrated by words."[26] For example, when we utter the word "pot" with regard to a jar placed before us, other knowledge concerning the ground or

---

23. *bhinnakālam katham grāhyam iti ced grāhatāṁ viduḥ* ।
hetutvam eva yuktijñā jñānākārarpaṇakṣamam ॥ — *PV*, II.247
śābdyāṁ buddhāvarthasya pratyakṣa iva pratibhāsābhāvān nāsti kalpanāyā arthasākṣātkāritvam iti siddham । — ibid.

24. *yadi punaḥ kalpanājñānam arthād upajāyeta tenāpi tadā ghaṭādir artho dṛśyeta* । *tataś cāndhasyāpi rūpadarśanaprasaṁgaḥ* । *na cāsti* । — *TBh*, 8.4-6.

25. *śābdyāṁ buddhāvarthasya pratyakṣa iva pratibhāsābhāvān nāsti kalpanāyā arthasākṣātkāritvam iti siddham* । — Ibid., 8.6-8.

26. *na so 'sti pratyayo loke yaḥ śabdānugamādṛte* ।
anabiddham iva jñānaṁ sarvaṁ śabdena bhāsate । — *VP*, I.123.

others is experienced as well, still they are not referred to by the uttered word.[27] In fact, the form of an object, which we see unconsciously and for which our sense organs are not operating with proper attention, is not manifested in consciousness in association with word. In other words, our cognitions are not always associated with words. This is also testified by the rule that two concepts cannot occur at the same time.[28]

In defining perception in *Nyāyabindu* as well as in *Pramāṇaviniścaya* Dharmakīrti uses the term "non-erroneous" (*abhrānta*) in addition to *kalpanāpoḍha* to rule out erroneous cognitions from the scope of perception. Later on Buddhist philosophers followed Dharmakīrti and included the word *abhrānta* in their definition of perception. Thus we find Mokṣakaragupta in his *Tarkabhāṣā* defining perception as being free from conceptual constructs and as non-erroneous.[29] However Diṅnāga defines perception as being free from conceptual constructs, and thinks that the phrase "non-erroneous" is redundant. In fact, he has criticized the Naiyāyikas for including in their definition of perception an analogous expression, viz. *avyabhicārin* since it is unnecessary. This indicates that Diṅnāga did not take into consideration errors caused by defective sense organs when he defined perception and discussed cases of erroneous perception as due to determination. Perhaps later on his views had been subjected to criticism on the ground that *manas* or mind is not the only cause of erroneous cognitions and this criticism forced

27. *tathā hi ghaṭe purovarttinyuccāryamāṇe tatsamīpavartti bhītalādijñānam uccāraṇarahitam anubhūyata eva* । *na ca tatra śabdānugamo 'sti* ।
— *TBh*, 8.11-13.

28. *na vikalpadvayaṁ sakṛd iti nyāyāt* । — Ibid., 8.13.

29. *tatra pratyakṣam kalpanāpoḍham abhrāntam* । — Ibid., 7.18.

Dharmakīrti to make an extended interpretation of Diṅnāga's thought. However, there were some commentators who did not follow Dharmakīrti and interpreted Diṅnāga in a different way. According to them the reason why Diṅnāga did not include the word *abhrānta* in his definition of perception was that even erroneous cognitions such as the cognition of a yellow conch-shell for what is really a white conch-shell, are to be recognized as *pratyakṣa* inasmuch as they are not inconsistent in producing effects (*arthakriyāvisaṁvāda*). Thus they interpret the term *sataimira* in Diṅnāga's verse on erroneous perception, as derived from *timira* in the sense of *ajñāna* but not as meaning *indriyopaghātajam jñānam.*[30] But Dharmakīrti himself felt the need to include the term "non-erroneous" in his definition of perception because of his way of relating epistemology to ontology in his philosophical framework.

In Diṅnāga's philosophy, perception is knowledge. That is, without being able to name it, one can have knowledge of an object. Such direct perception does not entail conception. Since we can detect the knowledge to be an error only after the object gets a name, Diṅnāga thought that "non-erroneous" is not necessary in the definition of perception. Dharmakīrti also did not include conception within perception like Diṅnāga. But he regarded reality to have causal efficiency. This idea distinguished him from Diṅnāga. This epistemology of Dharmakīrti is an idea of the Śautrāntika school of thinking. Dharmakīrti defined valid cognition as that which does not contradict with reality and not contradicting with reality, for him, is producing the useful action. In the philosophy of Dharmakīrti the relation between the world of cognition and

30. *pīta-śaṁkhādi-buddhīnāṁ vibhrame 'pi pramāṇatām* ।
artha- kriyāvisamvādād apare sampracakṣate ॥ — *TS*, 1324.

the reality of the outside world is very important. According to him, the object which serves our purpose alone is real. In his epistemology he recognized perception and inference to be the only means of obtaining true cognition. Perception is free from conceptions and is non-erroneous. Errors arise where the sense organs are affected by eye disease or other extraneous factors like rapid motion, speed of the boat, etc. Sense organs which are affected by such factors cannot present the object correctly; naturally from such presentation it is not possible to have satisfactory attainment of the object. In other words, knowledge which is produced by such erroneous perception cannot have causal efficiency. Thus even though there is no element of conception in perception it may be that one does not perceive the object correctly because of erroneous influence. To get rid of such knowledge of the object which does not entail *arthakriyā*, Dharmakīrti included the word *abhrānta* in his definition of perception.

Thus Dharmakīrti agreed with Diṅnāga in the following points: (1) perception is free from conceptual constructs (*kalpanāpoḍha*), (2) the object of perception is the bare particular (*svalakṣaṇa*), and (3) this knowledge is self-cognitive (*svasaṁvedana*). However, he did not believe that all self-cognitive knowledge is certain knowledge as Diṅnāga thought; his view, on the other hand, was that reality has causal efficiency and knowledge which corresponds with the real object is only valid. Since Diṅnāga considered that an object is knowledge itself and that there is no room for knowledge to contradict the object, for him there is no possibility of knowledge being erroneous. Consequently he did not feel any necessity to define perception in terms of "non-erroneous cognition" which Dharmakīrti did. It is the basic outlook towards knowledge that accounts for the difference of the two thinkers.

6

Varieties of Perception

PERCEPTION, according to the Buddhists, is of four varieties — sense-perception (*indriya-pratyakṣa*), mental perception (*mānasa-pratyakṣa*), self-consciousness (*svasaṁvedana*) and yogic apprehension (*yogījñāna*). These four varieties of perception are to be mentioned in the order as stated. Durveka Miśra has offered a justification for maintaining this sequence. Since sense-perception is a part of all our activities it is stated first in the list. Mental perception is stated second in the order because this mental perception originates by depending on sense-perception. Self-cognition is stated after it because it is apprehensible in itself and its existence can be determined with certainty. As the apprehension of the omniscient person occurs as a whole and it is the ultimate goal of human beings, it is stated last in the order. That is, there is a gradation towards certainty among the four varieties of perception. Hence, there is a definite reason for presenting the varieties of perception in such an order and it is not a matter of whims.[1]

1. *abhimataṁ caturvidhaṁ pratyakṣaṁ darśayitavyam* । *taccaikadā vaktum aśakyatvāt krameṇa vacanīyam* । *kramaścaivaṁvidho 'stvanyādṛśo vā kim atrādareṇeti indriyajñānādirīdṛśaḥ kramaḥ kṛtaḥ* । *athānyadapyasya nimittamastīti? anyad apyastītyucyate* । *tathā hi sarvasya sarvavyavahārāṅgam indriyajñānam iti tadādito 'bhihitam* । *tenaivendriyajñānena tathābhūtena, mānasaṁ janyata iti tadanu mānasaṁ vyākhyātam* । *tasya paścāt pratyātmavedyatayā 'stitvena* →

Sense-Perception

Of these four, sense-perception may be described as the perception by the senses or due to the senses.[2] To be specific, it is that variety of cognition which originates by depending on the five external sense organs[3] like eye, etc. and has as its object the five external qualities like colour, etc.[4] For example, visual cognition has colour as its object, the olfactory one has smell for its object, the gustatory one has taste for its object, the auditory one has sound for its object and the tactual cognition has touch for its object. The designation "sense-perception" is due to the fact that this variety of perception has sense organs as their "specific cause" (*asādhāraṇa-hetu*). "Having sense organs as their specific cause" is a very important expression, since otherwise the definition would have been overly inclusive as it would be applicable to inferences about the senses. Inferences about the senses are also a variety of knowledge and they are about the senses. So if "sense-cognition" meant "cognition of the senses (*indriyasya jñānam*) it would include that variety of inferences. But as the term is restricted for cognition having sense organs as their specific

→ *śakyaniścayatayā ca svasaṁvedanam uditam । tataḥ sarvajñajñānasya sāmagrīmātrapradarśanatayā 'ntimapuruṣārthatayā cānte yogijñānam upadarśitam iti ।* — *DhP*, 58.16-22.

2. *yadindriyeṇa janyate tad indriyasya bhavati* — *DhP*, 57.6.

3. Though the word "sense organ" (*indriya*) has been used very widely to include different faculties, both empirical and transcendental, in the Buddhist literature, when the term is used in the context of perception it is used to refer to what we regard as sense organ in our ordinary usage, viz. the visual, gustatory, olfactory, auditory and tactual ones.

4. *cakṣurādīndriyapañcakāśrayeṇotpanna-bāhya-rūpādipañcaviṣayālambanaṁ jñānam indriyapratyakṣam ।* — *TBh*, 8.23-24.

causes, there is no chance for such inclusion as such inferences do not have sense organs as their causes.[5]

Now, sense-perceptions are due to the sense organs as also due to the objects for their occurrence. Then why is it that this variety of cognition is named after the sense organs only[6]? It is in reply to such a query that Vasubandhu has offered two reasons. (1) According as the sense organ is strong or weak, the cognition or *vijñāna* becomes clear or dim. As such the sense organs are regarded as the basis of such cognitions. (2) The sense organ is the specific cause. When a person has a visual cognition, he can realize that his own sense organ is the specific cause of it; the object like colour, etc. can be the object of valid cognitions of other individuals also at the same time. So the object cannot be regarded to belong to him uniquely to give rise to his cognition. Because of these two reasons, sense-perceptions are named after the sense organs and not after the objects.[7]

In the text *Pramāṇasamuccaya* Diṅnāga, and later on Dharmakīrti in his text *Pramāṇavārttika,* have mentioned the second argument of the *Abhidharmakośa* to justify the name "sense-perception."[8] Dharmakīrti has said that a name is to be taken after its indicator (*gamaka*). For example, if a sprout is

---

5. *nanu ced indriyānumānam api kāryaprabhavaṁ bhavatīndriyasya jñānam* । *tatas tasyāpi pratyakṣatvaṁ prāptam ityāha — indriyāśritamiti* । *āśritaṁ janyatayā tasmin satyeva bhāvāt* । *na cendriyānumānam indriyeṇa sākṣaj janyate, yena tasya pratyakṣatvaṁ syād iti bhāvaḥ* । — *DhP*, 57.7-9.

6. *sākṣāc ca jñāna-janane samartho viṣayo 'kṣavat* ।
atha kasmād dvayādhīnajanma tat tena nocyate ॥ — *PV*, II.191.

7. *tadvikāravikāritvād āśrayāś cakṣurādayaḥ* ।
ato 'sādhāraṇatvāc ca vijñānaṁ tair nirucyate ॥ — *AK*, I.45.

8. *asādhāraṇahetutvād akṣaistad vyapadiśyate* । — *PV*, II.1.

named as "sprout of barley" it can be understood that it has as its specific cause barley and not rice, but if it were named "sprout of earth" this name could not specify what it is, for it can be applied to sprout of barley and sprout of rice in the same way. Hence, to point to the nature of the object the specific cause (*asādhāraṇa hetu*) is to be considered as the indicator (*gamaka*). This is the practice followed in the case of sense-perception.[9] This explanation also makes it clear that even if *indriya-vijñāna* is interpreted as *indriyasya vijñānam* (cognition of the senses), it does not signify that the sense organs (*indriya*) are the agents. It simply points to the sense organs' being the specific cause of such cognitions.[10]

This variety of perception is regarded as valid cognition or *pramāṇa* only in those cases where it can give rise to a determinate cognition (a moment later) which corresponds very much to the sensation. In other words, this sense-perception is considered as valid only because it can generate a determinate cognition about the sensation.[11] The very validity of sense-perception depends on the generative efficiency of itself and it can be regarded as an efficient cause of cognition only when it exercises functioning and this functioning is nothing but the generation of conceptual knowledge of itself.

Mental Perception

Mental perception is defined as the cognition which is generated by sense-perception, which immediately precedes

9. *samīkṣya gamakatvaṁ hi vyapadeśo niyujyate* ।
taccākṣavyapadeśe 'sti tad dharmaśca niyojyatām ॥ — *PV*, II.192.

10. *indriyasya jñānaṁ pratyakṣam iti kathayatā nendriyasya draṣṭṛtvam iti darśitam* । — *DhP*, 57.10-11.

11. *tasmād adhyavasāyaṁ kurvad eva pratyakṣaṁ pramāṇaṁ bhavati* । — *NBT*, 16.7-8.

it and is its homogeneous cause and which co-operates with the immediately succeeding facsimile, i.e. the second moment of its proper object. In respect of cognition and in respect of object, mental perception and sense-perception are the same since they are co-operative with each other.[12] It may be noted here that Diṅnāga in his *Pramāṇasamuccaya* has regarded self-awareness to be one variety of mental perception. There he says that mental perception is of two kinds — awareness of an external object and self-awareness of such subordinate mental activities as desire and the like, and both of them are free from conceptual construction.[13] Jinendrabuddhi, the famous commentator of Diṅnāga, holds that the expression *artha-rāga-saṁvittiḥ* is to be analysed as *arthasaṁvittiḥ* and *rāgādi-svasamvittiḥ*. But Prajñākaragupta interprets the expression *sva* of Diṅnāga as "*svarūp*" and presents the definition of mental perception thus: *mānasam apyartha-rāgādi-svarūpa-saṁvedanam-akalpakatvāt pratyakṣam anubhavākāraḥ pravṛtteḥ*. Dharmakīrti, however, distinguishes *svasaṁvedana* of mental states like attachment (*rāga*), etc. from the mental perception. It is following Dharmakīrti that Mokṣakaragupta regards perception to be of four kinds. Even Jinendrabuddhi while interpreting Diṅnāga was influenced by Dharmakīrti in his explanation of mental perception. According to him, mental perception is that whose object is a derivative from the object of the immediately preceding sense-perception, viz. a thing of colour, etc. and it operates in the form of immediate experience being free from conceptual construction.[14]

---

12. *viṣayavijñānābhyāṁ hi manovijñānam ekaṁ kriyate yatas tadanayoḥ parasparasahakāritvam* । — Ibid., 59.1.

13. *mānasaṁ cārtharāgādi-svasaṁvittir akalpikā* । quoted by Hattori, in *Dignāga on Perception*, p. 92.

14. *mānasam api rūpādiviṣayālambanam avikalpakam anubhavākāra-pravṛttam* । quoted by Hattori, ibid., p. 93.

Regarding mental perception some objections are raised. First, if the mind perceives the same object that had been known by the sense organs in the immediately preceding moment, such mental perception cannot be considered valid as they are going against the concept of *pramā* as *anadhigatārthaviṣaya* — that *pramā* should always be about objects not previously known. Secondly, if to avoid this difficulty it is suggested that mental perception is able to apprehend external objects without the mediacy of sense-perception, then it would be possible for even the blind and the deaf to have perceptions of colours and sounds, since their mind is not as defective as their senses. Thirdly, the knowledge of the *yogin* would also be mental perception, and lastly it is not commonly apprehended.

It is not clear as to whether Diṅnāga himself was aware of these problems or not. But his commentator Dharmapāla mentions the first two of these in his commentary on *Ālambanaparīkṣā*.[15] But Dharmakīrti in the *Pratyakṣaparicchedaḥ* of *Pramāṇavārttika* mentions the first two of these objections[16] and answers them in his own framework.[17] (1) What is perceived by means of mental perception is the object in the moment that immediately follows the moment of sense-perception; therefore, there is no chance of apprehending what has already been apprehended. Since mental perception occurs by causes which immediately succeeds sense-perception, it is not possible by the mind to apprehend the object of sense-perception; it always apprehends an object other than that

15. For details vide Hattori, *Diṅnāga on Perception*, p. 93.

16. *pūrvānubhūtagrahaṇe mānāsyāpramāṇatā* ।
adṛṣṭagrahaṇe 'ndhāder api syād arthadarśanam ॥ — *PV*, II.239.

17. *tasmād indriyavijñānāntarapratyayodbhavam* ।
mano 'nyam eva gṛhṇāti viṣayaṁ nānyadṛk tataḥ ॥ — *PV*, II.243.

apprehended by sense-perception.[18] (2) Mental perception is conditioned by the immediately preceding sense-perception as its *samānāntara pratyayaḥ*. As the deaf and blind persons do not have any sense-perception regarding word or colour, it is not possible for them to have the mental perception produced by sense-perception. Hence the charge that admission of mental perception will lead to the denial of deaf or dumb persons is not justified.[19] If, as stated in the first reply, it is admitted that mental perception has as its object something different from the object of sense-perception, then is it not possible for the mental perception to apprehend anything in the past or in the future?[20] In answer it can be said that it is true that the object apprehended by the mental perception is something different from the object of sense-perception, but it is not unrelated either. The object of mental perception is preceded by the sense-perception in the previous moment. That is, it is similar to the momentary object of the first moment apprehended by preceding sense-perception. Accordingly, it cannot be said that any object whatsoever is apprehensible by mental perception. (3) Some consider that mental perception is the intellectual intuition of persons who by repeated practice of meditation upon the true state of all objects, have attained omniscience. In such case mental perception may be conceived as identical with the knowledge of the *yogīs*. Dharmottara, however, observes that there is a

---

18. *yata evaṁ tasmādindriyavijñānam evānantara-pratyayas tasmād udbhavo yasya tanmano mānasaṁ pratyakṣaṁ indriya-pratyakṣagrāhyād viṣayād anyam eva viṣayaṁ gṛhṇāti* । — *PVV*, 147.12-13.

19. *tata indiriyajñānajanyatvāt mānasasyāndhānāṁ cakṣurvijñānavikalānāṁ dṛgdarśanaṁ rūpasya na bhavati* । — *PVV*, 147.14-15.

20. *yady anyaviṣayagrāhakaṁ mānasam, tadā bhūtabhaviṣyadgrāhakam api syād* । — Ibid., 147.16.

basic difference between mental perception and perception of the seer. The former perception is conditioned by the immediately preceding sense-perception whereas the latter is unconditioned. Sense-perception is the *samanāntara pratyaya* in the case of mental perception whereas it is *ālambana pratyaya* in the case of a seer — a seer can have a direct insight in what other persons perceive.[21]

The reason for postulating mental perception of external objects is discussed by the post-Dharmakīrti scholars in different ways. Some accept it only because it is canonically established. The following *āgama* is quoted in justification of mental perception. Lord Buddha had said "O Monks! there are two way by which colour can be apprehended — by the eyes and then subsequently by the mind."[22] Dharmottara clearly says that there is no means to establish this variety of perception. But he accepts it simply because he does not find anything wrong in accepting it insofar as its nature has been explained by Dharmakīrti.[23] Jitāri omits this variety from his classification of perception. Some, however, maintain that mental perception is to be admitted as intermediary between

---

21. *idṛśenendriyavijñānenālambanabhūtenāpi yogijñānaṁ janyate* ı *tannirāsārthaṁ samanantarapratyayagrahaṇaṁ kṛtam* ı

— *NBT*, 59.2-3.

idṛśenetyādinā samanantarapratyayagrahaṇasya vyavacchedaṁ darśayati ı *idṛśena svaviṣayānantaraviṣayagrahaṇasahakāriṇā* ı *ālambyata iti ālambanabhūtaṁ rūpam yasya tena grāhya-svabhāvena satā janyata ityarthaḥ* ı *tasya yogijñānasya nirāsārthaṁ mānasatvanirākaraṇārtham* ı

— *DhP*, 59.17-20.

22. *bhikṣavo rūpaṁ gṛhyate, kadācit cakṣuṣā tadākṛṣṭena manasā ca* ı

— *TBh*, 9.17-18.

23. *etac ca siddhāntaprasiddhaṁ mānasaṁ pratyakṣam* ı *na tvasya prasādhakam asti pramāṇām* ı *evaṁ jātīyakaṁ tad yadi syāt na kaścid doṣaḥ syāditi vaktuṁ lakṣaṇam ākhyātam asyeti* ıı — *NBT*, 63.1-2.

sense-perception and conceptual construction in the *pramāṇa vyavasthā* set-up. In the framework of *pramāṇa vyavasthā* which is the position of the Buddhist epistemology, sense-perception and conceptual construction belong to two extremes in the apprehension of objects. Sense-perception grasps the bare particular which is beyond any description while the conceptual construction deals with the universal which are mental objects lacking external reality. Mental perceptions are perceptions on one hand and mental on the other. So unless such mental perceptions were admitted in the system, data collected through the senses could not be combined with mental constructs and consequently human activities based upon perception with regard to objects could never be possible.[24] Thus in reply to the objection of the opponents that when such a variety of perception is not applicable to common discourse what is the necessity for admitting it, the Buddhist view is that there is no logical fault in admitting such perception and further it fits with the words of Lord Buddha. Hence it has to be admitted as a variety of indeterminate perception.[25]

Self-cognition

Mind and all the mental states are self-cognized.[26] The self-cognizant mind is the cognition which apprehends the object in its general aspect only.[27] That which occurs in the mind is

24. *iha pūrvaiḥ — bāhyārthālambanam evaṁvidhaṁ manovijñānam astīti kuto 'vaseyam ity āśaṁkya, tadabhāve tadbalotpannānāṁ vikalpānām abhāvād rūpādau viṣaye vyavahārābhāvaprasaṁgaḥ syād ityuktam.* — *DhP*, 62.29-31

25. *idṛglakṣaṇayuktaṁ yadi mānasaṁ pratyakṣaṁ syāt, na kaścid doṣaḥ syād ityāgamasyāpi śuddhir anena pratipāditeti prayojanam* ı — *TBh*, 9.19-20.

26. *sarva-citta-caittānām ātmasaṁvedanam,* — *NB*, I.10.

27. *svasaṁvedanaṁ cittaṁ vastumātragrāhakaṁ jñānam,* — *TBh*, 9.21-22.

called the *caittāḥ*. It refers to those states which apprehend the specific aspects of the object and is of the nature of pleasure, pain or indifference.[28] There is no mental state which cannot be cognized directly.[29] Thus self-consciousness stands for that cognition by which the mind and all the mental state is apprehended. It can be described that self-cognition or the cognition cognizing itself is the result of the act of cognizing. Every cognition is produced in a two-fold appearance, namely that of itself as to the subject (*svābhāsa*) and that of the object (*viṣayābhāsa*). The cognizing of itself as possessing these two appearances or the self-cognition (*svasaṁvedana*) is the result of the cognitive act. Such sort of self-consciousness is conceived as indeterminate cognition since it is free from conceptual constructs and is unerring because its nature consists in direct intuition of the nature of itself.

The word *svasaṁvedana* or *svasaṁvitti* stands for the idea that a cognition is cognized by itself and does not need any other cognition to cognize itself. When a man has cognition of something as blue, he has the awareness of the cognition of something blue. This awareness is caused by nothing other than the cognition itself. Thus the cognition, while cognizing the object cognizes itself just as a lamp illuminates itself while illuminating an object. In *Tattvasaṁgraha*, Śāntarakṣita defines self-cognition as such cognition which does not need any other cognizant to cognize itself, nor does it ever remain unapprehended.[30]

---

28. *citte bhavāś caittāḥ* I *vastuno viśeṣarūpagrāhakāḥ sukha-duḥkhopekṣālakṣaṇāḥ* I — *TBh*, 9.22-23.

29. *nāsti sa kācit cittāvasthā yasyām ātmanaḥ saṁvedanaṁ na pratyakṣaṁ syāt* I — *NBT*, 64.5-6.

30. *svarūpa-vedanāyānyad vedakaṁ na vyapekṣate* I
na cāviditam astīdam ityartho 'yaṁ svasaṁvidaḥ II — *TS*, 2012.

This theory of self-cognition is admitted by both the Sautrāntika and the Yogācāra schools alike. That consciousness itself appears as subject (*svābhāsa*) and object (*viṣayābhāsa*) is a principal doctrine of the Yogācāra school. In stating that self-consciousness is the result of the act of cognizing, Diṅnāga is expressing his affiliation to the Yogācāra school. In his *Ālambanaparīkṣā* Diṅnāga examines different theories regarding the object of cognition and ultimately comes to the conclusion that the object of cognition is nothing other than the appearance of the object in the cognition itself. When *svasaṁvitti* is regarded as the *pramāṇaphala*, the role of *pramāṇa* which takes the cognition as its *prameya* has to be attributed to the *svābhāsa* of the cognition itself. The Sautrāntika school of Buddhism also holds that *svasaṁvitti* is the *pramāṇaphala*. According to this school, when an external object (*bāhyārtha*) is brought to the cognition and the cognition comes to possess similarity to the form of the object, there arises the awareness of this cognition, viz. the *svasaṁvitti*. Inasmuch as the awareness is regarded as the *pramāṇaphala* the Sautrāntikas believe that the *prameya* in this case is the cognition itself and not the external object. The difference between the Yogācāras and the Sautrāntikas lies in the point that for the Sautrāntikas the external object is the *prameya*, the cognition's taking the form of the object is the *pramāṇa* and *svasaṁvedana* is the result; for the Yogācāras there is no external object. So cognition's taking the form of the object is the *prameya*, cognition's own form is the *pramāṇa* and the *svasaṁvedana* is the result.

Against self-cognition variety of perception, it has been objected that the theory of self-consciousness of cognitions and feeling is not tenable because the action of a thing towards its own self is a contradiction. For instance a dancing boy, however expert he may be, cannot climb on his own shoulder; the blade of a sword cannot cut itself; a body of fire cannot burn itself. Then how is it possible for a cognition or feeling to cognize or feel itself? The relation of the feeler and the felt is no other than the relation of the agent and the object (*kartr̥karma bhāva*); and the agent and object are well known to be distinct from each other. So the possibility of a cognition to apprehend itself is not justified. In reply, the Buddhists point out that the relation between the feeler and the felt in cognition is not to be understood as agent-object relation but as the relation of the determinant and the determinable one (*vyavasthāpaka-vyavasthāpya*). Just as a lamp illuminates itself, so is also knowledge considered to know itself. Knowledge because of its self-luminosity is distinguished from the insentient objects (*jaḍa-padārtha*), and so can be produced by its own cause.

Śāntarakṣita in his *Tattvasaṁgraha* has said that knowledge is opposed to insentient objects. This immateriality is nothing but the self-consciousness of the cognition.[31] Self-consciousness of knowledge is not to be understood as action and its agent, since knowledge being a single entity without compartment cannot be divided into knower, known and the knowing. In the *Pramāṇavārttikālaṁkāra* Prajñākaragupta has said that the agent, the object and the means are mere fictional constructs and not existent in reality. It is explained that the self touches itself by means of itself.[32] It is not possible that cognition and other mental states are illuminated by another cognition. For in order to be illuminated by another cognition, there are two possibilities — either that this other revealing cognition occurs simultaneously when those cognitions and feelings are

31. *vijñānaṁ jaḍarūpebhyo vyāvr̥ttam upajāyate* ।
iyam evātmasaṁvittir asya yājaḍarūpatā ॥ — *TS*, 2000.

32. *kalpitaḥ karmakartr̥ādiḥ paramārtho na vidyate, ātmānam ātmanaivātmā nihantīti nirucyate* । — *PVBh*, II.369.19.

occurring or that this cognition occurs at a different time. But none of these alternatives can be accepted as intelligible. If it is simultaneous, there can be no relation of the benefitting and the benefitted as in the case of the two horns of a cow. Nor can the revealing cognition be regarded as occurring later or at a different time, since by the time it has occurred, the former or that which is to be illumined has disappeared because of the momentary character of all things. In fact, the theory advocated by the Nyāya and some school of the Mīmāṁsā, that knowledge is cognized by another cognition is refuted by almost all the Buddhist thinkers. For example, Diṅnāga in his *Pramāṇasamuccaya* observes that if a cognition is held to be apprehended by another cognition there would arise the fallacy of infinite regress. Moreover, if knowledge were not regarded as self-cognizant then it would not be possible to state whether the object has been apprehended or not, for in order to apprehend the qualified, object the apprehension of the qualifier is essential. Nor in cognition, the object is the qualified one and the state of being known is the qualifier. Since "known" means "qualified by knowledge," if knowledge itself is not apprehended through its self-luminosity, how can the object qualified by the knowledge be apprehended? Just as if we do not know the stick, we cannot speak of the stick-holder, similarly unless knowledge were cognized we cannot speak of the object as known.

In support of the opponents anyone can argue like Trilocana that just as in the case of visual consciousness, it is possible to have the visual apprehension of colour even when the visual sense organ itself is not apprehended, similarly we can speak of the object apprehended even when we do not know the cognition. Such an argument will not be justified. For, the example does not fit in the present situation. For, the qualifier of colour is not the visual sense organ but the visual consciousness. Then when such visual consciousness is not cognized, how can colour be cognized? Thus the argument of Trilocana is not sound. In fact, when the realist philosophers of the Nyāya and Mīmāṁsā school argue that cognition makes known an object by keeping itself in the background, they offer sense organs as an example. But the analogy of sense organ is not a justified one as it ignores a fundamental difference between cognition and sense organs. The sense organ is the efficient cause, the *causa essendi* of cognition whereas cognition only reveals the object already in existence. It has no generative efficiency, it is a mere *causa cognoscendi* in regard to the object.

As the manifestation of cognition cannot be explained by any other means, therefore, it has to be admitted that whatever is manifested is manifested because it is produced out of its own causes.

Yogic Apprehension

Apart from these three types of perception, the Buddhists admit a fourth variety which is the mystic intuition. In his *Pramāṇasamuccaya*, Diṅnāga has said that "the *yogin*'s intuition of a thing in itself unassociated with the teacher's instruction is also a type of perception. Since the intuition of a mystic is not associated with any conceptual construction, even the authoritative words of the teachers, and apprehends only a thing in itself, it is regarded as a case of perception. The Jaina logician Akalaṁka objects that since Diṅnāga has defined perception as that which bears close relationship with the sense organs, he cannot speak of the yogic apprehension, since it has nothing to do with the senses. To meet this objection Dharmottara has already argued that the word *pratyakṣa* though etymologically means knowledge arising out of the senses, actually stands for direct or immediate apprehension. And since the yogic apprehension is a case of immediate apprehension of the particulars there is no difficulty in admitting such apprehension as a variety of perception. The term *yoga* means concentration (*samādhi*) and also wisdom (*prajñā*) and it is characterized by intent alertness of the mind on one particular topic (*cittaikāgratālakṣaṇaḥ*). This wisdom is that which discerns the truth of all objects totally without any termination.[33] A person possessing such wisdom is regarded as a *yogī*. Durveka Miśra in his commentary remarks that when Dharmottara and his followers have identified *samādhi* or concentration with *prajñā* or wisdom, they are following the usual practice. In the *Pramāṇaviniścayaḥ* another interpretation is offered. That is, it is the capacity to discriminate *viveka-karaṇaśakti*. So in the ultimate stage the mystic is not only able to apprehend the true nature of the objects, but make distinctions among the momentary particulars.[34]

The nature of such wisdom has been described as that which is produced after the termination of intensive meditation on a true object (*bhūtārthabhāvanā-prakarṣa-paryantajam*). This "true object" means "the object derived through valid cognition (*pramāṇopapannārthaḥ*). *Bhāvanā* or meditation means repeated ascription of the mind. The knowledge which originates after the termination of intensive meditation on the true nature of object is called the Yogic apprehension, and such apprehension is free from conceptual

33. *niḥśeṣa-vastutattva-vivecikā prajñā yogo asyāsti iti yogī.*
— *TBh*, 11.2-3.

34. *samādhiścittaikāgratā* । *iha dharmottareṇa lokaprasiddhir-āśritā* । *viniścayatīkāyāṁ tu śāstrasthitis tenāvirodhaḥ* । *yadvā samādhi-grahaṇasyopalakṣaṇatvāt prajñā ca viveka-karaṇa-śaktir draṣṭavyā 'sa yasyāsti sa nityasamāhito viveka-karaṇa-tatparaśca yogī* ।
— *DhP*, 72.19-22.

construction and is non-erroneous. The true nature of the object is the fourfold noble truth, suffering, the causes of suffering, extinction of suffering and the means of such extinction. We should concentrate on the nature of the object as constituted by the five *skandhas*, as momentary, as void, as devoid of any soul but full of suffering, etc. And this truth is also consistent with the truth that "what is real is momentary" obtained through inference.

In his commentary on *Nyāyabindu,* Dharmottara divides the meditation process into three stages — *bhāvanāprakarṣa* in which a *yogin*'s vision begins to be clear, *prakarṣaparyantāvasthā* in which the *yogin* contemplates the object as though it were veiled by a thin cloud just as when one looks at the object through a smoked glass, and *yoginaḥ pratyakṣam* in which the object is perceived as clearly as it were a small grain on his palm.[35] Thus the *yogin*'s contemplation proceeds through two stages and reaches its highest form in the third stage. The second stage continues till the *yogin* is able to reach his highest stage of enlightenment, when he is able to have a clear and distinct idea of the nature of all objects. The clarity of apprehension reaches its final form only in this third stage. As such the yogic apprehension is described to be borne out of *prakarṣaparyantyāvasthā* where the *yogin* has a direct apprehension of the object but with less clarity. In his commentary on the *Nyāyabindu,* Vinītadeva mentions certain other subdivisions in the first stage, i.e. *bhāvanāprakarṣa*. According to him this stage comprises four degrees *smṛtyupasthāna, uṣmagata, mūrdham* and *kṣānti;* the

---

35. *tadiha sphuṭābhatvārambhāvasthā bhāvanāprakarṣaḥ* । *abhraka-vyavahitam iva yadā bhāvyamānaṁ vastu paśyati sā prakarṣaparyantāvasthā* । *karatalāmalakavad bhāvyamānasyārthasya yad darśanaṁ tad yoginaḥ pratyakṣam* । — *NBT*, 68.4–69.2.

prakarṣaparyanta is the same as *laukikāgra dharma*. After that comes the decisive moment, the meditating man suddenly acquires the faculty of transcendental intuition, he changes completely, it is another *pudgala*, a saint, an *ārya*, a *bodhisattva*.

Such yogic intuition is regarded as a case of perception for it satisfies both the requirements of perception, viz. being free from conceptual construction and being unerring. Since it is a case of clear and distinct apprehension of objects, it is unerring. But why is it indeterminate? In the notion of the Buddhists what is unerring cannot be determinate. The possibility of determinate cognition arises when we are able to compare the present representation of the object with the past representations and this comparison is possible only in the second moment and by that time the object is no longer there. So just as our past knowledge is only apparently real, so also the object of the past knowledge is apparent and it cannot be actually real. So determinate cognition cannot give us a proper picture of the actual object. As such that which has been regarded as clear and distinct has to be indeterminate. In other words yogic apprehension is indeterminate because it is unerring.

7

Erroneous Perception

PERCEPTION, in general, is believed to give us definite knowledge regarding an object. Still it cannot be denied that perception does not always give us correct representation of the object. That is, there are cases where our perception is erroneous. Such erroneous perception may be of two types — perception of one object as another and perception of an object in a place where there is no such object at all. These two types of erroneous perception are technically known as illusion and hallucination respectively. Just as in respect of definition of perception Indian philosophers offer different views, in respect of erroneous perception also they offer explanations which differ from each other. Let us concentrate on the views of the Buddhist philosophers, especially those of Diṅnāga and Dharmakīrti, in this regard.

In the first chapter of *Pramāṇasamuccaya,* Diṅnāga after discussing perception as that variety of cognition which is free from conceptual construction in one verse, in the subsequent commentary, has referred to the cases of erroneous cognition:

> erroneous cognition, cognition of empirical reality, inference, its result, recollection and desire are not true perceptions and are accompanied by obscurity.[1]

1. *bhrāntis saṁvṛtisajjñānam anumānānumānikam* ।
smaraṇaṁ cābhilāṣaś cetyakṣābhāsaṁ sataimiram ॥ — *PS,* verse 8.

In his *Vṛtti,* Diṅnāga explains three types of *pratyakṣābhāsa* thus :

> erroneous cognition is not perception because it conceptually constructs such object as water out of vapour.

Cognition of empirical reality (*saṁvṛttisajjñāna*) is not perception as it superimposes (*āropa*) on empirical reality something else. In other words, it conceptually constructs empirical reality as absolute reality. Inference, its results are not true perceptions, as they are conceptual constructions of previous experience (*pūrvānubhūta kalpanā*).

To present his view: "The erroneous cognition of conceiving water in the case of mirage is a case of defective perception. The cognition of empirical object is not true perception for it superimposes something extraneous upon things which are only empirically true and thus functions through the conceptualization of the forms of those objects. Inference and its results are also not true perception since they result from the conceptualization of what had been felt previously."[2]

Jinendrabuddhi in his commentary observes that Diṅnāga has mentioned a fourth variety in addition to these three varieties of erroneous perception, namely, *satimiram* or cognitions due to the defects of sense organs, thus amounting to four varieties of *pratyakṣābhāsa.* The difference between the first three varieties of *pratyakṣābhāsa* and the fourth one lies in the fact that the first three sorts are produced by conceptual construction, while the fourth variety is free from conceptual construction. The word *satimira* is interpreted by

2. *atha marīcikādiṣu jalādikalpanāt bhramajñānaṁ pratyakṣābhāsam* । *saṁvṛtisatyaṁ hi svasmin arthāntaram āropya tatsvarūpakalpanāt pratyakṣābhāsam* । *anumānaṁ tatphalaṁ ca pūrvānubhavakalpanāt na pratyakṣam* । — *PSV*, p. 21.

Jinendrabuddhi as something caused by the defect of sense organ (*indriyopaghātajam jñānam*), as for example *timira* or the eye-disease which causes the perception of a white object as yellow. In enumerating these three varieties of erroneous perception, Diṅnāga is actually confirming the view of his predecessor Vasubandhu. Vasubandhu in his *Vādavidhi* has presented the definition of perception as the "cognition which originates from the object"[3] because it effectively rules out *bhrānti jñāna, saṁvṛtti jñāna*, and *anumāna jñāna*.

Regarding the number of *pratyakṣābhāsa*s really admitted by Diṅnāga there is a controversy among his modern interpreters. On the basis of Diṅnāga's own statement, Hattori holds that Diṅnāga accepted only three varieties of *pratyakṣābhāsa*s all of which are due to conceptual construction. Hattori interpreted "the word *satimiram* as an objective modifying *pratyakṣābhāsam* . . . and not as mentioning a separate kind of *pratyakṣābhāsa*". Alex Wayman, on the other hand, mainly relying on Kamalaśīla's writings on the subject, came to the conclusion that Diṅnāga actually accepted four *pratyakṣābhāsas*, there being four kinds of errors involved and they correspond with four kinds of perception. To support his analysis, Wayman puts forward the following association:

Causes of error	**Types of perception**
Error due to object (*viṣayagata*)	Mental perception (*mānasa pratyakṣa*)
Error due to place (*bāhyāśrayasthita*)	Perception of *yogin* (*yogipratyakṣa*)

3. *tato 'rthāj jātaṁ jñānaṁ pratyakṣam.*

Error found within (*adhyātmagata*)	Self-awareness (*svasaṁvedana*)
Error due to senses (*indriyagata*)	Sense perception (*indriya pratyakṣa*)

This interpretation of Wayman does not seem to be convincing to other writers, for example to Eli Franco. As regards the second variety of errors, which Wayman has associated with *yogīpratyakṣa*, it is really difficult to accept as to how moving trees seen from a boat can be associated with a *yogin* only since this is an illusion to which ordinary persons are subject. Secondly, Wayman takes it for granted that Diṅnāga accepted four varieties of perception, which is highly doubtful, since it is not based on Diṅnāga's own words, but on Dharmakīrti's reshuffle of them. Hence Eli Franco's observation in his paper "Once again on Dharmakīrti's deviation from Diṅnāga" (JIP, 14) is that Diṅnāga held only three *pratyakṣābhāsa*s rather than four.

Dharmakīrti, however, holds that there are actually four varieties of erroneous perception, three of which arise because of conceptual construction and the other one, though devoid of conceptual construction arises because of defects in the sense organs which are the seat of perception.[4] The first three varieties of erroneous perception are explained by his commentator Manorathanandi: The three varieties of erroneous perception which are conceptual cognition are — (1) erroneous cognition superimposing water in mirage, (2) empirical cognition superimposing reality to empirical objects, and (3) inferential

4. *trividhaṁ kalpanājñānan, āśrayopaplavodbhavam* ।
avikalpakam ekaṁ ca pratyakṣābhaṁ caturvidham ॥ — *PV*, II.288

cognition arising through the conception of identity between the present object and what had been perceived earlier. Thus all these three varieties of erroneous perceptions arise because of conceiving one thing for another. That is, the error in the three cases are due to the constructive part of the human thinking. Hence, Dharmakīrti clubs them together and regards them as *kalpanājñānam* or conceptual cognition. But there is another variety where the erroneous perception is not due to such conceptual capacity but to the defects of the sense organs themselves, which are actually the instruments of perception. Example of such non-conceptual erroneous perception is that of perceiving the white shell as yellow. Since the ailment of jaundice affects the eyesight, the individual suffering from that disease will perceive the white colour of the object as yellow. Thus Dharmakīrti's own words are clear enough to speak for themselves that there are four varieties of erroneous perception, three produced by conception (*kalpanā*) and the fourth produced by the defects of sense organs.

Dharmakīrti was explicitly aware of the distinction drawn between error due to sense organs (*indriyaja bhrānti*) and error due to conception (*vikalpaja bhrānti*). As such he insisted that *pratyakṣa* must be defined as *abhrānta*. Without the inclusion of this term *abhrānta*, the definition of *pratyakṣa* would have applied to cases of perceptual error which are not due to wrong interpretation by the intellect. In the case of *vikalpaja bhrānti*, that is when the conceptual capacity of the mind superimposes the concept of snake on the presented rope, the error is removed when one is convinced by reasoning that the object in front is a rope. But the experience of a double moon will continue as long as the defect of the eye remains. Even if a man is rationally convinced that there cannot be double moon in the sky, he will continue to have the illusion. Hallucinations of fiery columns in water are vivid visions.

They lack the vagueness which characterizes conceptual construction. Since vividness is a characteristic feature of sensory perception, such hallucinations must be regarded as sensory aberrations. They cannot be understood as misrepresentation of one thing as another, as there is no such "other thing."

In a later verse Dharmakīrti says that the word *satimira* had been stated by Diṅnāga to note an exception to his definition of perception as "free from conceptual construction" (*kalpanāpoḍha*). If perception were defined as being free from conceptual construction, then erroneous perception or *pratyakṣābhāsa* would have to be considered as genuine perception since they are also perceptions free from conceptual construction. So to exclude this variety, Diṅnāga has added the term *satimira* to suggest that erroneous perception is not only free from conceptual construction but at the same time is originated by the defects in the sense organs. In that case the term *satimira* stands for cognition arising out of the defects of the sense organs (*indriyopaghātajam jñānam*).[5]

This sort of difference of opinion arises because of Diṅnāga himself. While discussing the Nyāya definition of perception as the cognition that is produced by the contact of the sense organ with the object and which is inexpressible, non-contradictory and is of determinate character,[6] Diṅnāga had stated that there is no necessity for mentioning such attributes as *avyabhicārī* or *avyapadeśya*, etc. in the definition of perception since the cognition produced by sense-object contact (*indriyārthasannikarṣa*) is always free from error, while illusion

5. *apavādaścaturtho 'tra tenoktam upaghātajam* ।
kevalaṁ tatra timiram upaghātopalakṣaṇam ॥ — *PV*, II.293.

6. *indriyārthasannikarṣotpannaṁ jñānamavyapadeśyamavyabhicāri vyavasāyātmakaṁ pratyakṣam.* — *NS*, 1.1.4.

is caused by the conceptual capacity of the mind for the object. This indicates that in the opinion of Diṅnāga, errors are always caused by the mind through its conceptual construct. As perception is free from conceptual construction, there is no chance of error in the case of perception. This shows that in the opinion of Diṅnāga erroneous perceptions are due to the mind and not to the sense organs.

Dharmakīrti, however, justifies his own reading of Diṅnāga by saying that though Diṅnāga had highlighted the role of mind in the origination of errors in most cases, he did not ignore the role of the sense organs in the occurrence of illusion as is evident not only from his use of the word *sataimirika* but also from another passage where he has recognized that defects in the sense organs are responsible for the perception of yellow colour or of double-moon, etc. In verse 294 of the second chapter of *Pramāṇavārttikam*, Dharmakīrti says that there are some who hold that error is a mental phenomenon; but their view is refuted or contradicted since the causes of such cognition as of yellow or of double moon, etc. are the sense organs also.[7]

Dharmakīrti, himself, believes that erroneous perception does not always occur because of mind but also because of defects in the sense organ. He establishes this point with the help of the following arguments: If the erroneous perception of double-moon was due to mind, this would involve the following absurd conclusions. (1) The error would be removed even when the defect of the sense organ is not cured, just as the erroneous mental cognition of snake for a rope or silver

7. *mānasaṁ tad apītyeke teṣāṁ grantho viruddhyate* ।
nīla-dvi-candrādi-dhīyāṁ hetur akṣāṇyapītyayam ॥ — *PV*, II.294.

for a shell is removed simply by the close examination of the object. (2) The error would not be removed even when the defect of the sense organ is cured. (3) A man with a sound sense organ would also have the erroneous perception of double moon when he hears about it from a person who has such a defective sense organ. (4) It would not be immediate to the sense organs but mediated by memory, just as the illusion of snake in a rope depends on the memory of the formerly perceived snake and as such it would not be vivid (*parisphuṭana*) which it actually is.[8] Manorathanandi in his commentary on the *Pramāṇavārttikam* tries to make the argument of Dharmakīrti explicit by pointing out that if defect in the sense organs is not admitted, the erroneous cognition of yellow colour or of double moon would not be possible. These arise just like other results of the changing states of sense organs. Then, why are they regarded as errors? This is because the cognition of double-moon or of the yellow colour are the results of sense organs which are affected by particular disease of the eyes; and because of such defects the sense organ which has the nature of revealing physical objects cannot reveal the physical object and becomes the cause of error.[9]

Dharmakīrti believes that there are two types of erroneous perception — those which arise out of conceptual constructions

---

8. *sarpādi-bhrāntivac cāsyāḥ syād akṣavikṛtāv api* ।
nivṛttir na nivartteta nivṛtte 'py akṣaviplave ॥
kadācid anyasaṁtāne tathaivārpyeta vācakaih ।
dṛṣṭa-smṛtim apekṣeta na bhāseta parisphūtam ॥ — *PV*, II. 297-98

9. *na hīndriyavyāpāram antareṇa taimirikajñānam utpadyate* । *indriyavikāreṇa vikriyāvat jñānam aindriyaṁ cet? dvicandrādijñānānāṁ timirādi indriyavikāreṇa vikriyā, saiveyam abhūtārthopadarśanātmikā bhrāntatvanimittam uktāḥ asmābhiḥ kiṁ niṣidhyate* ।
— Manorathanandī, on *PV*, II.296.

and those which are free from mental construction but arise because of defects of the sense organs themselves. It is because of this that Diṅnāga has classified erroneous perception into two classes — indeterminate (*avikalpaka*) and determinate (*savikalpaka*).[10] This interpretation of Dharmakīrti is not, however, supported by modern scholars on Diṅnāga. Hattori in his *Diṅnāga on Perception* remarks that "Diṅnāga defines *pratyakṣa* simply as *kalpanāpoḍha* and regards the qualifier *avyabhicārin* in the Nyāya definition of *pratyakṣa* as unnecessary. As I see it, Diṅnāga did not take into consideration errors caused by defective sense organs when he defined *pratyakṣa* and mentioned *pratyakṣābhāsa* in the above verse. Perhaps later on Diṅnāga's definition was subjected to criticism when recognized that *manas* is not the only cause of erroneous cognitions and this criticism propelled Dharmakīrti into making an extended interpretation of Diṅnāga's thought.[11]

Thus according to Hattori's interpretation Diṅnāga did not admit cases of illusion caused by the defects of sense organs, rather they are all to be caused by the mind. Hattori's interpretation of Diṅnāga gets supported by the fact that Diṅnāga did not see any necessity to admit the epithet *abhrānta* or non-erroneous in the definition of perception. But Dharmakīrti could not remain content by taking into consideration the indeterminate character of perception alone; he felt the necessity to add the property *abhrānta* or non-erroneous also in the definition of perception. Thus his

---

10. *tasmāt 'kalpanāpoḍham' ityukte timirajñānasyāvikalpe nirvikalpakatve 'pi sati prāmāṇyaṁ pratyakṣātmakaṁ prāptaṁ 'sataimiram 'ityapavādena visaṁvādāt pratiṣidhyate; saṁvādalakṣaṇātvāt prāmāṇyasya* । *tadartham upaplutajñānanivṛttyarthaṁ cācāryadignāgena pratyakṣābhaṁ saṁkṣepato dvidhoktam — savikalpakam avikalpakañca* ।

— Ibid., II.300

11. *Diṅnāga on Perception*, p. 97.

definition of perception is — perception is that variety of valid cognition which is non-erroneous and free from conceptual construction.[12] In other words, perception, according to Dharmakīrti, stands for direct cognition of the object and which is free from mental construction and is non-erroneous.[13] However, regarding the import of the term *abhrānta* or non-erroneous in his definition, there is a controversy among the interpreters of Dharmakīrti. According to Vinītadeva the term "non-erroneous" means "not illusory", i.e. which is not contradictory in respect of the knowledge that makes one reach the object,[14] while Dharmottara interprets the term as "not contradictory to the causal efficiency feature of the object."[15]

In explaining what he considers to be *bhrama* or error, Dharmakīrti points to four cases — (1) defective vision (*taimirika*), (2) rapid movement (*āśubhrama*), (3) travelling on a fast-moving vehicle (*nauyāna*), and (4) physical disorder (*saṁkṣobha*). Commentator Dharmottara has given illustration of these four varieties to show that these four cases of erroneous perception are due to different causes. For example, (1) morbid vision is a kind of disease that affects the eyes. So it is a case of illusion whose cause is located in the sense organ. (2) Rapid movement is the movement of a circling fireband which makes one think that there is a fire circle. Accordingly the cause of this illusion is located in the object of knowledge. (3) Travelling on a fast-moving vehicle like a boat or a train, makes one feel that the

---

12. *tatra pratyakṣaṁ kalpanāpoḍham abhrāntam* — *NB*, 40.I.4.

13. *yat tat bhavatām asmākaṁ cārtheṣu sākṣātkārijñānaṁ prasiddhaṁ tat kalpanāpoḍhābhrāntatvayuktaṁ draṣṭavyam* — *NBT*, 40.8-9.

14. *na bhrāntam abhrāntam, prāpakaviṣaye avisaṁvādakam iti śeṣaḥ* I Vinītadevaṭīkā, p. 7.

15. *abhrāntam arthakriyākṣame vasturūpe 'viparyaṣṭam ucyate* I *arthakriyākṣamaṁ ca vasturūpaṁ sanniveśopādhivarṇātmakam* I *tatra yan na bhrāmyati tad abhrāntam* — *NBT*, 41.5–42.3.

trees on the side of the railway track or on the shore of the river are moving in the opposite direction. The cause of this illusion belong to the object where the knower is situated. (4) Physical disorder is exhaustion caused by the disturbance of the gaseous (*vāyu*) and bileous (*pitta*) elements of the body. Because of such disturbance the individual has the erroneous experience of a burning pillar. This illustrates the internal cause of illusion. Jitāri in his *Tarkasopāna* holds that knowledge is regarded as erroneous, when due to any of these four causes — eye-disease, rapid movement, or being in a fast-moving object or change in the physical elements — it does not reveal the true nature of the object.[16]

Elaborating all the four varieties of erroneous perception stated by Dharmakīrti, Dharmottara observes that the occurrence of the first three varieties of illusion is due to something external to the individual whereas the fourth one is due to cause within the individual himself.[17] However, all of these causes, finally affect the sense organs and as such the individual has erroneous experiences. If the sense organs were not at all affected, i.e. if the sense organs remained quite normal, there would not be any illusory perception. So the upshot is that disorder in the sense organs is the ultimate cause of erroneous perception.[18]

---

16. *bhrāntam api jñānaṁ timirāśubhramaṇa nauyāna-saṁkṣobhādyā hitavibhramam artharūpavisaṁvādakam* । *tat katham anyathāsthitam arthaṁ sākṣātkuryāt svarūpapratibhāsasya sākṣātkaraṇaśabdavācyatvāt tasmānnāsti vastusākṣātkaraṇaṁ vibhramasyāpi iti siddham* ।
— *Minor Buddhist Texts*, ed. G. Tucci.

17. *ādhyātmikāśrayasthā vibhramahetavo gṛhyante* । — *NBT*, 55.12.

18. *sarvaireva ca vibhramakāraṇair indriyaviṣayabāhyādhyātmikā āśrayagatair indriyam eva vikartavyam* । *avikṛte indriye indriyabhrāntyayogāt* ।
— *NBT* 55.7-8

Dharmakīrti in his *Pramāṇavārttika* has said that the appearance of hair is without an object.[19] Manorathanandi has elaborated it and said that the appearance of hair-tuft to a person suffering from the *timira* disease, is objectless for there is absence of hair in the actual world.[20] In his commentary *Pramāṇavārttikabhāṣya* another commentator of Dharmakīrti, Prajñākaragupta has offered an explanation as to why the appearance of hair-tuft is considered as a case of erroneous perception[21] since it does not satisfy the basic conditions of valid perception. According to him, perception of an object arises when the sense organ is influenced by that object. So in the absence of the object, the perception of that object would be contentless. This is the case with the perception of the hair-tuft. In the case of such variety of illusory perception, as the awareness occurs without object, one cannot have successful activity being guided by such perception.[22] Since success of activity is the determinant of the validity of knowledge, it follows that such variety of perception is not valid, rather erroneous.[23]

Dharmakīrti, thus, differs from his preceptor Diṅnāga by reintroducing the characteristic "non-erroneous" (*abhrānta*) in the definition to eliminate the cases of illusion caused by

19. *keśapratibhāsam anarthakam* । — *PV*, II.9.

20. *taimirika-keśa-pratibhāsaṁ jñānamanarthakaṁ bāhyakeśābhāvāt* ।
— *PVV*, 87.30-31.

21. *athaitad indriyajñānam arthābhāve bhramo mataḥ* ।
svasaṁvittis tu naivākṣāt tadvināpi pravartanāt ॥ — *PVB*, 181.3.

22. *tasmād indriyam artha eva pravarttate tadabhāve 'narthakaṁ tat syāt* । *keśajñānam anarthakaṁ na tatra keśaprāptiḥ* । *tato 'rthāpekṣayā 'narthakam iti niścayaḥ* । — *PVB*, 181.8-10.

23. *keśādiviṣayañcāpramāṇam eva vijñānam* । *tathā hi pramāṇaṁ avisaṁvādi jñānaṁ iti sāmānyalakṣaṇe kṛte viṣayabhedena tadbheda upapādyate* । — Ibid., 180.3-5.

defective sense organs. His point is that we have to distinguish between illusion of the sense organs and illusion of the understanding. When we mistake a rope for a snake or a shell for silver, this illusion is caused by the wrong interpretation of the object presented to the sense organs. This illusion ceases as soon as we bring light and discover that the object is a rope (or a shell) and not a snake (or silver). But if a man sees a double moon because of the eye disease, which makes him see everything double, this illusion will continue, even when he is convinced that the moon is single.

What we have so far noted is mainly the discussion of those erroneous perceptions where one thing is understood as something else. If we look again into the illustrations mentioned by Diṅnāga, viz. that of mirage, or that of empirical knowledge or that due to desire and other mental conditions, we notice that all of them are cases of illusion. Similarly the instances discussed by Dharmakīrti are cases of mistaking something for another. So the question naturally arises, do the Buddhist philosophers regard illusion as the only variety of erroneous perception? Or, do they admit hallucination as well? This is an important issue, because we find that the realist school of Indian philosophy, namely the Nyāya school does not admit hallucination. For, they believe that in the substantive part (*dharmī*), there can be no error. Error arises only in the case of attributes (*dharma*). The Yogācāra school of Buddhism are supporters of idealism; they do not admit the reality of external objects. So they can explain hallucination in their framework. But what about Dharmakīrti? Dharmakīrti is a supporter of the Sautrāntika school of Buddhism which may be described as a sort of Neo-realism admitting the reality of external objects. Then what will be his view of erroneous perception?

If we read the chapter on perception in the *Pramāṇavārttika* text along with the commentaries *Pramāṇavārttikabhāṣya* of Prajñākaragupta and *Pramāṇavārttikavṛtti* of Manorathanandi very carefully we find long discussion of the case of *keśondraka* or perception of hair-tuft or the vision of hair-tuft floating in the regions of the eye. In such perception, the individual perceives the hair-tuft when there is actually no hair-tuft in the external world. Even Dharmakīrti himself has recognized that perception of such hair occurs without an object. In *Pramāṇavārttikabhāṣya* commentator Prajñākaragupta has provided explanation as to why the appearance of hair-tuft is considered as a case of erroneous perception. According to him, perception of an object arises when the sense organ proceeds towards the object and so when there is no object knowledge due to the sense organs becomes objectless. In such cases the individual cannot attain the object with the help of the object. And as the success of an activity is the criterion of validity of knowledge, it follows that such perceptual awareness of the hair-tuft is not valid. This invalidity can be ascribed to the absence of the object in the actual world.[24] This suggests that Dharmakīrti and his commentator did not consider all cases of erroneous perception as illusion, but admitted the possibility of hallucinations also as cases of wrong perception.

---

24. *keśādiviṣayañcāpramāṇam eva vijñānam* । *tathāhi pramāṇam avisaṁvādijñānaṁ iti sāmānyalakṣaṇe kṛte viṣayabhedena tadbheda upapādyate* । . . . *indriyam artha eva pravarttate tadabhāve 'narthakaṁ tat syāt* । *keśajñānam anarthakam na tatra keśaprāptiḥ* । *tato 'rthāpekṣayā 'anarthakan iti niścayaḥ* । — *PVB*, 180.3–181.10

8

Inference

Its Nature

PRAMĀṆA or valid knowledge has been held by the Buddhists to be of two types — perception and inference. Of them perception is that variety of cognition where one can have direct apprehension of an object. Where the object cannot be directly perceived or directly apprehended, but can be only indirectly apprehended, then for that indirect apprehension of the object, one has to take recourse to inference.[1] Diṅnāga, however, had presented a definition of inference in his *Pramāṇasamuccaya* as — *nāntarīyakārthadarśanam tadvido 'numānam*. The experience of a thing which is inseparably connected with another thing is regarded as inference for a person who is cognizant of that inseparable connection. The meaning of this definition has been clarified thus — a thing which does not exist without another thing is regarded as being inseparably connected. The expression *nāntarīyakārthadarśanam* is to be analysed as the *darśana* or observation of the *nāntarīyakārtha* and the latter itself is a compound signifying that the *artha* or object here is *nāntarīyaka* or inseparably connected. In other words, *artha* is the subject whose attribute is *nāntarīyaka*, thus the compound as a whole is substantial. The word *tad* in the expression *tadvidoḥ* refers to the *nāntarīyakārtha* mentioned earlier.

---

1. *parokṣārthapratipatter anumānāśrayatvād eva* . . . — *HB*.

This definition has been quoted by Uddyotakara in his *Nyāyavārttika* (I.1.5). Though Uddyotakara has not mentioned the name of Diṅnāga as the formulator of this definition, but simply refers to it as *apare bruvate,* Vācaspati Miśra clearly attributes this definition beyond possibility of doubt to Diṅnāga[2] and seems to imply clearly that this definition has been offered in a passage immediately preceding that in which his famous formulation *anumeye atha tat-tulye* . . ., etc. occurs, that is in the Chapter II of *Pramāṇasamuccayaḥ*.[3]

This definition of Diṅnāga also is in consonance with the etymological analysis of the term *anumāna* as has been shown later by Dharmottara and others. From this, it may be said that while delineating the concept of inference the Buddhists are mainly relying on etymological analysis. Their impression may be that one who understands the very etymology of the term *anumāna* as "subsequent knowledge" does not need anything else to identify inference and distinguish it from the other *pramāṇa*s. But the case is different with *pratyakṣa,* the other variety of valid cognition. There the etymological meaning tells us merely that it is immediate apprehension (*sākṣātkārījñāna*). But the Buddhists intend to mean by *pratyakṣa* not merely this but also something more, namely that it is non-erroneous and that it is free from conceptual construction. These two features are not included in the etymological meaning. Accordingly it was necessary to present a separate definition of perception. In the case of inference if it is simply specified "to what it is subsequent to" the nature of inference can be grasped; hence, no need for any additional definition.

---

2. *tad anena dignāgasya lakṣaṇaṁ dūṣayitvā 'nyeṣāṁ lakṣaṇaṁ dūṣitam* . . . — *NVT.*
3. For detailed discussion vide Randle, *Fragments from Dignāga*, pp. 21–22.

In fact, if we take a look into the definition of inference as presented by other schools, like the Nyāya definition (*parāmarśajanyam jñānam anumitiḥ*) or the Jaina definition (*sādhanāt sādhyavijñānam anumānam*[4]) it can be seen that they are all relying on the etymological sense, since they are mentioning exactly from what knowledge does inference follow.

Nowhere in his different texts, Dharmakīrti has attempted to define inference. In his *Nyāyabindu* he starts the chapter on inference with classifying inferences into two varieties — inference for oneself and inference for others. Though he himself did not offer any reason for this, his commentator Dharmottara has provided us with an explanation. His argument is that these two varieties of inference are so different in nature from each other that it is not possible to present a definition which will be applicable to both of them.[5]

Without remaining satisfied by this excuse, if we insist on finding out what did the Buddhists really have in mind when they spoke about inference, we will have to look back in the introductory chapter of the text *Nyāyabindu*. There we find Dharmottara in course of explaining Dharmakīrti's classification of valid cognition into two types, offering an etymological analysis of the term *anumāna* and later on other Buddhist writers like Mokṣakaragupta, have simply followed that analysis of Dharmottara while explaining the nature of inference.

The term *anumāna*, according to Dharmottara, is derived from the two expressions *anu* and *mānam*. The term *mānam* is again a derivation from the root *mā* meaning "to know." Here

---

4. *Jaina Tarka Bhāṣā*, p. 12.

5. *tayor atyantabhedāt naikaṁ lakṣaṇaṁ asti* । — *NBT*, 87.4-5.

it is understood in the sense of instrumental cause (*karaṇa*)[6] of knowledge and in that sense as similar to knowledge.[7] The expression *anu* means later, subsequent. So taking the two expressions *anu* and *māna* together we obtain the sense "later or subsequent knowledge." But subsequent to what? In reply it is said by Dharmottara "subsequent to the apprehension of the probans and the rememberance of relation."[8] But simply by this the nature of inference is not made clear; for we have to say where the probans is to be apprehended and what is that relation. Accordingly Dharmottara spells out that we must have the knowledge of the probans as existent in the locus and also have memory regarding the relationship between the probans and the probandum, then subsequent to these two pieces of knowledge we can proceed to have inference. So, as inference is subsequent to these two knowledge-states, it is described as a subsequent apprehension.[9] To sum up, inference is the knowledge of an indirect object like fire (an object which is not directly apprehended at the time of inference) in a locus like a mountain (the standard Indian example of inference is "there is fire in the hill since we can perceive smoke there") and this knowledge arises subsequent to the apprehension of the probans, smoke, and also to the recollection of the relationship between the probans and the probandum both.[10]

---

6. *mīyate 'rtho 'neneti mānam* — *TBh.* 3.24.
7. *karaṇasādhanena mānaśabdena sārūpyalakṣaṇaṁ pramāṇam abhidhīyate* । — *NBT.*
8. *liṁgagrahaṇa-sambandhasmaraṇasya paścāt mānam anumānam* । — *NBT*, 39.6.
9. *gṛhīte pakṣadharme smṛte ca sādhya-sādhana-sambandhe 'numānaṁ pravarttata iti paścātkālabhāvyucyate.* — *NBT*, 39.6–40.1.
10. *liṁga-grahaṇa-liṁga-liṁgi-sambandha-smaraṇayoḥ paścāt yadvijñānaṁ parvatādau dharmiṇi parokṣavastvālambakaṁ tadevānumānaśabdenocyate iti rūḍhi-śabdād avagantavyam* । — *TBh*, 3.25-27.

Controversy Between the Nyāya and the Buddhists on Inference

There is a basic point of difference between the Buddhists and the Nyāya logicians regarding their attitude towards inference. For the former, inference or *anumāna* consists of a pure thought process, that is conceptual (*vikalpikā*); though it may be expressed through judgements when it is employed to convince others. It is possible to have inferences which are purely thought process and which is not verbally expressed. This variety of inference is regarded by the Buddhists as *svārthānumāna* or inference for oneself. When the inference is expressed in language, then they are sentential in nature and that form of inference is called *parārthānumāna*. Keith in his *Indian Logic and Atomism* holds that Diṅnāga was the first to introduce the distinction between inferences. But probably this distinction was prevalent in the older Nyāya school. However, so far as *parārthānumāna* is concerned, Diṅnāga admits like the Naiyāyikas that we have to take the help of propositions or judgements in order to make another person come to know of an unknown object. But in respect of understanding *svārthānumāna* the Buddhists' view is opposed to the Naiyāyikas. For the Naiyāyikas *svārthānumāna* is also judgemental or sentential for according to them no conceptual knowledge is non-verbal. The Buddhists, on the other hand, believe that there can be non-verbalized conceptual cognition and in *svārthānumāna* we have such cognition.

If we look for the conditions of inference, the Buddhists' view is different from the Nyāya view. Since the Naiyāyikas are believers in the *pramāṇasamplava* theory that one and the same thing can be known by different means, they believe that even if we already possess valid cognition regarding an object we may still be involved in inference if we have the desire to infer (*anumitsā*). So they believe that the only case where inference does not arise is when there is no desire to infer and at the same time there is the establishment of the probandum.[11] But such a view will never be admitted by the Buddhists. For, first of all they believe in *pramāṇa vyavasthā*, that is, they believe that objects of the different *pramāṇas* are always different. Moreover, they believe that *pramāṇa* always reveals something new,[12] so it is never possible according to the Buddhists that an object of which I already have certain knowledge, can be known again through inference.

There is, however, another important point of distinction between the Naiyāyikas and the Buddhists and that is regarding the issue of what is the object of inference. For the Nyāya philosophers *sādhya* is *anumeya* but for the Buddhists it is the locus (*pakṣa*) characterized by the *sādhya*. So in the example of the inference of fire on the basis of smoke, the Buddhists would maintain that the thought process is from smoky hill to fiery hill and not from smoke to fire. The later Naiyāyikas emphasize the co-existence of *hetu* and *sādhya* in the same locus, but the Buddhists would talk of the probans and the probandum as being co-properties of the *pakṣa*.

In fact, what is the *anumeya* of an inference has been a very debatable issue among the Buddhist logicians themselves. Generally it is taken to mean the knowledge which arises in the agent about an unperceived object in the locus on the basis of a probans possessing threefold character. According to some[13] it is the determination with certainty of the necessary connection of the probandum (with the probans) in a particular

11. *siṣādhayiṣā-viraha-sahakṛta-siddhyabhāvaḥ . . . Bhāṣāparicchedāḥ.*

12. *anadhigatārtha-viṣayaka.*

13. *tacca dharmiviśeṣa-sambandhitayā sādhyāvinābhāvitvaniścaya ityeke* |
— *TBh*, 13.7–8.

locus on the basis of the relation of the probans in it. But others hold that inference is the determination of the probandum like fire.[14] Dharmakīrti has presented the definition of *anumeya* as "the locus or subject whose property or determinations are under investigation."[15] In his *Pramāṇasamuccayavṛtti* Diṅnāga stated the first feature of the probans as existence in the *anumeya* (*anumeye 'stitā*) but the notion of *anumeya* has not been made clear by him — as to whether it stands for the locus or *pakṣa* only or for the locus as characterized by the property to be proved. In a later verse of the same text Diṅnāga himself says — *dharmaviśiṣṭo dharmy anumeyaḥ* which suggests that he is also thinking of *anumeya* in terms of the locus as qualified by the probandum. The commentators of Diṅnāga also seem to be in a sea regarding Diṅnāga's actual intention. Jinendrabuddhi in his *Viśālamālāvatī* commentary refers to an objection that as the existence of the property to be proved is not known when the probans is being perceived, *anumeya* cannot mean "the locus as characterized by the property" at least in the context of the first characteristic of the probans. Accordingly Jinendrabuddhi interprets Diṅnāga's definition as meaning *jijñāsitadharmaviśiṣṭo dharmī*. Diṅnāga himself was aware of this sort of objection. For in the *Vṛtti* of the third chapter of his *Pramāṇasamuccaya* he reports of an opponent who argues that Diṅnāga cannot speak of the characteristic of probans as "residing in the *pakṣa*" (*pakṣadharmatā*) when by *anumeya* he means "the locus qualified by the property-to-be-proved" and the locus being already established, is not to be proved. In reply to such an objection, Diṅnāga comments that though the word *anumeya* does not primarily mean the locus, *p*, or the property-to-be-proved, *s*, it metaphorically means that, since they constitute part of that

14. *agnyadhyavasāya ityanye* । — *TBh*, 13.8.

15. *anumeyo 'tra jijñāsitaviśeṣo dharmī* — *NB*, II.6.

compound "*p* qualified by *s*" which is to be proved. Prajñākaragupta in his *Pramāṇavārttikabhāṣya*, while replying to the same objection, states that Diṅnāga's intention in the definition of *anumeya* was: *anumeya* is the *p* qualified by *s*, where *s* is the property required to be determined. However, it seems that both Jinendrabuddhi and Prajñākaragupta were influenced by Dharmakīrti's definition. Dharmottara, while interpreting on the definition of Dharmakīrti points out that though one and the same word *anumeya* has been used, it does not convey the same sense in different contexts. In the context of the determination of the characteristic of probans the word *anumeya* means the locus *p* only; when the word *anumeya* is used in the context of the determination of the subject matter of inference, it means the locus as qualified by the probandum and the same word *anumeya* when used in the context of the determination of invariable concomitant relation between the probans and the probandum it means simply the property *s*. So when the meaning of the term *anumeya* is to be determined, it is to be done only with reference to the context in which the term is to be used and not in any general sense. For example, when Dharmakīrti proposes the definition of *anumeya* as *jijñāsitaviśeṣadharmī*, his objective was to state the characteristic of probans and not anything else. This is evident from his use of the word *atra* (here) in his statement of the *anumeya*.[16]

Another point of difference between the Buddhists and the Naiyāyikas is regarding the number of steps in an inference. For the Buddhists an inference consists of two statements only — one representing the pervasion relation between the probans

---

16. *atra hetulakṣaṇe niścetavye dharmī anumeyaḥ* । *anyatra tu sādhyapratipattikāle samudāyo 'numeyaḥ* । *vyāptiniścayakāle tu dharmo 'numeya iti darśayitum "atra" grahaṇam* । — *NBT*, 97.1-3.

and the probandum and the other representing the presence of the probans in the locus. These two statements are respectively referred to as *vyāpti* and *pakṣadharmatā*.[17] This view stands as opposed to the view of the Nyāya school where inference is believed to consist of five members — thesis (*pratijñā*), the logical ground (*hetu*), the corroborative example (*dṛṣṭānta*), the application (*upanaya*) and the conclusion (*nigamana*). Thus the standard form of an inference, according to the Nyāya school, will be: The mountain has fire (*pratijñā*), since it has smoke (*hetu*); wherever there is smoke there is fire, as for instance in the kitchen (*dṛṣṭānta*); the present case is like this (*upanaya*); therefore, there is fire here (*nigamana*). The Buddhists hold that only inference for others requires sentences for their expression, and for this what is necessary is the statement of the probans with the three characteristics. Since these characteristics are stated through the *anvaya* and *vyatireka* form of *vyāpti* and the *pakṣadharmatā*, these are the only two statements required. There is no need to have any other statement. In his *Vṛtti*, Diṅnāga observes that the fault of incomplete statement (*nyūnatā*) arises from the omission of any of the three characteristics of the probans and not from the non-statement of the *pratijñā*, etc. In *Nyāyamukha* also Diṅnāga refutes the theory of those logicians who consider the thesis, application and the conclusion as separate members of a syllogism.[18] Dharmakīrti in his *Pramāṇavārttika* has pointed out that since the probandum is proved through compatibility even when the *pakṣa* is not stated; so the fallacy of incompleteness does not result from the omission of thesis, but from the non-statement of any of the three characteristics

---

17. *vyāpti-pakṣadharmatāsaṁjñakaṁ dvyavayava-sādhanavākyaṁ saugatānām* । — *TBh*, 14.19-20.

18. Tucci, *The Nyāyamukha of Dignāga*, 45.

of the probandum. In the *Nyāyabindu* text also Dharmakīrti upholds the same position that the statement of the characteristics of the probans is sufficient for an inference; and there is no necessity to state the thesis.[19] Dharmottara elaborates this view of Dharmakīrti by pointing out that whether the probans is related to the probandum by invariable concomitant relation or not is the only essential condition for inferring the probandum from the probans. So the statement of the characteristic of the probans is needed for an inference. When this relationship is known and the probans is found to be existing in the locus, there is no necessity to state the other members.[20]

Accordingly the Buddhists criticize the view of the Naiyāyikas regarding the five members of a syllogism. Regarding the first member of the syllogism they point out that we cannot understand a probandum through the mere statement of a thesis having nothing to do with logical necessity or connection. As the Buddhists do not admit that there is any direct or indirect relationship possible between a word and its object, there is no need for the thesis. Since the thesis is refuted there is no use to state a reason putting it into ablative case. Apart from the reason, the corroborative example and the application become insignificant. Lastly when there is no thesis, there is no chance for the conclusion which is just a

---

19. *dvayor apyanayoḥ prayogayor nāvaśyaṁ pakṣa-nirdeśaḥ* | — *NB*, III.34.

20. *yataś ca sādhanaṁ sādhyadharmapratibaddhaṁ tādātmya-tadutpattibhyāṁ pratipattavyaṁ dvayor api prayogayoḥ tasmāt pakṣo 'vaśyam eva na nirdeśyaḥ* | *yat sādhanaṁ sādhya niyataṁ pratītaṁ tata eva sādhyadharmiṇī dṛṣṭāt sādhyapratītiḥ* | *ato na kiñcit sādhyanirdeśeneti* | — *NBT*, 172.8-10.

repetition of the thesis. Thus all the five members admitted by the Naiyāyikas turn out to be irrelevant.[21]

To sum up, the difference between the Buddhists and the Naiyāyikas lies in respect of the nature of inference, object of inference, conditions for the occurrence of inference, statement of inference as well as the classification of inference.

Classification of Inferences

Inference, according to Buddhist logicians, is of two types — inference for one's own (*svārtham*) and inference for others (*parārtham*). Here the criterion of distinction is, for whose sake the knowledge, viz. inference, is being made. If the agent uses this inference for his own apprehension of an object which is not directly apprehended, it will be regarded as inference for one's own.[22] It is the knowledge by which the individual himself is apprehending whereas in the case of inference for others, the objective is not the apprehension of one's own apprehension but to make another individual apprehend the object. So it is for the sake of others.[23]

Though it is primarily with regard to the intention that the two varieties of inference are differentiated, there is

---

21. *etaccāyuktaṁ pratijñāvacanamātrāt sambandharahitāt sādhyapratipatter ayogāt | sambandhābhāvastu śabdārthayoḥ sambandhadūṣaṇe pratipāditatvān na punar ucyate | pratijñām antareṇa pañcamy-antahetuprayogo 'pyayuktaḥ | hetuṁ vinopanaya-dṛṣṭāntāṁ tāva pyayuktou | yatra pratijñaiva nāsti tatra pratijñāyār vacanaṁ nigamanaṁ kuto bhaviṣyatīti sarvam ālūnaviśīrṇam |* — *TBh*, 14.23-27.

22. *svasmai yat tat svārtham,* — *TBh* 13.1.
also
yenānumānena karaṇa-bhūtenānumātā svayaṁ pratipadyate parokṣam artham iti śeṣaḥ, prakaraṇa-labhyaṁ vā | tat svārtha-jñānam-ātmapratipatti-prayojanam iti yāvat — *DhP*, 88.25-26.

23. *parasmāyidaṁ parārtham | yena paraṁ pratipādayati tat parārtham,* — *NBT*, 88.3-4.

another very important aspect or feature by which the two varieties are distinguished and this is with regard to the essence or nature of the two. Inference for oneself is of the nature of knowledge while inference for others is judgemental in nature. That is, in the case of the first variety of inference, as the objective is one's own knowledge, it occurs to that agent who has the direct knowledge of the probans in the locus and also the knowledge about the close relationship between the probans and the probandum.[24] By means of this knowledge he himself comes to comprehend the object which he could not directly perceive. Since he needs the knowledge for himself and not for anyone else, he does not need to employ any other means. But the case is different with the other variety of inference. Here the objective is to enable another individual apprehend through inference, what he cannot directly apprehend. So the agent needs to take recourse to propositions so that the other individual can have the knowledge. Hence this variety of inference is propositional in nature expressed through propositions depicting the threefold properties of the probans.[25]

It may be asked by the opponents that since inference for others is one variety of inference and inference is a variety of valid cognition, how can it be judgemental in nature?[26] To put it differently, if inference for others is judgemental in nature, how can it be regarded as inference. In reply it has been said

24. *parvatādau dhūmādikaṁ dr̥ṣṭvā yasya pratipattur jñānam utpadyate sa eva tena jñānena parokṣaṁ arthaṁ pratipadyate nānyaḥ iti svārthānumānam ucyate* II — *TBh*, 13.2-5.

25. *yena vākyena karaṇena paraṁ prati vācyaṁ pratipādayati parokṣamarthaṁ bodhayati tat trirūpaliṁgākhyānaṁ vākyaṁ parārthānumānam* I — *DhP*, 89.5-7.

26. *nanu ca samyag-jñātmakam-anumānam uktam* I *tat kim arthaṁ saṁprati vacanātmakam anumānam ucyata ityāha . . .* — *NBT*, 150.7-8.

by the Buddhists that here the word "inference" is used in a secondary sense (*upacāra*). Since inference for others stated in terms of three propositions expressing the threefold characteristic of the probans actually produces knowledge in the mind of the other individual, it is regarded as inference in the secondary sense.[27] Here the sense of the effect, viz. knowledge, is applied to the cause, viz. the propositions[28] since these propositions give rise to the knowledge of the unperceived object in another.

By naming the twofold varieties of inference as inference for oneself and inference for others, the Buddhists are highlighting the fact that they are admitting only this sort of classification and not any other sort.[29] In Indian philosophy we find that different systems try to classify inference into different types on the basis of different criteria; even within a single school we notice different types of classification. For example, the Nyāya school of thinkers along with the Buddhists classify inference into two varieties — inference for one's own and inference for others. But in addition to that, they speak of two other alternative classifications — (1) classifying inferences as *pūrvavat, śeṣavat* and *sāmānyatodṛṣṭa,* and (2) classifying inferences as *kevalānvayī, kevalavyatirekī* and *anvayavyatirekī* types. In the case of the first variety of

---

27. *trirūpa-liṅga-pratipādakaṁ vacanaṁ paraṁ pratipādayati jñāpayatīti kṛtvā vacanam apy-anumāna-śabdenocyate upacārāt* । — *TBh,* 13.4-6.

28. *kāraṇe kāryopacārāt* । — *NB* III.2.
also
kāraṇe vacane kāryasya jñānasyopacārāt samāropāt । — *DhP,* 150.19.

29. *dvidhaivaivam ātmakam iti kathaṁ nāma pratīyateti* । *itaratheha tāvad etāvad eva vyutpādyatayā prastutam, anyatra punar anyad apyanumānaṁ vyutpādyam astītyāśaṁkā nāhatya nirākṛtā syād iti* ॥ *pūrvavac cheṣavadādirūpeṇa anyathā 'pi dvaividhyasambhavāt saṁśayānaḥ pṛcchati — kiṁ punar iti* । — *DhP,* 88.18-21.

classification the criterion is whether we are proceeding from the cause to the effect or from the effect to the cause or not in any fixed order. In the case of the second variety of classification the criterion is on what basis we can apprehend the invariable relationship between the probans and the probandum. If the relation is established simply on the basis of affirmative instances and where no negative instance is available at all, the inference is regarded as *kevalānvayī;* where the relation is established on the basis of negative instances there being no affirmative instance available at all, it is regarded as *kevalavyatirekī;* and where both affirmative and negative instances are taken into consideration it is regarded as *anvayavyatirekī*. Of these, three the last one is the most commonly accepted form of inference by the Buddhists as well as the Naiyāyikas. The standard example of this variety is — the hill has fire on it because there is smoke; the positive example is the kitchen and the negative example is the lake full of water. The other two forms of inference are not accepted by the Buddhists. Since they believe in the docrine of *trairūpya* of the probans, they cannot regard the invariable relation to be established by the affirmative instances or the negative instances alone. Between the other two varieties — *kevalānvayin* and *kevalavyatirekin* — we might think of a possibility in which the universally positive variety of inference may have been accommodated in the Buddhist framework, though the second one could never be. In fact, the second variety was explicitly declared to be wrong or inconclusive by them. Let us elaborate on this point. The basic principle of the universally positive form of inference is that an example is nowhere to be found in which both the inferable property (e.g. knowability) and inferential mark (e.g. nameability) are absent. Since the Buddhists believe in the doctrine of impermanence we cannot find in their metaphysics anything which is neither impermanent nor a product. Hence in Buddhist parlance, we cannot find an example, a non-fictional one, where both impermanence and being a product are absent. Such an example is a fictional entity. One of the three necessary conditions says that the probans should be absent from the place which lacks the probandum. But if there is no such place in actuality the condition seems to be automatically fulfilled. That is, *vipakṣe nāsti — vipakṣo nāsti.* In this way, the universally positive form of inferences might be included in the Buddhist system. But the major problem for the Buddhists occurs with regard to the universally negative form of inference or *kevalavyatirekin* variety. Example of such inference is — "The earth is nothing but earth since it has smell," "A triangle is nothing but a triangle because it is a plain figure bounded by three sides." All of them are correct forms of inference, but it is not possible to show their validity in the Buddhist scheme. For, one condition in the Buddhist theory is that we must find an example where the inferential mark/probans *a* and the inferable property/probandum *b* are found to occur together. But such an example cannot be found in the cases outside the actual inferable case, i.e. the locus or the *pakṣa*. Hence, such correct inferences cannot be covered by the above theory of the triple condition. Accordingly, the Buddhists challenge the correctness of the Naiyāyika account of the universal negative form of inference.

Again, with regard to the Nyāya classification of inference into *pūrvavat, śeṣavat* and *sāmānyatodṛṣṭo* variety, it may be said that though the Buddhists believe in the doctrine of causality, they will not admit any distinction among inferences on the basis of causality. For them we can only proceed to infer the cause on the perception of the effect and not the other way round, since it is not possible to infer the effect from the cause always. Even though we have observed the cause there is no certainty that the effect will occur later. For example, if mangoes are never seen in any tree where mango-blossoms do not grow, could we then infer without doubt that the tree with mango-blossoms will have mangoes later on? This is uncertain because it is quite possible that bad weather had destroyed all the mango-blossoms. The example that Dharmakīrti offers is *dehād rāgānumānavat*. It is generally observed that the embodied existence of a human being is the cause of such qualities as attachment, love, hatred, etc. But inference of such attachment, etc. from the observation of body cannot be absolutely certain; for instance when an *arhat* or a saint practises meditation regularly to get rid of such attachments, the inference in the above manner will fail. Dharmakīrti accordingly holds — "Since our teacher (Diṅnāga) has said : mere non-observation of the reason in the example where *sādhya* is absent delivers a pseudo-reason, not a proper cognition of reason, as in the case of attachment in the body; we conclude that invariable concomitance (between *sādhya* and *hetu*) cannot be established simply on the basis of non-observation. For deviation is possible, just as one grain of rice may by chance remain uncooked in a rice-cooking pot. Hence, our teacher has illustrated the *śeṣavat* inference as a doubtful case because here simple non-observation of the reason is taken to be proving the correctness of the inference."[30] Accordingly, the Buddhists do not admit the first variety of classification done by the Naiyāyikas also.

While winding up our discussion on the nature of *anumāna* let us concentrate on the issue whether the Buddhist theory of inference can be viewed in the light of the standard deductive, inductive division. To be precise in respect of

30. *PV*, I.12-14; also, B.K. Matilal, "Dharmakīrti and the Universally Negative Inferences."

formulation, can the Buddhist way of classifying inferences into *svārthānumāna* and *parārthānumāna* varieties be looked upon as deduction, induction, both or neither? This issue goes long back to the days of Stcherbatsky who conceived "inference-for-someone else" as *syllogism* having the same form as that of the first mood of the first figure of Aristotle's categorical syllogism. Following this practice almost all modern Indian writers on the subject, including S.C. Vidyabhusana, S.N. Dasgupta, Radhakrishnan, S.C. Chatterjee and D.M. Datta have regarded the *parārthānumāna* or inference for others syllogism and used Aristotle's terms in characterizing it. As BARABARA is the standard example of deductive argument, it follows that, according to these thinkers *parārthānumāna* is deductive in character. There is a second line of thinking which holds that the *parārthānumāna* is not a BARABARA form of argument at all, though it is "a formal deductive inference with some built-in checks and balances which disallow the use of any false premise, and the deduction of a false conclusion from true premises." Emphasizing these two features of the *parārthānumāna* or inference for others, modern interpreters locate the distinctiveness of Indian theory of inference and consider it to be both deductive and inductive at the same time. According to them, *parārthānumāna* is a kind of inference to which the distinction between deduction and induction does not apply.

In face of such theories, the question becomes pertinent to discuss — what sort of argument is an *anumāna* — deductive, inductive, both or neither? In reply, it needs to be pointed out first that to ask such a question is to mischaracterize *anumāna* as an argument. *Anumāna* is a hybrid enterprise involving both logical and epistemological considerations of propositions, but of cognitions the study of *anumāna* is better thought of as an epistemological and not a logical investigation. When *anumāna* is understood in the sense of *parārthānumāna,* its constituents are statements whose contents are the state of affairs to which the statements refer. Given the ways in which the contents of these constituents are fixed, they cannot fail to be veridical. They are not the sorts of things that can be either true or false. Accordingly, *anumāna* cannot be regarded as an argument, rather it is an inference. Though not an argument, if we look into the nature of an inference seriously, we will find that the epistemic virtue of an *anumāna* consists partially in the fact that it instantiates a deductively valid argument pattern, a *modus ponens.* But it is not a deductively valid argument: since it does not consist of propositions, it is not an argument at all. Its epistemic virtue consists also in part in the efforts that the cognizer has made to have her beliefs caused by the facts that adhere to the *modus ponens* pattern. Since virtue in performance is always a matter of degree, these efforts may always come up short. But this does not make the *anumāna* an inductive argument. There is no such thing as an inductive argument. There are just those epistemic processes whereby we seek to acquire knowledge of new facts indirectly. When these efforts succeed — through a combination of skill and luck — then we have an *anumāna.*[31] A cognitive exercise is a specimen of *parārthānumāna* or even *svārthānumāna* because of the fact that the object cognized by means of it is mediately or indirectly cognized (*parokṣa artha*) through the mediation of the triple-charactered logical reason or probans. The different types of inference — *svabhāvahetuka, kāryahetuka, anupalabdhihetuka* — are called differently by him on the basis of the different types of *hetu* figuring in them, and not on the basis of the source of cognition, perception or inference, deduction or

31. For details vide Mark Sideris, "Deductive, Inductive, Both or Neither."

induction, by means of which any of its premises are known. That the example of an inference given above is deductive, is explicitly admitted by Dharmakīrti when he says that the inference for others is nothing but the *hetuvākyas*, the assertion or statement of the triple characteristic of the probans and that it is not necessary to state the conclusion because the *hetuvākyas* or premises entail it. For Dharmakīrti, to tell anyone the *hetuvākya* or the premises of a *parārthānumāna* is also to tell him by implication its conclusion. From this it can be said that the *parārthānumāna* is deductive and not inductive in nature, since the premises of an inductive reasoning do not entail the conclusion. To say all this is not to suggest that Indian logicians do not have any theory of induction, but is to point out that their theory of *parārthānumāna* is in no way an inductive inference. By calling it deductive or non-inductive, we are not under-estimating the logical value of such *anumāna* or ignoring the creativity of the philosophers who have formulated the theory of *parārthānumāna* or *svārthānumāna*. In fact, both *parārthānumāna* and *svārthānumāna* are *vyāpti*-using, *vyāpti*-based and not *vyāpti*-establishing inferences. The methods of establishing *vyāpti*, at least some of them, are inductive in character; but they are neither *svārthānumāna* nor *parārthānumāna*. The attitude of the Buddhist logicians regarding *anumāna* may be considered as scientific in outlook. The scientist makes an induction, deduces a conclusion from it, tests its truth and finding it to be false, modifies his generalization or induction, etc. Similarly the Buddhists apply the *vyāpti* relation to a particular case and tries to provide new information. But just as in the scientist's case the same act of inference is not regarded as both deductive and inductive since it involves the technique of both deduction and induction, the Buddhist view of *anumāna* cannot be regarded as inductive and deductive both though they have an inclination towards deduction.[32]

32. For detailed discussion on this topic, vide R. Prasad, *Dharmakīrti's Theroy of Inference : Revaluation and Reconstruction.*

9

The Threefold Characterization of the Probans

In Buddhist philosophy each inference is believed to consist of three terms — probans, probandum and the locus. Of them the probans or the *liṅga* is that by which we are able to cognize an object.[1] In Indian philosophy a probans or a *liṅga* is known by different names like *sādhana* (a logical mark), *jñāpaka* (which makes something known), *hetu* (logical ground), and *vyāpya* (the pervaded).[2] According to the Buddhists, such a probans is said to possess three characteristics. Before considering the three characteristics let us first concentrate on what is a probans. Diṅnāga said that any property can be the probans or mark of a second property provided that it has been observed to be with the second property at least once and no example of the contrary possibility has been observed. A contrary possibility would be one where the instance of the probans is seen but not the property signified by it, i.e. the probandum. Diṅnāga used this above procedure of probans to show how inference and linguistic utterance can lead to knowledge in the indirect manner. For example, in a particular place when we see a body of smoke with a body of fire, that might suggest to our mind that one is the sign or mark of

1. *liṁgyaste gamyate 'nenārthaḥ iti liṁgam.*
2. *sādhanaṁ jñāpakaṁ hetur vyāpyam iti liṁgāparanāmāni* ।
— *TBh,* 14.17-18.

another. That is, on the perception of smoke we might think that there might be fire, but we may not be sure of it. For this sureness, Diṅnāga thinks that we need a third condition, namely the exclusion of other possibilities — this is the elimination of any case where the probans is present but the thing to be proved is not. Hence in his *Pramāṇasamuccaya* he states that every valid probans must satisfy three characteristics — its definite existence or presence in the locus of inference as also in all the members of the class similar to the locus and its absence in the members of the class dissimilar to the locus.[3] Following Diṅnāga, Dharmakīrti in his *Pramāṇavārttika* makes the cryptic statement — *pakṣadharmas tadaṁśena vyāpto hetuḥ* — the probans is the property of the locus, and has invariable concomitant relationship with a part of it, viz. the probandum which is part of the object of inference. In this statement of Dharmakīrti the first part refers to the first characteristic while the second part refers to the last two characteristics of the probans. In his *Nyāyabindu* Dharmakīrti spells out the three characteristics in the following manner — (1) the definite presence of the probans in the *anumeya,* (2) the definite presence of the probans in the *sapakṣa* or similar instances, and (3) the definite absence of the probans in the dissimilar instances.[4]

Let us now consider the three characteristics of probans in detail. The first characteristic is known as *pakṣadharmatā,* while the second and the third features are known respectively as *anvaya* and *vyatireka.* Dharmottara while commenting on the three characteristics points out that though Dharmakīrti has placed the word "definite" (*niścitam*) at the end of the

3. *anumeye 'tha tattulye sadbhāvo nāstita 'sati* । — *PS,* II.5.

4. *trairūpyaṁ punar liṁgasyānumeye sattvam eva, sapakṣa eva sattvam, asapakṣe cāsattvam eva niścitam* । — *NB,* II.5

sūtra after stating all the three characters, it has to be added to each part[5] to signify that the ascertainment of the existence of the probans in the locus and the ascertainment of the joint occurrence of the probans and the probandum both in respect of presence and in respect of absence are to be necessarily done[6] as they are the essential conditions of the probans in respect of the determination of the indirect object.[7]

Each of the terms in the statement of the characteristic is essential. For example, the word "existence" (*sattvam*) is offered to avoid the fallacy of unproved probans (*asiddha*).[8] In the argument "Word is eternal because it is visible" the probans is visibility. Such a probans never exists in the locus "word" nor in any member of the class of words. Hence this is not a proper probans. To avoid such cases the word "necessary existence" is recommended. By the particle *eva* (real), partial non-existence of the probans in the locus (i.e. the non-existence of the probans in some members of the class of locus) is avoided. For instance, the Digambara Jainas argue that "Trees have consciousness because they sleep," where by "sleep" is meant the state of shrivelled leaves. But this sort of shrivelling state is not found among all trees; so it is a case of partial non-existence of probans. Hence sleeping cannot be regarded as a proper probans to prove the consciousness. The word *niścitam* or definite is added to eliminate the cases of dubious existence

5. *yadyapi cātra niścitagrahaṇaṁ na kṛtaṁ tathāpi ante kṛtaṁ prakrāntayoḥ dvayorapi rūpayor apekṣaṇīyam* I — *NBT*, 91.11-12.

6. *ato 'nvaya-vyatireka-pakṣadharmatvaniścayo liṁgavyāpārātmakatvād avaśyakartavya iti sarveṣu rūpeṣu niścitagrahaṇam apekṣaṇīyam* I — *NBT*, 92.4-5.

7. *parokṣapratipādane gamakasya vyāpārasya* . . . — *DhP*, 92.19.

8. *atra sattvagrahaṇenāsiddhasya nirāsaḥ* I *yathā nityaḥ śabdaḥ cākṣuṣatvāt* I *cākṣuṣatvaṁ cakṣur vijñānagrāhyatvam* I — *TBh*, 13.11-13.

of the probans in the locus. For example, "There is fire in the mountain because of the existence of a mass of smoke-like elements which is suspected to be vapour." The significance of stating the particle *eva* after the word *sattva* is that by it the fallacy of the probans subsisting in the locus alone, technically known as *asādhāraṇa*, is avoided. For instance, in the inference "Word is eternal because it is audible," the probans "audibility" belongs to the locus "word" alone and not to anything else. Hence with such a probans the existence of the probandum cannot be established. Such cases are avoided by the use of the word *eva* after *sattva*.

The second characteristic of the probans is that the probans should be present definitely in all the *sapakṣa* instances.[9] By *sapakṣa* is meant instances similar to the locus in respect of the possession of the property to be proved. Thus *sapakṣa* actually stands for all the instances in the example (*dṛṣṭāntadharmī*)[10] similar to the locus in respect of possessing the property of the probandum in general and not the property of the probandum specific to this inference.[11] By the expression "in general" what is actually meant is that of fire in general. The specific fire which is found in this particular mountain at this particular moment of time will be considered as the "probandum specific to an inference." This interpretation of Dharmottara is based on the view of Dharmakīrti as found in *Pramāṇaviniścayaḥ*. There Dharmakīrti says that homologous

9. *sapakṣa eva sattvaṁ niścitam iti varttate* I — *TBh*, 13.19.

10. *samānaḥ pakṣaḥ sapakṣaḥ* I *pakṣeṇa saha sadṛśo dṛṣṭāntadharmī tyarthaḥ* — *TBh*, 13.19-20.

11. *kiṁ tat pakṣa-sapakṣayoḥ sāmānyaṁ yena samānaḥ sapakṣaḥ pakṣeṇetyāha — sādhyadharmasāmānyeneti* I . . . *na ca viśeṣaḥ sādhyaḥ, api tu sāmānyam* I *ata iha sāmānyaṁ sādhyam uktam* I *sādhya-dharmaścāsau sāmānyaṁ ceti sādhyadharmasāmānyena samānaḥ pakṣeṇa sapakṣa ityarthaḥ* I — *NBT*, 98.1-4.

instances are similar to the locus or *pakṣa* in respect of their having the common property, the probandum.[12]

In this definition the word "existence" is used to avoid the fallacy of incompatible probanses (*viruddha*) as for instance in the following inference — "Sound is eternal because it is a product." Here the probans "being a product" cannot be regarded as a proper one for it does not exist in any of the homologous instances like sky, etc.; on the contrary it exists in all the heterogeneous instances like pot, etc.[13] The word *sattva* in the definition is to eliminate the possibility of using such incompatible probans. The word *eva* is used to avoid the fallacy of being overly inclusive (*sādhāraṇa-anaikāntikaḥ*) as in the inference "Word is eternal because it is an object of knowledge." The probans "being an object of knowledge" means "being the object of conceptual constructs" (*vikalpaviṣayīkr̥tatva*) which can be found in everything, in all the members of the homologous class like ether and also in all the members of the heterogeneous class like pot, etc. To avoid this fallacy the probans is said to be non-exclusive. The word *eva* if it were placed before "existence" would mean that the probans pervades not all the members of the homologous class but only some members of the homologous class. In that case the probans "being produced immediately after human effort" would have to be regarded as valid in such inferences as "Word is non-eternal since it is produced immediately after human effort like the jar." Jar is similar to word in respect of possessing non-eternity but the same similarity can be found in other cases like lightning, etc. So lightning might be regarded as

12. *sādhyadharmasāmānyena samānaḥ pakṣaḥ sapakṣaḥ tadabhāvo 'sapakṣaḥ* ।
— *DhP*, 98.9.

13. *kr̥takatvaṁ nitya-vipakṣeṇānityatvena vyāptam iti viruddham ucyate* ।
— *TBh*, 13.21-22.

sapakṣa or homologous instance of the locus, but the probans "being produced immediately after human effort" cannot be found in the case of lightning. So the probans will be existent in some cases of the homologous instances and not in all instances, which will be against the spirit of the second characteristic of the probans. The force of this difficulty, however lies in the fact that if the word *eva* were placed before *sattva* it would have excluded all cases of probans as effect (*kārya hetu*) like "This has fire since this has smoke;" for smoke exists only in some cases of fire like oven, etc. but not in other instances like electric heater, etc.[14] So to avoid such possibility, the probans is to be understood, according to Dharmottara as the probans whose essence consists in existence in the homologous cases (*sapakṣe sattvam eva yasya sa hetuḥ*). In that case it would exclude "being produced immediately after human effort" as probans when it does not apply to all homologous cases. The word "definite" is also essential to avoid the cases of dubious affirmative connection (*sandigdhānvaya*) with respect to the probans as in the following inference "This man is non-omniscient for he speaks as other persons do." In such an inference we are not sure whether for any person, who belongs to the class of human beings, being a speaker is pervaded with non-omniscience or not. Hence to avoid such cases the word *niścitam* is added — for using a probans we have to be sure that it certainly has the affirmative form of pervasion relation with the probandum in all the homologous instances.

---

14. *prayatnānantarīyakatvam apyanityatvasiddhau samartho hetur iti darśayituṁ sakala-sapakṣāvyāpi prayatnānantarīyakatvam udāhṛtam iti draṣṭavyam* I *vastutas tu sarva eva kāryahetu-dhūmādiḥ sapakṣaikadeśavṛttir boddhavyaḥ* I *itirebam arthe* I *evaṁ sati prayatnānantarīyakatvam upalakṣaṇatvād asya dhūmādikam api na hetuḥ syāt* I — *DhP*, 94.14-17.

The third characteristic of the probans is that it must be definitely non-existent in all the instances heterogeneous to the locus, i.e. in all the instances which do not possess the probandum.[15] The *asapakṣa* is described to be such which is not the co-member of the locus. In other words, it is a class which is incompatible with the probandum. Dharmakīrti himself defines a heterogeneous class or *asapakṣa* as that which is not the homogeneous class,[16] that which is other than the homogeneous class,[17] that which is the contradictory of the homogeneous class,[18] and that which has the absence of the homogeneous class.[19] Thus Dharmakīrti explains that the *asapakṣa* is to be understood as the other of or in opposition to the *sapakṣa*. Since we know that *sapakṣa* means cases similar to the locus in respect of possessing the probandum, so *asapakṣa* would amount to absence or lacking or not possessing the property of probandum.[20] In other words the third characteristic of the probans amounts to the absolute absence of the probans in all the heterologous or *asapakṣa* instances. This characteristic of the probans is designated as *vyatirekaḥ* or negative pervasion.

Here also the word "absence" (*asattvam*) is used to avoid the incompatible probanses (*viruddha hetu*), the word *eva* to exclude over-inclusive (*sādhāraṇa hetu*) probans like "Sound is produced immediately after human effort because it is

---

15. *asapakṣe cāsattvam eva niścitam* — *TBh*, 14.1-2.
16. *na sapakṣo 'sapakṣaḥ* — *NB*, II.8.
17. *tato 'nyaḥ* — *NB*, II.9.
18. *tadviruddhaḥ* — *NB*, II.9.
19. *tadabhāvaś ceti* — *NB*, II.9, *tasya ca sapakṣasyābhāvaḥ* — *NBT*, 99.2.
20. *sapakṣābhāvo 'sapakṣaḥ* । *sādhyadharmavān yo na bhavatītyarthaḥ* । *sādhyadharmābhāvārthatvād asapakṣa-śabdasya* — *DhP*, 99.11–12.

impermanent like a jar." In this case the probans "being impermanent" is found in some heterogeneous instances like lightning, etc. and so cannot be regarded as a proper one. By the word "absence" such probanses will be excluded.

The word "definite" (*niścita*) is for avoiding the fallacious probans whose non-occurrence in the heterogeneous case is doubtful (*saṅdigdha-vipakṣa-vyāvṛttika*). An example of such probans is "This man is not free from passions since he is a speaker like the man on the chariot." Here all cases in which being not free from passions is absent are cases in which "being a speaker" is absent as for example in stones. But such an inference cannot be correct, since though both the qualities are absent in a stone, we cannot be sure that the absence of the property "being a speaker" in stone is caused by the absence of the state of being free from passions; or the absence has occurred simply because of its own nature. Thus this is a case of inconclusiveness due to dubious negative pervasion.[21] The word *eva* is added to avoid that probans which occurs in part of the heterogeneous instances. For example "Word is produced immediately after human effort because it is non-eternal." Now the probans "being non-eternal" does not exist in some heterogeneous instance as ether, though it exists in some other heterogeneous instance like lightning, etc. Thus, this is a case of probans which being existent in part of heterogeneous instances cannot be a proper one. To eliminate these cases the word *eva* is added.

The Buddhists are very reluctant to point out that all these three characteristics are essential for a proper probans. It may be argued that when the second characteristic is stated there is no necessity to state the third characteristic for it follows by implication from the second one. If it is known that the

21. *tataḥ sandigdha-vyatireko 'yam anaikāntikaḥ* — *TBh*, 14.8-9.

probans definitely exists in the homogeneous cases, it follows that if a case is not homogeneous, the probans will not be existent in it. So what is the necessity of stating the third characteristic when the second one has already been stated? In reply it has been said that the logicians of early times like Diṅnāga and others have stated both the second and the third to determine the heterogeneous instances.[22] In fact, these logicians held that *vipakṣa* is of three kinds — the simple absence of the probandum, what is just different from the probandum and what is opposed to the probandum. These three interpretations of the term *vipakṣa* had been pointed out by Dharmakīrti in the second chapter of his *Nyāyabindu.* There he first states that the heterogeneous case *asapakṣa* is one which is not the *sapakṣa,* meaning thereby that which lacks the probandum. Then he classifies them into three kinds — that which is different from that, that which is contradictory to that, and that which is the absence of that. Here *tadabhāva* is to be understood in the sense of *prasajyapratiṣedha* and constitutes the basic idea of *vipakṣa,* representing the direct absence of *sapakṣa.* But the other two are those which are affirmed through the negation and represent the absence of *sapakṣa* only indirectly. In other words *tadabhāva* or the contradictory of the probandum connotes (i) those different from the probandum, and (ii) those contrary to it, both. Thus all the three kinds are the species of *vipakṣa.* Mokṣākaragupta refers to this view when he describes *vipakṣa* to be of three types. So it is quite possible that he might be referring to Diṅnāga, Dharmakīrti, Jinendrabuddhi, Dharmottara as *pūrvavṛddhāḥ* by overlooking the subtle differences between them.

There are some who hold that it is for determining the appropriate nature of the *vyāpti* relation between the probans

22. *vipakṣaniyamārtham iti pūrvavṛddhāḥ* — *TBh,* 14.13.

and the probandum that both the affirmative and the negative forms of the *vyāpti* is stated.[23] If this were not so stated then *post hoc ergo propter hoc* type of arguments would have to be regarded as valid. For example, "He must be black because he is his son like the other sons of that person" will be valid. Dhartmottara, thus specifically mentions that for the beginners, i.e. for those who do not have the knowledge of the necessary relationship between the probans and the probandum, statements of the affirmative pervasion and of the negative pervasion are absolutely essential. But for the persons who have already knowledge of this, they can infer one form of pervasion to the other; and so can be led to valid cognition about the unperceived object from the perception of the probans.[24] So for such persons statements of both the forms are not essential. But as this is not the case with the learners, so at the stage of learning, both the forms are to be stated.[25]

This view of the Buddhist regarding the characteristics of the probans is different from the view about the features or characteristics stated by the Nyāya school. The Nyāya logicians propose that a proper or valid probans (*sadhetu*) must have five features — *pakṣadharmatva, sapakṣasattvam, vipakṣāsattvam, abādhita-viṣayatvam* and *asatpratipakṣatvam.* Of them, the first feature holds that the probans must be a property of the locus. The second characteristic highlights that the probans must be present in all the instances where the probandum is

---

23. *tasmān niyamavator evānvayavyatirekayoḥ prayogaḥ kartavyo yena pratibandho gamyeta sādhanasya sādhyena* I — *NBT*, 96.1-2.

24. *prayogadarśanābhyāsāt kaścit prayogabhaṅgyaiva svayam api parokṣam arthaṁ pratipadyata iti svārthe 'pyanumāne nirṇītam idaṁ lakṣaṇa-kathana-prasaṁgena* I *tato na doṣa iti draṣṭavyam* . . . I — *DhP*, 96.28-30.

25. *niyamavatoś ca prayoge 'vaśyakartavye dvayor eka eva prayoktavyo na dvāv iti niyamavān evānvayo vyatireko vā prayoktavya iti śikṣaṇārthaṁ dvayor upādānam iti* I — *NBT*, 96.2-3.

present. The third feature points out that the probans must be absent in all the instances where the probandum is absent. The fourth feature holds that the probans should not be such as to be contradictory to or incompatible with the probandum. This is because the main function of the probans is to establish the probandum, so if it is incompatible with the probandum that function cannot be performed. The fifth characteristic states that a probans should be such that there is no other rival probans which is competent enough to invalidate it.

The Naiyāyikas point out that in some cases all these five characteristics may not be simultaneously present. As for example, in the case of *kevalānvayī anumāna* the third feature is not possible. Similarly in the cases of *kevalavyatirekī anumāna* the second feature is not admissible. Hence, they hold that a valid reason must satisfy the five conditions or at least four conditions.

If we compare the list of characteristics of a valid probans as proposed by the Buddhists with the list provided by the Naiyāyikas, we will see that the first three features are common to both. Of course, the details of the three characteristics as admitted by the two schools are different — there can be said to be only rough correspondence between them. But the last two features stated by the Naiyāyikas will be never acceptable to the Buddhist school. There are definite reasons for such non-acceptance. In the first place the Buddhists believe in *pramāṇavyavasthā,* while the Nyāya school believes in *pramāṇasamplava* thesis. Thus the latter can believe that the verdict of one inference can be contradicted by some other *pramāṇa,* but the former school cannot believe that the verdict of one inference can be contradicted by another *pramāṇa.* That is why the Buddhists do not feel any necessity to include the fifth condition for the probans. Secondly, the basis of inference according to the Buddhists is *liṅga-liṅgī-bhāva* between two concepts. Such relation cannot exist if the two concepts were incompatible or opposite in nature. Hence there is no necessity to add *abādhitaviṣayatva.* Thirdly, by the addition of the word *eva* with the second and third characteristics of the probans the Buddhists want to emphasize that there is necessary connection between the probans and the probandum. Thus when the necessary connection between the probans and the probandum is established, there remains no possibility that one probans can be counterbalanced by another probans or be refuted by any other *pramāṇa.* As such the Buddhists, in their own philosophical framework, do not feel any necessity to add the extra two conditions/features of the probans as have been done by the Naiyāyikas.

10

Classification of Probans

THE probans or the logical mark possessing these three characteristics is said to be of three types — probans as effect (*kārya-hetu*), probans as essence (*svabhāva-hetu*) and probans as non-apprehension (*anupalabdhi-hetu*). Each of them possesses the threefold characteristics. That is, the probans as effect has three characters, the probans as essence has three characters and the probans as non-apprehension also has the three characters.[1]

The Probans as Effect

The probans as effect is in the form of an effect; it necessarily presupposes its cause. Thus *kārya* as *liṅga* necessarily leads to its *kāraṇa*, which is the *liṅgin*. The relation between seed and sprout, between fire and smoke are examples of the relation of causality. This relation is given to us in our experience. We always find that whenever there is smoke there is fire, and whenever there is no fire there is no smoke. The causal relation is a relation of succession.

The apprehension of necessary connection between a cause and an effect is based on perceptual experience, but the relation as such is a matter of mental construction. The causal connection is so well known to all individuals that the Buddhist

1. *pratiṣedhyasya sādhyasyānupalabdhis trirūpā* | *vidheyasya sādhyasya svabhāvaś ca trirūpaḥ kāryam ca* | — *NBT*, 100.9-10.

logicians did not feel any urge to define or lay out this causal relationship.[2] From the very fact that two objects are related by causal relationship, when one sees the effect one can pass on to the cause.[3] In the Nyāya tradition it is accepted that the process of inference may proceed from cause to effect and from effect to cause, both ways. As such they draw a distinction between *pūrvavat anumāna* and *śeṣavat anumāna*, where the former is based from the effect to the cause while the latter from cause to effect. The Buddhists, however, recognize the inference from effect to cause as valid and not the inference from cause to effect. For, whenever there is an effect there must be a cause, but it is not necessary that whenever there is a cause there is an effect.

The probans as effect is classified into three kinds because of the differences in the terms (*viṣaya*) related to it.[4] In the inference where the object to be proved is fire and the probans is smoke, this smoke and the like can be proved by means of threefold cognition consisting of perception and non-perception of fire and smoke. In the inference where the object to be proved is sense organ like eye, etc. the probans is the effect, namely knowledge like visual cognition, etc. and this is to be determined through the fact that the effect occurs occasionally only when that particular sense organ is active.[5] In the inference

2. *kāryakāraṇabhāvo loke pratyakṣānupalambhanibandhanaḥ pratīta iti na . . . kāryasya lakṣaṇam uktam* I — *NBT*, 107.5-6.

3. *kārya-kāraṇa-bhāvena gamya-gamakabhāve sarvathā gamya-gamakabhāvaprasaṁga ityādikāyāṁ vipratipattāvapi na kāryasya lakṣaṇe vipratipattiḥ* I *kintarhi? tasya gamakatve* I *sā cānyatra nirākṛtā 'trāpi prājñaiḥ svayaṁbhyūhyā prājñajanādhikāreṇāsya prārambhād iti* I — *DhP*, 108.24-27.

4. *ayam kāryahetur viṣayabhedena trividhaḥ* I — *TBh*, 14.27-28.

5. *agnādau sādhye dhūmādistrividhapratyakṣānupalambhena niścetavyaḥ* I *cakṣurādau sādhye jñānaṁ kadācitkakāryyotpādān niścīyate* I — *TBh*, 14.28–15.1.

when colour of an orange is the object to be proved and the taste of the orange is the probans, this is a probans as effect, since both the colour and taste of the orange are dependent on one and the same set of causes as is the case of inferring the taste of the orange from its colour.[6] In the latter case the colour of the preceding moment is the material cause of the colour of the second moment, and the taste of that preceding moment which is the material cause of the taste of the second moment, is the auxiliary cause for the production of the colour of the second moment. This is the logical relation involved in the production of the orange at the subsequent moment from that of the preceding moment. Actually the theory operative here is that inference of colour from taste is possible because colour and taste both are the co-products of the self-same set of causes. Just as in the case of an ordinary cause-effect relationship like fire and smoke, from the perception of the effect we can pass on to the causal efficiency, similarly in the case of the orange, from the effect we can infer its cause. The cause of taste which produces the taste at t_2 being the material cause of taste at t_2 is the auxiliary cause which co-operates with the material cause in the production of colour at t_2. Thus while we infer the cause of taste from its effect, viz. the present taste, we can infer the present colour with whose cause the cause of taste must have been co-operating. Let us explain this third variety of inference a bit elaborately.

Since the taste (x_1) is the product of its material cause (x_0), the taste x_1 as the reason, from which the material cause x_0 is inferred, is determined as reason as *kārya*. This material cause of taste x_0 while producing its own effect functions as co-

---

6. *rūpādau sādhye rasādir ekasāmagryadhīnatayā niścīyate yathā mātuluṅge rūpānumānam* ǀ *atra rūpe janayitavye pūrvakam rūpam upādānam* ǀ *rasas tu sahakārikāraṇam* ǀ *pūrvapuñjād uttarapuñjasyotpattau nyāya eṣaḥ* ǀ — *TBh*, 15.1-3.

operating condition for the production of another effect form y_1. In other words, when the material cause of taste x_0 and the material cause of form y_0 gather they can produce their effect, form y_1. Therefore, these two material causes become a sufficient complex of causes for the production of form y_1. Here we find the possibility to apply the logical relation "sufficient complex of causes $\rightarrow$ fitness for the production of effect" to this causal relation. In the case of inference of form y_1 by the reason of taste x_1, however, as long as the consequence to be inferred from the complex of causes x_0 and y_0 is restricted to the particular form y_1 which is simultaneous with the other effect, i.e. taste x_1 which plays the role of reason, one can say that the effect itself, form y_1 is inferred from the complex of causes (x_0 and y_0) without taking into consideration the qualification "fitness" because at the point in time t_1 of taste x_1 from y_1, the effect of the complex of causes, is not an effect to be produced, but an effect already produced. Consequently, through the medium of logical relation "viewed at the point in time of an effect x_1 produced from the complex of causes x_1 and y_0, when there is this sufficient complex of causes, there is the other effect y_1" we can infer the form y_1 from the taste x_1: at first from the taste x_1 as reason as *kārya* its material cause x_0 is inferred. Then from the factual relation that the latter x_0 constitutes together with the material cause of form y_0 the sufficient complex of causes for two effects x_1 and y_0 the following logical proposition is drawn: viewed at the point in time of the taste as an effect x_1, when there is the complex of causes (x_0 and y_0), it is self-evident that there is necessarily the form as the other effect (y_1) which is simultaneous with the taste x_1. Accordingly the taste x_1 as reason as *kārya* can imply indirectly the existence of the form y_1. In this sense, the taste

x_1 as reason, from which the form y_1 is inferred, is considered as reason as *kārya*.

In the same manner the reason "smoke" for the inference of ash and coal is to be reduced to reason as *kārya*: by the reason smoke (x_1) as *kārya* its cause fire (x_0) is inferred.[7] Fire (x_0) and firewood (y_0) constitute a sufficient complex of causes for the production of ash and coal (y_1); so that it is self-evident that when there are fire (x_0) and firewood (y_0) at a point in time (t_1) of smoke (x_1) there is ash and coal (y_1). Since, in this way, from smoke (x_1) as reason as *kārya* fire (x_0) is inferred, and the latter implies ash and coal (y_1), smoke (x_1) implying indirectly ash and coal (y_1) is considered as reason as *kārya*.

However, it may be asked, what is the difference between a material cause and auxiliary causes, when both function equally to the concomitance of the effect affirmatively as well as negatively? The Buddhist answer is that when something x is produced because of the transformation of y in one and the same stream of entity, then y will be regarded as the material cause of x. But when something x is produced because of the transformation in other stream of entity like z, z will be regarded as the auxiliary cause in respect of x.[8] Thus, for example, in the production of a rice shoot, the rice-seed is regarded as the material cause while earth, water, air, etc. are regarded as auxiliary causes.

---

7. *ekasāmagryadhīnasya rūpāde rasato gatiḥ* ı
hetudharmānumānena dhūmendhanavikāravat ıı — *PV*, I.9.

8. *syād etat, sarveṣām anvaya-vyatirekāvanuvidhīyete tadā . . . kuto 'yaṁ bhedaḥ — ihopādānabhāvenedam upayujyate, anyatra tu sahakāri-bhāveneti?. . . tasmād avasthā 'bhede 'pi yad ekākāraparāmarśapratyayani-bandhanatayā svasantati-patita-kāryaprasūti-nimittaṁ tad upādāna-kāraṇam* ı *yat santānāntare prāgavasthāpekṣaviśeṣodayanibandhanaṁ tat sahakārikāraṇam* ı — *HBT*, 94, 26-95, 9.

Thus the probans as effect is based on the relation of causality and therefore can function as the logical mark (*gamaka*) in an inference. Dharmakīrti does not feel any necessity to spell out this causal relationship, as he does in the case of essential identity (*tādātmya*), because it is evident to all individuals on the basis of observation and non-observation of two entities.[9]

Probans as Essence

The nature of probans as essence is defined as the one whose existence is sufficient for the establishment of the probandum. For example, in the judgement "It is a flower because it is a rose," the probans, namely the rose, is sufficient for proving the *sādhya* or the probandum, namely the flower. Here the terms "rose" and "flower" have one and the same object for their reference. This sameness of reference which is known as *tādātmya* is responsible for the existential tie between rose and flower.

The nature of probans as essential identity has been presented by Dharmakīrti thus: A property (*bhāva*) is a probans for an essential property (*svabhāva*) which follows the mere existence of the former property (*bhāvamātrānurodhin*).[10] To put it thus, the nature of the property *s* is such that it is the *h* of the property to be proved (i.e. *s* itself) when the latter (i.e. *h*) depends for its existence on the essence of that *s* alone; in that case *h* is said to be the *svabhāva-hetu*.[11] The *svabhāva* is that property of something which is not caused by something else,

9. *kāryakāraṇabhāvo loke pratyakṣānupalambhanibandhanaḥ pratīta iti na svabhāvasyeva kāryasya lakṣaṇam uktam* । — *NBT*, 107. 5-6.

10. *svabhāvaḥ svasattāmātrabhāvini sādhyadharme hetuḥ* । — *NB*, II.15.

11. *yo hetor ātmanaḥ sattām apekṣya vidyamāno bhavati* । *na tu hetusattāyā vyatiriktaṁ kañcid hetum apekṣate sa svasattāmātrabhāvī sādhyaḥ* । *tasmin sādhye yo hetuḥ sa svabhāvaḥ tasya sādhyasya nānyaḥ* । — *NBT*, 106.5-7.

but is given with the thing itself. It is an inseparable property (*avyatirikto dharma*) of the thing. And as such it is a particular necessary characteristic of a real thing without which the thing could not exist. Thus *svabhāva* is in a logical context the concept of an essential property of real things. The stock example of a *svabhāva-hetu* inference is "This is a tree because it is a *śiṁśapā*," which actually means that "This can be called a tree because it can be called *śiṁśapā*." In this inference "this" refers to a thing in front of the inferring person, "being a tree" or "can be called a tree" refers to the property to be inferred and "being a *śiṁśapā*" or "can be called a *śiṁśapā*" refers to the probans. What is the meaning of "because it can be called a *śiṁśapā*"? It means the application of the name *śiṁśapā* which connotes particular branches, leaves, height, form, etc. In the *Hetubindu* text, Dharmakīrti presents the definition of *svabhāva-hetu* thus: An essential property (*svabhāva*) is the logical reason, when the property to be inferred follows only the existence of the inferring property (*sādhana dharma*).[12] He adds in explaining this definition — although the two properties are different by virtue of that difference which consists in the differentiation from the respective other properties, the inferring property is factually (*vastutaḥ*) nothing but the essence (*svabhāvaḥ*) of the indicated property (*liṅgī*).[13] In this way Dharmakīrti points out that the difference between the probans and the probandum is due to the particular process of abstraction alone, but they both mean the same real.[14]

---

12. *tatra sādhanadharmabhāvamātrānvayinī sādhyadharme svabhāvo hetuḥ* I — *HB*, 55.1.

13. *aparāpara-vyāvṛttibhedena dharmabhede 'satyapi vastutaḥ liṁgisvabhāva eva* I — *HB*, 55.2-3.

14. *paramāthasatā rūpeṇā 'bhedas tayoḥ* I *vikalpa-viṣayas tu yat samāropitaṁ rūpam* I *tadapekṣaḥ sādhyasādhanabhedaḥ* I — *NBT*, 113.6-7.

And the logical relation between the two concepts is one of identity (*tādātmya*), that is, the fact that the reality corresponding to one concept is the same as the reality corresponding to the other concept. What Dharmakīrti tries to highlight by the *svabhāva-hetu* is that the concept of an essential property is a reason for the concept of another property when this other concept means no other reality than the concept which serves as the reason.

The opponents might object that if two things are identical, they cannot be related to each other by the relation of probans and probandum, because in this case both of them would be one and the same part of the thesis.[15] In answer it has been pointed out that this objection is not tenable. It is true that both of them are not different in reality. But it is quite possible that there is a person who seeing a certain thing applies the name *śiṁśapā* which he learnt once, but does not identify it with the name "tree"; since he imagines through the name *śiṁśapā* not the essential qualities of a tree but something else, for instance the tall height, owing to confusion. Such a person may be now persuaded by means of this inference on the basis of identity. As such even though they are one in reality they appear distinct when they appear in our conceptual construction (*vikalpikā buddhau*) which depends on distinction from others. Their difference is due to the particular process of abstraction alone, but they both mean the same real. And the logical relation of the two concepts exists only because of their real identity, that is, the fact that the reality corresponding to the one concept is the same as the reality corresponding to the other concept. In other words, though the two concepts are in reality identical, in our conceptual construction they

15. *nanvekatve sādhya-sādhana-bhāvo na yuktaḥ pratijñārthaikadeśatvāt* ।
— *TBh*, 15, 14-15.

appear as different on the basis of their distinction from other objects. Hence, there is no difficulty in their acting as probans and probandum.[16]

Probans as Non-apprehension

This third variety of probans is distinguished from the earlier two varieties in respect of its fundamental nature. Both probans as effect and probans as essential identity are positive inasmuch as they help in proving the existence of a thing,[17] while this third variety is negative in nature. It helps in proving the absence or non-existence of an entity.[18] *Anupalabdhi* has been defined as the non-cognition of such an object that otherwise fulfils the conditions of cognizability.[19] For example, a pot by nature is such that it fulfils the conditions of cognizability. In other words a pot is by nature perceptible in normal condition. Now, if in a particular place in spite of the presence of all the normal conditions of perception like light, etc. the pot is not perceived, then from such non-apprehension we can infer that the pot is non-existent in that particular place. So the non-apprehension of the pot is the probans (*liṅga*) and the non-existence of the pot is the probandum (*liṅgī*).[20]

The non-apprehension of the object is regarded as the *liṅga* or probans for the non-existence of the object (*liṅgī*), on the

16. *tasmād etayoḥ paramārthata ekatve 'pi vikalpabuddhau vyāvṛttisamāśrayeṇa samutpannāyāṁ bhedena pratibhāsanāt sādhya-sādhanatvaṁ na virudhyate* । — *TBh*, 15.17-19.
17. *atra dvau vastusādhanau* । *ekaḥ pratiṣedhahetuḥ* । — *NB*, II.18.
18. *ekaḥ pratiṣedhasya hetur gamakaḥ* । *pratiṣedha iti cābhāvo 'bhāvavyavahāraś cokto draṣṭavayaḥ* । — *NBT*, 108, 5.
19. . . . *upalabdhi-lakṣaṇaprāptasyānupalabdheḥ* । *upalabdhilakṣaṇaprāptasyeti dṛśyasyetyarthaḥ* । — *TBh*, 15, 20-21.
20. *tatrānupalabdhir yathā na pradeśaviśeṣe kvacid ghaṭa upalabdhi-lakṣaṇa-prāptasyānupalabdher iti* । — *NB*, II.12.

logic that when all the conditions necessary for the perception of an object are present then if the object were there it would have been perceived. The existence of the object is one of the conditions for the perception of the object, the other conditions are eye, light, etc. But in spite of the presence of all the other conditions needed for perception, the object is not perceived.[21] Hence it can legitimately be inferred that the object is not there. In other words from the non-apprehension of the object the non-existence of the object is inferred.

It may be asked that if the object were non-existent, how can it be perceived? In reply it is said that when the place and other things are being cognized by one and the same perception, if the jar were present it would have been necessarily perceived.[22] That is to say, it is hypothetically supposed as perceptible on the ground that all the other conditions necessary for its perception are present. It is actually not perceived. Thus its actual non-apprehension is regarded as the probans. This is ascertained by means of the actually present objects comprised in one and the same cognition by which a jar, if it existed, would be also perceived (*ekajñāna-saṁsargī-padārtha*) or the knowledge of the objects comprised in one and the same cognition (*ekajñāna-saṁsargī-padārthopalambhaḥ*); thus these two, standing in the relation of agent and object (*karma-kartṛ-bhāva*) are each called non-cognition in the mode of the affirmation of what is excluded through the negation of a term.

---

21. *pratipattṛpratyakṣe kvacideva pradeśa iti dharmī* । *na ghaṭa iti sādhyam* । *upalabdhir jñānam* । *tasyā lakṣaṇam janikā sāmagrī* । *tayā hi upalabdhir lakṣyate* । *tat prāpto 'rtho janakatvena sāmagryantarbhāvāt* । *upalabdhilakṣaṇaprāpto dṛśya ityarthaḥ* । *tasyānupalabdheḥ ityayaṁ hetuḥ* ।
— *NBT*, 101, 6-9.

22. *yatra yasmin upalabhyamāne niyamena yasyopalabdhiḥ sa tatsaṁṛṣṭaḥ, ekajñānasaṁsargāt* । *tayoḥ sator naikarūpaniyatā pratipattir, asambhavāt* ।
— *HB*, 64, 27–65, 2.

This expression "negation of a term" is important. For it indicates that this form of inference is valid for only one form of negation, viz. the *paryudāsa* variety and not the *pratiṣedha* form of negation. The distinction between these two forms of negation is very important in Indian philosophy. In the field of Buddhist philosophy, Bhāvaviveka of the Mādhyamika School first pointed to this distinction to highlight the absolutist standpoint. Dharmakīrti in his *Hetubindu* also refers to this distinction. Arcaṭa in his commentary on the *Hetubindu* makes the distinction clear by pointing out that in one case where the negation occurs as a part of a sentence or a compound expression, though negation is used the main motive is affirmation and negation is understood only as implication. For example, when it is said "He is a non-brāhmaṇa" it is actually intended that "He is a kṣatriya." This variety of negation is called *paryudāsa*. But in the variety of negation called *prasajya pratiṣedha* it is just the other. There negation is applied to a proposition and the main intention is negation and affirmation is understood by implication. Here the negation conveys a different sense from the affirmative proposition related to it. For instance when it is said "Do not eat curd at night" it does not mean "Eat curd at night." The object to be negated is expressed by its own word, is connected with the negative. This distinction has been applied by Arcaṭa in the explanation of *anupalabdhi anumāna*. His point is that the negation in the case of non-apprehension is of the *paryudāsa* type, i.e. though negation is used the cognition of other things is implied. Mokṣakaragupta in his *Tarkabhāṣā* follows this view of Arcaṭa and recommends that non-apprehension is to be understood as negation with reference to a word and not with reference to a proposition. The non-apprehension of a pot must not be understood as the simple absence of cognition, the negation being construed by *prasajya pratiṣedha*, but as the apprehension of things other than the pot, e.g. the cognition of the locus, and other associated things. In other words in the non-apprehension of the pot the negation is to be understood as a case of *paryudāsa*. The reason is that if we took the negation to be *prasajya pratiṣedha* variety, then it itself will not be anything, as such it cannot act as the probans of anything. Even if we take non-apprehension in the sense of *paryudāsa*, i.e. as the apprehension of other things, it cannot be the apprehension of other things in general except that whose absence is going to be proved. For, in that case the negation of one object, like "the orange is not sweet" will mean the presence of the colour of that orange which will be absurd. Therefore, it is clear that either of the two things distinguished in the way characterized above from what is negated, i.e. either the locus or the knowledge of the locus is called non-apprehension.

It is because of this reason that the Buddhist logicians hold that the absence itself is not proved by inference, the absence of an object like the absence of jar can be proved by perception of the place without the jar. But non-apprehension as a logical probans is admitted only for practical activities, like convincing another person about the absence of an object. Dharmakīrti holds that the non-existence of an object is established by perception alone, but the function of inference of non-apprehension consists in persuading an ignorant person who cannot realize the absence. So, according to Dharmakīrti what is negated by such negative inference is the subjective function, i.e. knowledge, verbal expression or doubt regarding an object which is falsely believed to exist. This, however holds in the case of *svabhāvānupalabdhi* which is the principal form of non-apprehension. Regarding the other two varieties of non-apprehension, viz. *kāryānupalabdhi* and *vyāpakānupalabdhi*, the non-apprehension aims to prove either the *abhāva* itself or the application of absence (*abhāvavyavahāra*). This is because, when we infer the absence of smoke from the non-apprehension of fire or the absence of elmness from the non-apprehension of tree, we not only prove the negative activities concerning them, but also the absence itself. In the case of *svabhāvānupalabdhi*, i.e. in the case of direct negation of a perceptible object, the absence itself is proved by perception alone without being dependent on inference.

When looked at from the objective mode as the locus without the pot, the non-cognition is to be understood as the relation of identity with the locus. But when it is considered from the subjective mode (*kartṛdharmapakṣa*) as the knowledge of the locus without a pot, the relation between non-apprehension and the locus is one of causality; since the locus without the pot or the apprehension of the locus is the probans. So the capacity of the jar to be recognized as non-existent (*asad-vyavahāra-yogyatā*) is the essential nature of the locus without the pot. The knowledge of the locus without the jar is the effect of the locus itself. So when the apprehension of the locus is considered as the probans, we are proceeding from the effect to the cause.

It may be pointed out by the opponents that what has been exhibited just now is that non-apprehension is reduced to essential identity or causality. If that is so, how is the probans as non-apprehension differentiated from the probans as effect or probans as essential identity? In reply it has been said by the Buddhists that the difference is made on the basis of the difference between affirmation and negation, and not in reality. This has been stated very explicitly by Dharmakīrti in his *Nyāyabindu* as also in his *Pramāṇavārttikam* that of the three probanses two are for establishing the existence of an object and the other one is for establishing the absence.[23]

In the context of probans as non-apprehension it has been said that the object "must be such that it is by nature perceptible," and this phrase is very important. For, if the object were such that it is inaccessible in space, time and essence, then from the non-occurrence of such an object it will not be possible to explain the practical activities regarding the concerned object. As examples of such objects the Buddhists refer to the mountain Sumeru which is inaccessible in respect of space, the future emperor Śaṁkha who is inaccessible in respect of time and a ghost which is inaccessible in respect of essence. In his autocommentary on *Pramāṇavārttika* Dharmakīrti makes a distinction between two kinds of non-apprehension — non-apprehension of an imperceptible object and the non-apprehension of a perceptible object. Both these non-cognitions have the same effect, viz. negating the practical activities referring to an object wrongly supposed to be existent. However, their mode of approach is different — the former leads to the result through the absence of a proof while the latter through the presence of a counterproof. As such in the former case one cannot be assured of the existence of an imperceptible object like a ghost and so its existence is neither denied nor asserted. Because of this doubt one negates the positive assertion of its existence. But one can be sure of the absence of a perceptible object when it is not apprehended, and so its existence can be definitely negated. Thus though both the non-cognition leads to the same result, they differ in respect of certainty.

23. *atra dvau vastusādhanau । ekaḥ pratiṣedhahetuḥ ।* — *NB*, II.19.

This also refers to another important point regarding non-apprehension. Non-apprehension can lead to valid cognition only with regard to the present experience or with regard to that past experience about which we have vivid memory. About future experience non-apprehension is doubtful and cannot lead to valid cognition. This has been very clearly pointed out by Dharmakīrti in his *Nyāyabindu* that non-apprehension, i.e. the fact that perception does not occur to an observer with regard to a past object which he keeps in clear memory-impression or with regard to a present object, establishes practical activities referring to the absence of the object.[24]

The number of this sort of non-apprehension probans varies from logician to logician. Even Dharmakīrti himself in his three different texts has mentioned the classification in three different ways. In his *Hetubindu* he speaks of three varieties of non-apprehension, in his *Pramāṇavārttikam* he adds one more and speaks of four varieties, and in his *Nyāyabindu* he mentions eleven varieties of non-apprehension. Mokṣakaragupta in his *Tarkabhāṣā* adds five more to this list, and thus there are total sixteen varieties of non-apprehension. These differences are due to the fact that sometimes we are to establish the negation of an object which is situated at a distant place and inaccessible and to which the non-apprehension of an *ex hypothesi* perceptible object is not directly available. In such situation we have to take into consideration the non-apprehension of an effect or other indirect forms of negative inference. Hence, regarding the variety of applied formulae there is variation in the form of negative inferences.

24. *amūḍhasmṛtisaṁskārasyātītasya vartamānasya ca pratipattṛ-pratyakṣasya nivṛttir abhāva-vyavahāra-pravartanī* | — *NB*, II.28.

1. ***svabhāvānupalabdhi***: where the object which is perceptible in nature is not perceived. Here there is no smoke because it, by nature perceptible, is not perceived.
2. ***kāryānupalabdhi***: where from the non-apprehension of the effect, the non-existence of the cause is inferred. There is no efficient cause producing smoke here, for there is no smoke.
3. ***kāraṇānupalabdhi***: from the non-apprehension of the cause the non-existence of the effect is proved. For example, there is no smoke here for there is no fire.
4. ***vyāpakānupalabdhi***: where the non-existence of the pervaded is inferred from the non-perception of the pervader. There is no oak here for there is no tree.
5. ***svabhāvaviruddhopalabdhi***: There is no sensation of cold here for there is fire. Here the sensation of cold is denied on the basis of the apprehension of fire which has a nature contradictory to the sensation of cold.
6. ***kāryaviruddhopalabdhi***: There is no efficient cause of the sensation of cold for there is fire here. The causes giving rise to the sensation of cold are denied here on the basis of the apprehension of fire which as an effect is contradictory to the effect generated by the causes of the sensation of cold.
7. ***kāraṇaviruddhopalabdhi***: He exhibits no symptom such as the bristling of the hair of the body caused by cold, because he is near fire. The cause of the symptoms of such bristling of the hair of the body is cold. Fire is contradictory to cold. So when fire is apprehended, the effect of its contradictory, viz. cold cannot exist.

8. ***vyāpakaviruddhopalabdhi***: Here there is no sensation of freezing because there is fire. Sensation of freezing is to be negated. The *vyāpaka* or pervader of such sensation is cold. Fire which is the contradictory of such cold is perceived here. So from the apprehension of such fire, the sensation of freezing is negated.

9. ***svabhāvaviruddhakāryopalabdhi***: Perception of the effect of something which is contradictory to the nature of the thing to be negated. Here there is no sensation of cold because there is smoke here. Smoke is the effect of fire and fire has a nature incompatible with the sensation of cold, so from the apprehension of smoke, the sensation of cold is negated.

10. ***kāryaviruddhakāryopalabdhi***: Perception of the effect of something which is contradictory to the effect of the thing negated. Here there is no cause of cold because there is smoke. Smoke is the effect of fire and fire is contradictory to the effect of the cause of cold, i.e. to cold. So from the apprehension of smoke, the cause of cold is negated.

11. ***kāraṇaviruddhakāryopalabdhi***: Perception of the effect of something which is contradictory to the cause of the thing to be negated. There is no one exhibiting the symptom of cold because there is smoke here. The effect of smoke is fire which is contradictory to cold which is the cause of the symptom of cold. So from the observation of smoke, the symptom of cold is negated.

12. ***vyāpakaviruddhakāryopalabdhi***: Apprehension of the effect which is contradictory to the *vyāpaka* of the thing to be negated. There is no sensation of freezing because

there is smoke. Smoke is the effect of fire. Fire is contradictory to cold which is the pervader (*vyāpaka*) of the sensation of freezing. So from the apprehension of fire, the sensation of freezing is negated.

13. ***svabhāvaviruddhavyāptopalabdhi*:** Perception of the pervaded which is incompatible with the nature of the thing to be negated. There is no fire because of the sensation of freezing. Sensation of freezing is pervaded by cold. Cold is contradictory to fire, which is to be negated. So when there is sensation of freezing there can be no fire.

14. ***kāryaviruddhavyāptopalabdhi*:** Perception of what is pervaded of the thing incompatible with the effect of the thing to be negated. Here there is no cause of fire because there is sensation of freezing. Sensation of freezing is pervaded by cold which is contradictory to fire and fire is the effect of the cause of fire. So from the sensation of freezing, cause of fire is negated.

15. ***kāraṇaviruddhavyāptopalabdhi*:** Perception of what is pervaded of the thing incompatible with the cause of the thing to be negated. There is no smoke here because of the sensation of freezing. Sensation of freezing is pervaded by cold which is contradictory to fire, which is the cause of the thing to be negated, viz. smoke.

16. ***vyāpakaviruddhavyāptopalabdhi*:** Perception of what is pervaded of the thing incompatible with the pervader of the thing to be negated. This is not permanent because it produces the effect only occasionally. Production of the effect occasionally is pervaded by changeability. Changeability is the

contradictory of changelessness which is the pervader of permanence. So from the apprehension of the occasional production of effect, permanence is negated.

11

Nature of Vyāpti
as Avinābhāva and as Svabhāvapratibandha

INFERENCE regarding an unknown object on the basis of some known fact is possible on two conditions, first if the probans exists in the locus, and secondly, if the probans has invariable connection with the probandum. Such invariable concomitance is technically known as *vyāpti* relationship in Indian logic. The significance of *vyāpti* is indicated by the fact that there can be no inference in the absence of such a relation and that every definition of *anumāna* directly or indirectly has to bring it in.

The concept of *vyāpti* can be traced to the *Caraka-Saṁhitā*, but it was Diṅnāga who first emphasized the necessity of *vyāpti* in an inference along with the condition of *pakṣadharmatā*, viz. the existence of the probans in the locus of the inference. In the *Pramāṇasamuccaya* Diṅnāga holds *grāhyadharmas tadaṁśena vyāpto hetuḥ* and states the invariable concomitant relation of *B* with *A*, which legitimizes the inference of the probandum *A* from the probans *B*, as follows:

> When the probans occurs, there the probandum, that of which it is the probans, has to occur as well. And if the probans has to occur somewhere, it has to occur only where the probandum occurs.[1]

---

1. *liṅge liṅgī bhavatyeva liṅgīny evetarat punaḥ* ।

This verse has been quoted frequently by logicians belonging to the Nyāya, Jaina and other Indian traditions. It actually amounts to saying that all cases of *B* are cases of *A*, and only cases of *A* could be cases of *B*.

In one of his articles on *svabhāvapratibandha*,[2] Prof. Katsura has identified four different stages in the development of the notion of logical connection which constitutes the basis or foundation of inference. The first of them has been represented in the *Vaiśeṣikasūtra* (*c.* second and third century CE) as well as in *Ṣaṣṭhitantra* (*c.* CE 300) where different concrete relations between the probans and the probandum have been identified as the foundation of inference. A similar view has been upheld by Asaṅga. The second stage may be referred to by Vasubandhu's time (CE 400–480) when an abstract relation called inevitability or *nāntarīyakatva* or *avinābhāva*, between the probans and the probandum, was considered as the foundation. It was during the time of Diṅnāga, that is in *c.* CE 480–530, the notion of *vyāpti* attained its third stage. Diṅnāga conceived *vyāpti* or the notion of pervasion of the probans by the probandum to be the foundation of the inevitable (*avinābhāva*) relationship. From this time onwards the notion of *vyāpti* was gradually accepted by most Indian logicians. The final and fourth stage of *vyāpti* was attained with Dharmakīrti (CE 600–660) who introduced the concept of *svabhāva pratibandha* to give the logical relation of inference a solid and natural foundation. In the writings of previous writers we did not find any discussion regarding the relation between *vyāpti* and reality, i.e. how *vyāpti* was related to reality; Dharmakīrti tried to provide a solution to this problem by his concept of *svabhāva pratibandha*. Let us now try to

2. "Svabhāvapratibandha Revisited," in *Journal of Indian and Buddhist Studies*, 1992.

understand these notions *avinābhāva* and *svabhāva pratibandha* a bit elaborately.

Etymologically the word *avinābhāva* means *a* + *vinā* + *bhāva*. *Vinā* means "without," i.e. "without the probandum" or "in the absence of the probandum." *Bhāva* means "existence," i.e. "existence of the probans," and *a* means "not". Taken together, the whole expression *avinābhāva* amounts to saying "it is not the case that in the absence of the probandum, the probans exists." Thus it implies the absence of the probans (*hetu*) in the absence of the probandum (*sādhya*). Apparently it seems to have a negative meaning, but it has a positive implication also. *Avinābhāva* is a relation between two things which are such that one cannot be present in the absence of the other.

Dharmakīrti also uses the expression *svabhāva pratibandha* to designate the relationship of *vyāpti*. The word *svabhāva pratibandha* means "the existential tie." Existential tie means the existence of one thing tied to another, in other words it stands for dependent existence. The idea is that a probans can prove the probandum because it stands in a necessary relationship to the probandum. In other words, the existence of the probans is not possible without the existence of the probandum. For example, smoke cannot exist independently of fire. This is called *anvaya* which may be regarded as similar to the concomitance in agreement. It may be noted that the probandum may exist without the probans but the probans cannot exist without the probandum. The probandum is regarded as the *vyāpaka* or pervader and the probans as the *vyāpya* or the pervaded. The probandum can exist in the locus of the probans though not exclusively. It may exist independently of the probans. But the probans can exist only in the locus of the probandum. That is to say, it cannot exist in a place where the probandum does not exist. So, if probans is represented by *M* and probandum by *P* the relation between the two may be stated thus —

1. Where *M* exists *P* exists,
2. *M* does not exist where *P* does not exist.

The former is called *anvaya* or concomitance in agreement and the latter *vyatireka* or concomitance in difference. Thus while Diṅnāga pointed out the *vyāpti* relation between smoke and fire by the fact that the domain of smoke is pervaded by the domain of fire in the universe of discourse, Dharmakīrti justified the inevitable relation between smoke and fire on the ground of *svabhāva pratibandha*, i.e. such relation is supported by the fact that in reality smoke arises from fire. The reason why there is a universal connection between smoke and fire in the universe of discourse is that in reality the two entities are essentially connected in such a way that smoke arises from fire. Similarly we can successfully infer the existence of a flower from the existence of a lotus flower because in reality there is one and the same essence which is called flower as well as lotus.

Thus the Buddhists believed that if there is a real and natural relationship between two objects then it can be said that there is a necessary concomitant relationship between the two terms and then the existence of one can necessarily lead to the existence of the other. This natural relationship is possible if the terms under consideration are related by the relation of causality or essential identity. Dharmakīrti believed that only those terms which are related by causality and identity can be considered as valid grounds of inference. In other cases, the relation between two terms cannot be regarded as universal and necessary. The proof of the necessity of the relation is furnished by the consideration that the opposite possibility cannot be entertained without contradiction. Such relation can subsist in the case of effect and cause. Effect cannot be thought to exist without a relevant cause; that is, we cannot conceive that an effect has occurred without a cause. For example, smoke is an effect of fire and as such the former cannot come into existence in the absence of the other. Thus the relation between cause and effect is necessarily thought to be universally valid, and so also with regard to terms that stand in the relation of identity.

In the case of essential identity, an entity is possible only with that which follows from it (viz. the probans) and not with any other which is dependent upon another external fact. That is, if two entities *A* and *B* are such that the entity *B* was not present when the other *A* was present, then at subsequent moment the existence of *B* cannot necessarily be guaranteed by *A* with logical necessity. There is no ontological necessity that the cause should have the effect as its concomitance, since a cause can occur without the effect accompanying it. The Buddhists point out that though *tādātmya* or essential identity is different from *tadutpatti* or causality, both of them are considered to give rise to necessary connection. The effect is dependent upon and necessarily related to or concomitant with the cause but not vice versa. The effect does not come into being in the moment the cause occurs but after the occurrence of the cause, and that also is not necessary. An impediment may occur and the effect in that case may not materialize. Thus the nature of concomitance is different in two cases, — in essential identity the probans and the probandum are necessarily present together because they are ontologically identical and their difference is conceptual and logical; whereas in causality the cause may occur independently without producing the effect, if a counteracting agent supervenes. In short, in essential identity concomitance is bilateral, whereas in causality it is unilateral.

Since the Buddhists define reality in terms of causal efficiency (*arthakriyākāritva*), everything real is subject to causation. Thus a lotus flower is said to be existent because of its preceding causes. So in the ultimate analysis, the principle which governs the real world of our experience as understood by Dharmakīrti is the principle of causality. Causal relation can be determined by identifying the "cause" and the "effect." Understood thus, there is virtually no difference between the *svabhāva-hetu* and the *kārya-hetu,* as has been pointed out by Richard Hayes and supported by Prof. S. Katsura.

In Dharmakīrti's philosophy the concept of *svabhāva pratibandha* has been treated both in the ontological and logical levels. In his *Pramāṇavārttikasvavṛtti,* Dharmakīrti pointed out that only on the basis of the essential connection (*svabhāva pratibandha*) the probans can make the probandum known. And this connection is characterized by either causality or essential identity. That connection is also known as inevitable relation (*avinābhāva*) and is demonstrated by both affirmative and negative examples. To quote directly from his auto-commentary *Svavṛtti* —

> *tasmāt svabhāvapratibandhād eva hetuḥ sādhyaṁ gamayati* । *sa ca tadbhāvalakṣaṇas tadutpattilakṣaṇo vā* । *sa evāvinābhāvo dṛṣṭāntābhyāṁ pradarśyate* ॥[3]

This passage implies

1. *tādātmya/tadutpatti = svabhāvapratibandha = avinābhāva* → *sādhya-sādhanabhāva*

In an earlier passage of the same commentary Dharmakīrti appears to put an altogether different view where he differentiates the above three terms and puts them in logical order:

3. *PVSV,* 11.8-9.

> If there is an essential connection there can be no variation between one object and another, i.e. one object does not deviate from the other. And the connection exists because of essential identity between the two objects. An effect has an essential connection, because its essence arises from the cause.[4]

This passage presents the chain as follows —

2. *tādātmya/tadutpatti* ⟶ *svabhāvapratibandhaḥ* ⟶ *avyabhicāraḥ*

This view of *Svavṛtti* is also comparable to what is found in *Nyāyabindu.*

> When there is essential connection, one object can imply another (can make another object known), since, if two objects are not essentially connected, there can be no assurance that one object does not deviate from the other. Such essential connection exists between the probans and the probandum, if in reality the former is either identical with or caused by the object to be inferred. If *A* neither takes *B* as its essence nor arises from *B*, *A* is not essentially connected with *B*. Further, since both identity and causality principles exist only in *svabhāva-hetu* and *kārya-hetu* respectively, they alone can establish the existence of the object.[5]

---

4. *svabhāvapratibandhe hi saty artho 'arthaṁ na vyabhicarati* ı *sa ca tadātmatvāt . . . kāryasyāpi svabhāvapratibandhaḥ* ı *tatsvabhāvasya tadutpatter iti* ı —Ibid., 2.6-11.

5. *svabhāvapratibandhe hi sati artho arthaṁ gamayet* ı *tadapratibaddhasya tadavyabhicāraniyamābhāvāt* ı *sa ca pratibandhaḥ sādhye arthe liṅgasya* ı *vastutas tādātmyāt tad utpatteś ca* ı *atat-svabhāvasyātad-utpatteś ca tatrāpratibaddhasvabhāvatvāt* ı *te ca tādātmya-tadutpatti svabhāva-kāryayor eveti tābhyām eva vastusiddhiḥ* ı —*NB*, 2.19-24.

The implication of this passage is —

3. *tādātmya/tadutpatti* → *svabhāvapratibandha* → *avyabhicāraniyama* = *avinābhāvaniyama* → *gamya-gamakabhāva*

Another interesting aspect of *svabhāva pratibandha* is observed in the *Svavṛtti* commentary where Dharmakīrti declares that when there is no essential connection, there is no determination of *anvaya* and *vyatireka*.[6] This passage indicates the implication to be

4. *svabhāvapratibandha* → *anvaya-vyatireka-niścaya*

Commentator Manorathanandi in his commentary on verse 203 of the *Parārthānumānaparicchedaḥ* identifies *svabhāva pratibandha* with *tādātmya* (essential identity) and *tadutpatti* (causality) — *parābhimateṣu hetuṣ yeṣu pratibandhaḥ tādṛśaḥ tādātmya-tadutpatti-lakṣaṇo nāsti. . . .*[7] If this passage is taken note of the relation among the different terms will be:

5. *tādātmya/tadutpatti* = *svabhāvapratibandha* → *avyabhicāra* → *gamya-gamakabhāva*

In the fourth chapter, i.e. in the chapter on Inference for Others, Dharmakīrti identifies *avinābhāva* with *niyama* (*niyamo hi avinābhāvo . . .*[8]); in fact this had earlier been done by Diṅnāga in his *Pramāṇasamuccaya*. Diṅnāga, there, not only identified *avinābhāva* with *niyama*, but further identified it with *avyabhicāra*, i.e. non-deviation and *vyāpti* or pervasion. In the next line of the subsequent verse, i.e. verse 205,[9] Dharmakīrti

6. *na hy asati pratibandhe 'nvaya-vyatirekaniścayo 'sti* ।
— *PVSV*, 7.10.

7. *PVV*.

8. *PV*, verse 204.

9. *aikāntikatvaṁ vyāvṛtter avinābhāva ucyate*, — Ibid., verse 205.

proceeds to identify *avinābhāva* with *vyāvṛtter aikāntikatvam*, i.e. "absolute certainty of exclusion of *X* from where *Y* is absent." Thus we meet with a new form of equation:

6. *avinābhāva-niyama* (= *avyabhicāra* = *vyāpti*) = *vyāvṛtti-aikāntikatva*

Dharmakīrti then shows that it is on the basis of *svabhāva pratibandha*, *tādātmya* and *tadutpatti* that we can establish the positive and negative concomitance (*anvaya-vyatireka*) between the probans and the probandum.[10] That is

7. *svabhāvapratibandha* = *tādātmya/tadutpatti* ⟶ *anvaya-vyatireka-sthiti*

This, of course, is a repetition of what has already been stated in the *Nyāyabindu*. Now, the equations (5), (6), (7) taken together will lead us to say.

8. *svabhāvapratibandha* = *tādātmya/tadutpatti* ⟶ *anvaya-vyatireka-sthiti* ⟶ *avinābhāvaniyama* = *vyāvṛttyaikāntikatva* = *avyabhicāra* = *vyāpti* ⟶ *gamya-gamaka-bhāva*[11]

The upshot of the whole discussion is that, while Diṅnāga could locate the invariable character of *vyāpti* relation as essential basis for an inference, he was not able to account for the reason for such invariability. Dharmakīrti was able to identify *svabhāva pratibandha* in the form of identity and causality to be the basic reason for the *avinābhāva-niyama*. He could point out the logical necessity character of *vyāpti* relation and explain satisfactorily how and why the probandum can follow satisfactorily from the probans in a valid inference. It may be

---

10. . . . *tacca nāpratibaddheṣu tata evānvaya-sthitiḥ* ॥
svātmatve hetubhāve vā siddhe hi vyatirekitā । — Ibid., verses 205-06.

11. For details see, Katsura — "*Pramāṇavārttika* IV. 202-206 — towards the correct understanding of *svabhāvapratibandha*," *Journal of Indian and Buddhist Studies*, vol. 40, no. 2, March 1992.

noted here that in some early texts like the *Ṣaṣṭhitantra* ascribed to the Sāṁkhya philosopher Vṛṣagaṇa, it was recognized that there is a certain connection at the root of inference, since inference was defined as the establishment of something not perceived from something perceived/perceivable on account of a certain connection.[12] Though in that text, immediately after the definition, attempt had been made to specify that connection by enumerating seven different types of relation along with examples, the defect of that account became evident when in another part of the same *Ṣaṣṭhitantra* it had been implied that in some cases the mere connection is not sufficient for the validity of inference. Because of this discrepancy between the two parts of the same text, the earlier account of the constitution of connectedness was given up long before Dharmakīrti; and it goes to the full credit of Dharmakīrti to spell out that relationship which lies at the basis of inference. Dharmakīrti gave the discussion of *vyāpti* a new dimension by confining it not as a mere logical relation but giving it a footing in reality itself. In one of the oft-quoted verses of the *Svārthānumānaparicchedaḥ* of *Pramāṇavārttika*, namely —

> *kārya-kāraṇabhāvād vā svabhāvād vā niyāmakāt* ।
> *avinābhāvaniyamo 'darśanān na na darśanāt* ॥[13]

We have an explanation of the dependence of logical connections on connections in reality by specifying the two instances in reality eligible for being the cause of *avinābhāva niyama* in that they both are of restrictive character (*niyāmaka*).

---

12. *sambandhād ekasmāt pratyakṣac cheṣasiddhir anumānam* ।
13. *PV*, I.33.

12

Ascertainment of Vyāpti

THE question that arises in connection with the validity of inference is regarding the ascertainment of *vyāpti*. Since *vyāpti* is a universal proposition, the classical Indian logicians claim that the example mentioned in the premises cannot provide the truth of the universal proposition it exemplifies. It can only indicate that the universal proposition has been formulated on the basis of confirmative or supporting instances. Though this may be quite correct and acceptable to other school of thinkers, for the Buddhists it would be quite problematic to accept the *vyāpti* statement as an inductive generalization. For in that case it cannot claim to be uncontradictable or never contradicted by experience which it should be in order to be a piece of knowledge. It can claim to have only probability which, however high it may be, would not amount to absolute certainty. And if the *vyāpti* statement is not certain, then the conclusion drawn on its basis would also not be uncontradicted by experience. The consequence of this will be that inference which involves the application of such *vyāpti* cannot be regarded as *pramāṇa* in the sense accepted by the Buddhists themselves. Accordingly the Buddhists feel a special urge to ascertain the necessary character of *vyāpti* statement. In the Buddhist logical framework inference can be claimed to yield knowledge uncontradicted by experience only if its premises are uncontradicted by experience which it cannot do if the *vyāpti* is viewed as an inductive generalization. For the Naiyāyikas, it is not a problem at all, since they believe that with the help of a variety of extraordinary perception known as *sāmānya lakṣaṇa pratyakṣa* (perception of universals or concepts) we can directly cognize how one universal is related to another. For example, by perceiving in instances of fire and of smoke, how the universal of smokeness (*dhūmatva*) present in the latter is related to that of fireness (*vahnitva*) present in the former, we can apprehend that "All cases of smoke are cases of fire." But such a view is not acceptable to the Buddhists as they do not admit the reality of universals. So the Buddhists in their framework have no other alternative but to establish the *vyāpti* statement as a universal generalization on the basis of individual instances. But how can certainty be achieved in the process is the burning problem.

It may be noted here that the question of establishing the truth of a universal proposition on the basis of some particular cases was noted by the Western logicians also. For instance Hempel in his "Studies in the Logic of Confirmation" claims that it would be impossible to develop an account of rules of induction which "would enable us to infer, from a given set of data, that hypothesis or generalization which accounts best for all the particular data in the given set." In that paper Hempel accordingly discusses several criteria by which a hypothesis *H* may be confirmed or corroborated on the basis of a given body of evidences *E*. Regarding the confirmation of the hypothesis "*A* entails *B*" the criterion which had been offered by Nicod was that we have to observe *B* in the presence of *A*, since the hypothesis is invalidated if we do not observe *B* in the presence of *A*. Hempel notes two difficulties in Nicod's criterion. First, it only applies to hypothesis which either can be put in a universal conditional form or which involves both universal and existential quantifiers. Thus the hypothesis "There exists life on other planets" could not be confirmed using Nicod's criterion. But the second difficulty of Nicod's criterion is that it sets the stage for actual raven paradox. The raven paradox arises from the combination of both Nicod's criterion and the equivalent condition, namely $(x)\ (Ax \rightarrow Bx) \rightarrow (x)\ ({\sim}Bx \rightarrow {\sim}Ax)$. Nicod's criterion still applies in cases where we have straightforward confirmation of a hypothesis. Such an example would be the case when a white chalk confirms the hypothesis "All non-black things are non-ravens" which is logically equivalent to "All ravens are black." So according to the equivalent condition, it ought to confirm the latter hypothesis by confirming the former. From this it follows that since one cannot dispense with the equivalent condition, the hypothesis "All ravens are black" can be confirmed even without satisfying Nicod's criterion of confirmation.

In the Indian philosophical structure we find that the Nyāya school of thinkers are coming closer to Nicod's criterion in respect of confirmation of hypothesis. They suggest that it is through repeated observation (*bhuyodarśana*) of two things occurring together and non-observation of any contrary case that we can speak of confirming a universal proposition. The Buddhist logicians reacted against this view by pointing out that the lack of togetherness of *A* with non-*B* does not ensure the togetherness of *A* with *B*. For to say that "Every *A* is *B*" is to presuppose that "there are *A*-s"; but "No *A* is non-*B*" may not presuppose that there is at least one *A* which is also *B*. Hence the doctrine of repeated observation between two events is not the basis of *vyāpti* relation. This problem is also connected with the problem of induction. For Diṅnāga insisted that to confirm that "All products are perishable" we need not only a perishable product such as a pot as a positively supporting example, but also a non-perishable non-product such as the sky as a negatively supporting example, i.e. *vaidharmya dṛṣṭānta*. The puzzle is similar to Hempel's puzzle in a similar context, viz. confirmation of an induction. Just as each black raven tends to confirm the hypothesis that "All ravens are black" so each green leaf, being non-black and non-raven, should confirm that "All non-black things are non-ravens" which are logically equivalent to "All ravens are black."

Diṅnāga[1] might suggest a solution to the problem by saying that "All ravens are black" is not equivalent to "All non-black things are non-ravens." The equivalence does not hold since the latter may not imply the former always though the former implies the latter. For let us suppose that all black ravens are destroyed from the earth. Then it will still be true that "All non-black things are non-ravens" as other things of the world like the brown table or the green leaves will make it true, but we cannot say that they will make the sentence "All ravens are black" true (for there are no ravens to confirm the proposition). This means that in Diṅnāga's system we will have to assume that universal affirmative propositions carry existential presupposition. It is because of this that Diṅnāga insisted that both a positive and a negative example are needed to confirm a hypothesis.

Richard Hayes as such says that while speaking of a universal affirmative proposition "Every *A* is *B*" in the context of *hetu*-possessors and *sādhya*-possessors we have to

---

1. For a detailed discussion on this vide (a) Tuske, "Diṅnāga and the Raven Paradox", *Journal of Indian Philosophy*, vol. 26, 1998. (b) B.S. Gillon — "Dharmakīrti and the Problem of Induction" in *Studies in the Buddhist Epistemological Tradition*, ed. E. Steinkellner, 1991.

presuppose that the subject term *A* names a class that is non-empty. In this respect it differs from a proposition that states a *vyatireka* relation. The propositional form that best captures a state of affairs in which a *vyatireka* relation holds between classes *A* and *B* is the obverse of a universal affirmative proposition, that is a proposition of the form "No *A* is non-*B*." When the class *A* has no member this latter proposition is true, for it simply says that there exists non-member of the class *A* that is non-*B*. Thus, if the class A has members, then "Every *A* is *B*" and "No *A* is non-*B*" are logically equivalent. But if *A* has no members then we can regard "No *A* is *B*" and "No *A* is non-*B*" as true, but "Every *A* is *B*," will be indeterminate in truth-value. Diṅnāga's views on the conditions necessary to warrant asserting a universal proposition would rest upon the intuition that we are not likely to believe that one property always occurs with a second property unless the two following conditions occur — (1) there is some precedent of the two properties' actually occurring together, and (2) there is no reason to deny that the first always occurs with the second. The *anvaya* relation between a class *H* and a class *S* serves to justify our entertaining the possibility that every member of *H* is also a member of *S*, although it is of course not a sufficient ground for asserting that every *H* is *S*. If there is also a *vyatireka* relation between *H* and *S*, then there is no reason to deny that every *H* is *S*. If the *anvaya* relation fails to hold while the *vyatireka* relation holds, then we have no warrant to assert a universal affirmative proposition.

Let us consider the case "Sound is perishable because it is audible," here the *pakṣa* is the class of sounds. So the induction domain is the class of non-sounds but the property of being audible fails to occur at all in this induction domain, for only sounds are audible. Hence the *anvaya* relation between *sādhya dharma* and *hetu dharma* fails to hold. So we have no justification to believe that every *H* is *S* nor deny that no *H* is *S*; but the *vyatireka* relation does hold in this case; since it is not the case that some audible non-sound is *S* and so we have no justification either to deny that every *H* is *S* nor to believe that every *H* is non-*S*. If there is no reason either to affirm or deny either the universal affirmative or its contrary we must simply suspend judgements altogether on the relation between this *hetu* and other properties.

Accordingly Diṅnāga says that a "negative" example is not enough and a positive example is needed for the required certainty. So he must deny that "All ravens are black" is in any way implied by "All non-black things are non-ravens." This denial forces us to search for a possible situation which may not have been eliminated. Suppose "non-black" in my dictionary means "white." It will still be true that all non-black things are non-ravens, which may be confirmed by a white crane. Further suppose that I have never seen a raven and that I imagine that they are neither black nor white but gray. Only an actual black raven can remove my doubt in this case. The oddity implicit in such a consideration is not any more serious than the oddity in assuming that a green leaf confirms the rule "All ravens are black." Thus Diṅnāga's point is that a positive example is necessary even when there is a negatively supporting example. It is obvious from his writings that he was not comfortable with simple negative examples where no positive example was at all available, as for instance in the *kevalavyatirekin* or universally negative inferences.

In fact, his doctrine of the triple characteristics of the probans is suggestive of the circumstances under which it is rational to make an inference. According to him, not every probans *H* has to be included in the probandum *S*. It suffices if every known H is included in every known S. If $K(h)$ stands for the class of objects which are known to be h, then to say that all H is S, amounts to say that $K(h) \subset K(s)$. This is clearly an inductive statement. So the idea is that if one never observes an exception to a rule, then one is allowed to believe that the rule holds universally. Diṅnāga in his *Hetucakraḍamaru* points out that there are nine alternative combinations possible from the presence of the probans in (1) all, (2) some or (3) none of the class of homogeneous and heterogeneous entities. Out of these nine possibilities only two inferences are good, viz. (1) when the probans is present in all of the homogeneous and none of the heterogeneous entities, and (2) when the probans is present in some of the homogeneous entities and none of the heterogeneous entities. But Diṅnāga's views had been criticized by the Naiyāyika Uddyotakara who pointed out that it is quite possible to conceive the class of homogeneous entities or the heterogeneous entities as empty. Accordingly Uddyotakara extended the wheel of reason from nine to twelve. Dharmakīrti later on tried to solve the whole problem related to induction by pointing out that Diṅnāga's conditions are not clearly stated. The problem with Diṅnāga's formulation is that where the locus or *pakṣa* is a class, it is not clear from his formulation whether the probans has to be present in every member of the class or in only some. The same problem arises with homogeneous class or *sapakṣa* cases also — does the probans need to be present in every member of the class or in only some members? Dharmakīrti resolves this problem by introducing the particle *eva* with each of the three characteristics of the probans, meaning thereby that the probans has to be present in every member of the *pakṣa* class but only in some members of the class of homogeneous objects and no member of the heterogeneous objects.

Dharmakīrti in his *Pramāṇavārttika* points out that if "Each *A* is *B*" is true and is supported on the basis of some positive examples then "All non-*B*'s are non-*A*" may be taken to be true although we may lack a real example which is both non-*A* and non-*B* to support it. This proves that if "each *A* is *B*" is true "All non-*B*-s are non-*A*-s" is true but not vice versa; for the former presupposes that there are *A*'s but the latter need not presuppose that there are non-*B*-s. Dharmakīrti holds that "An example announces the co-presence of the probans and the probandum for those who have not comprehended their natural relation; for those who have comprehended it only the probans should be stated to prove the probandum and no example is needed." In this verse Dharmakīrti seems to suggest that the citation of an example to certify the invariable concomitant relationship between the probans and the probandum may not be essential for the system of Diṅnāga. For otherwise why did not Diṅnāga take negative examples seriously?

Dharmakīrti's own view is that there must be natural concomitance (*svabhāva-pratibandha*) or invariable connection between the probans and the probandum in order that one can be the appropriate sign of the other. In his *Svavṛtti* commentary he categorically asserts that simple observation and non-observation of positive and negative examples will not be enough. Dharmakīrti thinks that Diṅnāga also intended to speak of such natural invariance to be there between the probans and the probandum although he articulated it in terms of positive and negative examples.

Dharmakīrti wanted a sort of necessary connection between the probans and the probandum obviously in order to avoid the contingencies of an inductive generalization based purely upon observation. This is underlined by his insistence on *svabhāva-pratibandha* or natural invariance. The naturalness lies in its being necessary, i.e. in its opposite's being impossible. He says, with regard to the probans there is its invariance with the probandum, for if the probandum were not present the probans by virtue of its non-difference from the probandum would not be present either.

When we look at Dharmakīrti's cautious way of formulating the triple characteristics of the probans in detail we have the impression that he was aware of the problem of induction. He formulated the three types of probans in order to distinguish between accidental and law-like generalization. Only when a probans satisfies one of the three conditions set down for a valid probans the generalization in question will be deemed law-like and not a real "law." The first condition is called probans as effect (*kārya-hetu*) where the probans is the effect of the property which is to be inferred. The inference "The hill has fire because it has smoke" is an example of this variety of probans. The idea is that if the causal relation holds between the probans and the property to be inferred, then the smoke will not occur when fire has not occurred. The cause is necessary for the occurrence of the effect. The second condition is that of probans as essence. This comprises what is often called metaphysical necessity. An example of such an inference will be "This must be a material object since it is a table." The relation between being a material object and being a table is not causal but it is not accidental either. The final condition is reason based on non-apprehension (*anupalabdhi-hetu*), which may be compared to counterfactual statements. Example of such an inference is "there is no pot here because it is not observed"; the idea being that had there been a pot here it would have been perceived.

Dharmakīrti's own view regarding the method of ascertaining *vyāpti* is exhibited in the famous verse of the *Pramāṇavārttikam* where it has been said —

kāryakāraṇabhāvād vā svabhāvād vā niyāmakāt |
avinābhāvaniyamo 'darśanān na na darśanāt ||[2]

This verse summarizes the major contribution of Dharmakīrti to Buddhist logic, namely the foundation of inseparable logical relation on reality. It points out that the logical connection is dependent on connections in reality by specifying the two instances in reality which can be the cause of such invariable connection (*avinābhāva niyama*).

Dharmakīrti's argument to establish this "natural" connection is somewhat a priori and involves modalities. This does not mean that we do not in practice establish such a connection by looking at experience or by empirical examples. In general we establish the said connection in this way but that is because we are in general those who have not comprehended the natural connection. For those who have so comprehended the examples would be useless. This means that for Dharmakīrti this so-called "natural" connection is actually a necessary connection, ontologically based, although it need be neither a priori nor analytic. It may be said that the natural invariance between being a product and being impermanent (expressed as "All products are necessarily impermanent") is a necessary proposition which we know a posteriori. In this way the Buddhist view is not incompatible with some modern account of necessity, as for example exhibited in synthetic a priori propositions.

Dharmakīrti thus says that the very existence of a thing is called its own nature. That itself is its real being. How can it exist having discarded its own self? Therefore whatever is a product is also impermanent, for there is no real difference between the two. But then how can we account for the difference between the probans and the probandum? The

2. *PV*, 1.33.

answer is that since all things are naturally established in their own nature and thereby are differentiated from all other similar and dissimilar objects, different class-properties which supply the basis for the differentiation of a group of things from other things are imagined to be anchored in the particulars. Therefore, the exclusive nature (*viśeṣa*) that is understood in terms of one feature cannot be understood in terms of other features. Thus the probans and the probandum can be differently understood in spite of their essential non-difference.

To wind up, Dharmakīrti's view on the *svabhāva-pratibandha* can be seen in two modes or forms — it may be a case of "production-from-that" (*tadutpatti*), termed by Dunne as "production mode"[3] or it may be a relation of identity (*tādātmya*), which Dunne regards as "identity mode." These two relations provide the basis for Dharmakīrti's two forms of affirmative assertions (*vidhi*). They are respectively *kārya hetu* or probans as effect and *svabhāva hetu* or probans as essence. In his *Pramāṇavārttika* Dharmakīrti delineates the two types of probanses in the following manner:

> An effect is evidence for a cause in terms of that number of *svabhāvas* without which it could not occur (*avinābhāvī*). Also a *svabhāva* is evidence for a *svabhāva* that is invariably consequent from its mere presence.[4]

Dharmakīrti here states that one may use either an effect (*kārya*) as probans for its cause, or an essence (*svabhāva*) as probans for a *svabhāva*. The accuracy (*avyabhicārī*) or non-contradictory character of these two modes of probans are based upon the

3. John D. Dunne, *Foundations of Dharmakīrti's Philosophy*, pp. 152-53.

4. *kāryaṁ svabhāvair yāvadbhir avinābhāvi kāraṇe* ।
hetuḥ svabhāve bhāvo 'pi bhāvamātrānurodhinī ॥ — *PV*, I.2.

two modes of *svabhāva-pratibandha*, production and causality. That is, an effect can serve as the probans or evidence for the cause because, on the relation by production, certain *svabhāva*s of the effect (such as smoke) cannot occur without certain *svabhāva*s in the cause (such as fire). Likewise a *svabhāva* can serve as evidence because, on the identity relation, the *svabhāva* offered as the probans or evidence (such as "being a table") necessitates the presence of the *svabhāva* to be proved (such as "being a material object"). In other words, it is not possible for the entity in question to "be a table" if it is not also a "material object."[5] In other words, for Dharmakīrti the *svabhāva-pratibandha* is of *niyata* (restrictive) character since it is the ultimate and only cause for the fact that a logical relation is restricted to certain logical reasons or probanses, namely the three kinds only, but is absent in other kinds, which therefore are regarded by him as "spurious" (*hetvābhāsa*). In this way Dharmakīrti explains how it is possible that a "logical connection" exists at all. By additionally prescribing methods for ascertaining the *svabhāva-pratibandha* as the real basis of the logical connections, he also explains how the latter can be known with certainty. In this way he is able to explain both why a probans does not deviate from a property to be proved and how we can know that it does not deviate from it. In any case it seems that during the time of Dharmakīrti the development of logic, especially discussion on inference, had reached such a level of sophistication that it may be used in the case of the discussion of induction and of the raven paradox in particular.

---

5. It may be noted here that these notions of *bhāva* and *svabhāva* had undergone several changes in the later works of Dharmakīrti. We are not concerned with those later developments here. Our concern here is with what is found in the text *PV, NB* and also in *PVSVT*.

13

Antarvyāpti
A Buddhist Perspective

ALL the schools of Indian philosophy who accept inference as a valid source of knowledge believe that *vyāpti* or the invariable concomitant relation between the probans and the probandum is the essential condition of inference. But regarding the question where such *vyāpti* relation is to be apprehended — is it in the subject or the locus of the inference or in some other instances — there is a difference among them. The most popular answer, which seems also to be the view of common sense, is that the *vyāpti* is apprehended in external instances. This view is known as "external concomitance" (*bahirvyāpti*) and is distinguished from the other view of internal concomitance (*antarvyāpti*) which holds that *vyāpti* need not be apprehended in any other instance. That is, there is *bahirvyāpti* or external concomitance when the concomitance is apprehended in a corroborative example (*dr̥ṣṭānta*) whereas there is *antarvyāpti* "internal concomitance" where it is apprehended in the subject locus (*pakṣa*) of the inference. In the case of *bahirvyāpti,* a corroborative example is cited to show the commonality of abode of the probans and the probandum, and hence the inseparable relationship between them. In the standard example:

1. This hill has fire (probandum)
2. Since this has smoke (probans)
3. As in the kitchen (example)

the kitchen, which forms no essential part of the inference is introduced from outside as the common abode of fire and smoke to ensure the essential connection between them. In the case of *antarvyāpti,* on the other hand, the locus (*pakṣa*) of the inference itself as the common abode of the probans and the probandum shows the invariable relationship between them. Thus in the example —

1. This hill (locus) has fire (probandum)
2. Because this has smoke (probans)

the inseparable connection between fire and smoke is shown by the hill, the locus, which is their common abode.

Some logicians point out that that which is to be proved, viz. the probandum can be established by internal concomitance (*antarvyāpti*) alone. So, the pointing out of the inseparable connection between the probans and the probandum in external instance is superfluous. In the above mentioned example —

This hill has fire
because it has smoke
as in the kitchen

the example "kitchen" has no role to play in asserting the relationship between fire and smoke. Hence, the example is superfluous.[1]

---

1. *tataś ca antaḥ pakṣamadhye vyāptiḥ sādhanasya sādhyākrāntatvam antarvyāptis tasyaiva sādhya-saṁgamya-saṁsiddheḥ pratīteḥ bahir vivakṣita-dharmiṇo 'nyatra dṛṣṭāntadharmiṇī udāhṛtiḥ vyāptidarśanarūpā vyarthā niṣprayojanā । tad asadbhāve 'pyeva sambandhād grahaṇād antarvyāptyabhāve 'py evam iti vyarthaiva bahir udāhṛtḥ ।*

— *Nyāyavatāraviv̥ṛtti,* 8.1-4.

Some logicians go even further and argue that the locus or the *pakṣa* even is not needed in an inference. Even if the locus is not stated, there will be no impossibility in establishing the probandum. For instance, it can quite intelligently be said,

1. There is fire,
2. Because there is smoke.

Thus not only the example, even the locus is not needed to apprehend the *vyāpti* relation. It was the Jainas who upheld the theory of internal concomitance most resolutely. The Jaina argument in favour of internal concomitance is quite easy to understand. It follows from their discussion of the characteristic of the probans. As opposed to the Buddhist doctrine of the triple character (*trairūpya*) of the probans or the Nyāya position of fivefold characters, the Jainas insist on only one character of the probans, viz. definite non-apprehension in contrary instances — *niścitānyathā anupapattiḥ* — that is, the probans should be definitely non-apprehended in instances where the probandum does not exist. So, if in a certain place, the probans is definitely apprehended, it is implied that probandum is existent there. In other words, the invariable relationship between the probans and the probandum is apprehended by apprehending something as the probans in a particular inference. Hence there is no necessity to look for any other case to apprehend the *vyāpti* relation. The probans and the probandum themselves are sufficient enough to establish the *vyāpti* relationship. The case is different for the Buddhists as well as the Nyāya school. Since they believe that the probans has at least three features — presence in the locus, presence in similar instances and absence in dissimilar instances — the probans by itself cannot entail the probandum and hence the invariable relationship cannot be demonstrated from the nature of the probans. Accordingly the Nyāya and the Buddhists have to depend on external conditions for its demonstration and therefore are supporters of the external concomitance theory. In other words, the Jainas emphasize that the relation between the probans and the probandum must be a natural constitutional relation appertaining to the inherent nature of things, and so wherever the concomitance is apprehended, the concomitance is to be understood in respect of the probans and the probandum *per se*, without reference to the place of occurrence which is an accidental coincidence.

But why did the Jainas have to admit such a unique view? The answer seems to be that it was the necessity to establish their own philosophical position which led them to invent it and it was the same necessity which impelled some later Buddhist logicians to accept it. The Jainas wanted to establish their philosophical thesis — All things are possessed of many characters (*anekātmakaṁ vastu*) from the probans "existence" (*sattā*). Now, the doctrine of triple characters of the probans (*trairūpya*) entails that the concomitant relation, positive and negative, between the probans and the probandum has to be apprehended in external examples, homogeneous (*sapakṣa*) and heterogeneous (*vipakṣa*). Such a doctrine was not suitable for such inferences. The probans "existence" according to this theory, would be fallacious in being inconclusive (*anaikāntika*), since it is a property peculiar to the subject (all things) with respect to which no extraneous example is possible. In order to make the probans valid, one had therefore to give up the option of taking recourse to examples and conceive the concomitant relation to be "internal," viz. something that can be apprehended in the locus itself.

Buddhist logicians, in general, were supporters of the external concomitance theory. At the later stage of Buddhist logic we find Ratnākaraśānti upholding the doctrine of internal concomitance in the text *Antarvyāptisamarthanam.* Though traditional Buddhist logicians like Diṅnāga, Dharmakīrti, etc. did not explicitly speak of *bahirvyāpti,* later logicians like Jñānaśrīmiśra and Ratnakīrti upheld the theory of *bahirvyāpti* categorically. The latter two logicians recognized the necessity of corroborative example even in the inference of the Buddhist theory of momentariness. In the *Citrādvaitaprakāśavāda* Ratnakīrti speaks of external concomitance in connection with the inference for existence (*sattvānumāna*).[2] In the external concomitance thesis existence is found to be invariably related to momentariness in the corroborative example "jar" by the force of the proof *viparyāye bādhakapramāṇa.* On the basis of that concomitance, momentariness is proved in the locus from existence. Thus though it seems that Ratnākaraśānti was the only Buddhist logician to argue explicitly in favour of internal concomitance, the seed of Ratnākaraśānti's thesis can be traced in the philosophy of Dharmakīrti. In support of this the following arguments may be offered. First, the basic principle on which the theory of internal concomitance rests is the proof that contradicts the presence of the probans in the absence of the probandum, a principle that the Jainas represent as *anyathānupapatti* or impossibility otherwise. This principle originated with Dharamakīrti who enunciated it for the first time in the later phase of his philosophical career to establish the concomitance between existence and momentariness. Moreover, the other concept that has been mentioned by Ratnākaraśānti, viz. the all-inclusive pervasion, had been the creation of Dharmakīrti. These two points suggest that if any Buddhist logician had paved the way for Ratnākaraśānti to

2. *tataś ca yathā bahirvyāptipakṣe ghaṭe dṛṣṭāntadharmiṇī viparyyaya-bādhakapramāṇa-balāt sattvaṁ kṣaṇikatva-niyatam avadhārya sattvāt pakṣe kṣaṇabhaṅgasiddhiḥ.*

propound the doctrine of internal concomitance that was no other than Dharmakīrti himself. That example is of less importance in the apprehension of pervasion had been said by Dharmakīrti in his *Pramāṇavārttika*. There he declares that example is necessary only for those ignorant persons who are not able to apprehend the concomitant relation between the probans and the probandum. But for the intelligent persons who can apprehend the relation of identity and causality as the basis for the concomitant relation in an inference, the statement of the probans is sufficient and there is no need to mention the example.[3]

The view of Dharmakīrti in short is as follows. Although he adheres to the doctrine of triple characteristics as formulated by Diṅnāga, he modified it. Inference has ceased to be an affair of examples. Concomitance for him is universal law expressed either affirmatively or negatively in a universal proposition without reference to a concrete example.[4] Arcaṭa while commenting on Dharmakīrti's concept of *vyāpti* observes that by the expression *sarva* in his statement Dharmakīrti is rejecting "external concomitance."[5] From Arcaṭa's comments it seems as if Dharmakīrti is upholding the doctrine of *antarvyāpti* while rejecting the doctrine of external concomitance. But the rejection of external concomitance does not necessarily imply[6] the acceptance of internal concomitance.

3. *tadbhāvahetubhāvau hi dṛṣṭānte tadavedinaḥ* ।
khyāpyete viduṣām vācyo hetur eva hi kevalaḥ ॥ — *PV*, 1.27.

4. *sarvopasaṁhāreṇa vyāptipradarśanalakṣaṇau sādharmya-vaidharmyaprayogau uktou* । — *HB*, 55.

5. *atra sarvagrahaṇena cāśeṣaparigrahād bahirvyāpter nirāsaḥ* ।
— *HBT*, 62, 8-9.

6. *anena sarvopasaṁhāreṇa vyāptipradarśanaṁ kathayati* । *kimartham? vipratipattinirāsārtham* । *tathā hi pakṣa-sapakṣāpekṣayāntarvyāptiḥ bahirvyāptiś ca pradarśyate ity eke vipratipannāḥ* । *tac ca na yuktam, bastubalāyātatvād vyāpteḥ* । — *Vipañcitārthā*, 8.

Śāntarakṣita in his commentary on the *Vādanyāya* observes that by using the word *sarvam* in his formulation of the concomitance relation Dharmakīrti is actually pointing to the all-inclusive character of concomitance and this is to indicate that concomitance is neither internal nor external but something natural (*svābhāvika*) between the probans and the probandum without any reference to the locus of the inference or something similar to it. For Dharmakīrti what was important was how to show the universal character of *vyāpti* or *avinābhāva* relation. Once he has proved the all-inclusive character of concomitance by grounding it on the two laws of causality and essential identity, the question of where it is to be apprehended in the subject or outside the subject becomes immaterial. Accordingly the triple characteristics of the probans emphasizes the concomitant relation in its two aspects — positive and negative, but remains silent with respect to where such concomitance is to be apprehended. Thus in the conceptual framework of Diṅnāga and Dharmakīrti inferential cognition is not possible without the statement regarding the triple characteristic of the probans and as the statement regarding the triple characteristic of the probans seems to be redundant in the theory of internal concomitance, their scheme of logic made no provision for such theory of internal concomitance.

Following the tradition of these two master logicians, later Buddhist logicians, Jñānaśrīmitra and Ratnakīrti, also did not accept such theory of internal concomitance. However, later on Ratnākaraśānti in his text *Antarvyāptisamarthana* argues in favour of the internal comitance theory and holds that neither an inference nor the triple characteristics becomes redundant in the internal concomitance theory. On the contrary external concomitance is not possible on the case of the probans "real" with regard to the probandum "transitoriness" (*kṣaṇikatva*).

Mahāmahopādhyāya Haraprasāda Śāstrī in the Prefatory note to his *Six Buddhist Nyāya Tracts* points out that in the standard example of inferring fire on the hill-top on the basis of smoke, invariable concomitant relation is established in the example given, viz. kitchen. From there it is transferred to the mountain which proves the existence of fire in the mountain. "But in the case of proving momentariness of all things, you do not get an example, and so the invariable relation between the thing which is to be proved and the thing by which it is to be proved, cannot be established outside. This is a difficulty which the author has to face, and he faces it by declaring that such a relation need not be proved outside in all cases of inference."[7]

To ascertain necessary concomitance between the probans and the probandum, both of them must be known to us. Focusing on this aspect the supporters of the external concomitance argue that as the probandum is already established while ascertaining necessary concomitance in the locus, there remains no role to play for the probans and as such inference collapses in the theory of internal concomitance. Ratnākaraśānti opposing such contention of the opponents, holds that this exactly is an advantage in his theory of internal concomitance.[8] There may be two possible answers to the question, whether the probandum is established by the source of knowledge which ascertains necessary concomitance in the locus of inference. One may answer that the probandum is established by the same source of knowledge which ascertains necessary concomitance. Ratnākaraśānti argues that in case

7. *Six Buddhist Nyāya Tracts*, p. vi.

8. *yadi hi dharmiṇī vyāptiḥ sidhyantyeva sādhyasiddhim antarbhāvayati* । *nanu lābha evaiṣaḥ* । *vyāptiprasādhakād eva pramāṇāt sādhyasiddheḥ sattva-hetvapāśrayaṇāprayāsaya nirasanāt* । *na hi vyasanam evaitalliṅgāntarānusaraṇaṁ nāma* । — *Antarvyāptisamarthanam*, p. 193.

knowledge of the probandum is ensured while ascertaining necessary concomitance, then we are relieved from the necessity of considering the logical mark "real" in the subject other than the locus. He says that to consider the probans as different from the one which subsists in the locus, is only a matter of convention. If necessary, we may change the logical convention of considering the probans at two places — one in the corroborative example and the other in the locus of inference. Another possible way of answering the above question is to say that the probandum is not established by the source of knowledge which enables us to ascertain necessary concomitance. Ratnākaraśānti argues that in this case the probans cannot be declared to be redundant in the theory of internal concomitance. Hence the opponents need not try desperately to prove the redundancy of the probans in the theory of internal concomitance.[9]

If the *pramāṇa* which ascertains the necessary cocomitance in the locus is not able to prove the probandum in the locus, we need to prove the presence of the probans in the corroborative example as well as in the locus, in order to show the necessary concomitance between the probans and the probandum, and the *pakṣadharmatā* (existence of the probans in the locus) respectively. Otherwise it will not be possible to establish the probandum in the locus. The question that has to be considered at this point is — where is the object that is disputed to be proved, is it in any particular object like a pitcher or a table, etc. or is it in all objects that we want to prove the probandum? If the probandum is asked with regard to one particular object, say pitcher, but the necessary concomitance between the probans and the probandum is shown in

9. *na tarhy antarvyāptau heturvaiyartham iti kiṁ akāndakātaratayā bahutaram āyāsam ābiśasi* I — *Antarvyāptisamarthanam*, pp. 193-94.

something outside the pitcher, viz. table, then the probans established in the table becomes useless to establish the probandum in the pitcher. But if the dispute regarding the probandum lies not in one particular thing but in all things, then both the theorists have to establish the presence of the probans not in one particular thing but in all things. As dispute regarding the probandum even for the external concomitance theorists lies in all things the probans cannot be regarded as redundant/useless in the theory of internal concomitance. Since the locus where one ascertains necessary concomitance, is the place where there is dispute regarding the probandum, and where there is dispute regarding the probandum is called the locus of inference, so the locus where one ascertains necessary concomitance is the locus of inference. Hence, Ratnākaraśānti argues that as the probandum is proved in the locus while ascertaining necessary concomitance there, the probans cannot be regarded to be useless, and the necessary concomitance so ascertained is internal concomitance and not an external one.[10]

If dispute regarding the probandum lies in all things, then our knowledge of the probans and necessary concomitance will establish the probandum not in one particular subject but in all subjects. So particular subject must be mentioned for determinate reference. Ratnākaraśānti was aware of this

10. *dvayaṁ hi bhavataḥ sādhyaṁ dr̥ṣṭāntadharmiṇī vr̥ttiḥ sādhyadharmiṇī ca yathākramaṁ vyāptipakṣadharmatvayoḥ siddhyartham* । *nanu yadā pratiniyate dharmiṇī vivādaḥ tadbahirbhūte ca dharmiṇī vyāptigrahaṇam tadānīṁ bhaved vaiyarthyam* । *yadā tu vastumātre vivādaḥ tadā sarvavastuṣu hetorvr̥ttis tvayāpi sādhyā mayāpi ceti katam asmin dharmīṇī hetor vr̥ttisādhanam mama vyarthaṁ bhaviṣyati* । *katham idānīṁ bahirvyāptir vivādādhikaraṇaṁ bhūta evānyatamasmin vyāptisādhanāt* । *tāvan mātralakṣaṇatvāc ca sādhyadharmiṇaḥ* ।
— *Antarvyāptisamarthanam*, p. 194.

problem and so he held that necessary concomitance is always ascertained with reference to that particular locus where the probans is observed. The dispute regarding the probandum cannot arise in the subject where the probans "real" is unestablished, since the dispute regarding the probandum in the locus cannot arise unless the probans is established there. Thus Ratnākaraśānti says that necessary concomitance can be ascertained in the locus simply on the basis of one's knowledge of the probans in the locus (*pakṣadharmatā*). If it cannot be ascertained in the locus, then it cannot be ascertained in the corroborative example either. Necessary concomitance is ascertained in the subject on the basis of our knowledge of presence of probans there along with our knowledge that presence of a logical mark is contradictory in the absence of the probandum. The probans "real" is seen in the locus, otherwise dispute regarding the probandum would not have been there. So necessary concomitance ascertained there is certainly an internal concomitance and it has determinate reference.

The problem that seems to arise with regard to internal concomitance is how the theory of internal concomitance is consistent with regard to the triple characteristic of the probans as admitted in the framework of Buddhist logic? The second and third characteristics of a proper probans are respectively definite existence of the probans in similar instances and definite non-existence of the probans in dissimilar instances. These two characteristics imply that the probans exists in instances other than the locus or subject of inference which entails that necessary concomitance is ascertained in instances other than the locus. So the triple feature of the probans seems to justify external concomitance and not internal concomitance. Ratnākaraśānti as a follower of Diṅnāga-

Dharmakīrti tradition cannot go against the *trairūpya* feature. So he interpreted them to suit his purpose. He first states the threefold characteristic and then holds that to say that the probans is present only in similar instances and is absent from dissimilar instances actually amounts to saying that wherever positive or negative concomitance can be ascertained, that has to be ascertained in the locus/subject of inference.[11] Necessary concomitance in the positive and negative forms must be ascertained to ensure the validity of the probans. Hence, there is no hard and fast rule as regards where such necessary concomitance should be ascertained — it can be ascertained wherever possible. As necessary concomitance either in agreement or in difference is ultimately the same, one aspect implies the other, so there is no problem with regard to establishing the necessary concomitance between "real" and "transitoriness" by internal concomitance. One can establish "Whatever is real is momentary" (*yat sat tat kṣaṇikam*) by establishing concomitance in its negative form — in the absence of transitoriness there is absence of reality. This is ascertained in the locus of inference by establishing exclusion of reality from non-transitory in every case on the basis of the contradiction involved in assertion of presence of the probans in the absence of the probandum. As necessary concomitance is ascertained with regard to the probans which is seen in the locus, so the subject different from the subject of inference is impossible. Hence, even if it is possible to find an instance which is different from the locus, it is useless to go after it.[12]

11. *sādhyadharmayuktaḥ sarvaḥ sāmānyena sapakṣaḥ, atadyuktaścāsapakṣa iti* । *tasmin sapakṣa eva sattvam asapakṣe cāsattvam eva yathākramam anvayavyatirekau tau punar yatra tatra vā dharmiṇī grahītavyau yatra śakyau grahītum* । — *Antarvyāptisamarthanam*, p. 195

12. Ibid.

14

Sādhanābhāsa

Fallacies of Inference

In the history of Indian logic, the concept of *hetvābhāsa* occupies a fundamental position. An inference is accepted as a valid source of knowledge by almost all the schools of Indian philosophy. Any serious discussion on inference brings in the discussion of *hetvābhāsa,* for by knowing when an inference becomes wrong or incorrect, one is able to be cautious enough to avoid them and make the inference correct or valid. The initial statement of the auto-commentry of *Pramāṇavārttika* explicates the utility of valid inference (*anumāna*) in the following way — *arthānarthavivecanasyānumānāśrayatvāt tadvipratipattes tadvyavasthāpanāya āha* — In so far as the discrimination between what is meaningful and what is meaningless in epistemology and logic is made on the basis of correct inference, and since there is conflicting or perplexing opinions about correct inference, therefore Dharmakīrti in the first verse clearly determines the nature of inference. Since in Buddhist logic inference is considered as a second *pramāṇa* along with *pratyakṣa,* Dharmakīrti felt it necessary to refute the conflicting and contradictory opinions on inference by clearly describing the correct process of drawing inferences and the circumstances in which an inference can be valid. The first verse of the *PV* runs thus:

pakṣadharmas tadaṁśena vyāpto hetustridhaiva saḥ ।
avinābhāvaniyamād hetvābhāsas tato 'pare ॥ — I.1

The probans is a property of the subject pervaded by a part, namely another property of the subject. Such a probans possesses three properties due to the restriction of the invariable which are mainly concomitance between the probans and the probandum. Probans other than this one will be considered as fallacious. If a probans conforms to the definition of the probans presented in terms of the characteristic features it will be regarded as a correct probans, while if it does not it is a false one. The statement "other kinds of probans than this one are fallacious probans" means that probanses other than the stated three varieties of correct probans are fallacious probans.

This short introductory verse of the *PV* signifies a very important feature of the Buddhist analysis of *hetvābhāsa* as distinguished from the Nyāya conception. For the Naiyāyikas the definition of *hetvābhāsa* is roughly presented in terms of the statement of having that object the knowledge of which prevents inferential cognition — *yadviṣayakatvena jñānasya anumitivirodhitvaṁ tattvam* । Thus the knowledge of deviation, etc. prevents inferential knowledge and so they are fallacies. As for example, the inferential knowledge "lake has fire" (*hrado vahṇimān*) is prevented by the knowledge "lake has the absence of fire" (*hrado vahṇyabhāvavān*). Hence the state of having the absence of fire as object (*vahṇyabhāvavad hradaviṣayakatva*) is the determinant of the state of being the preventing agent of inferential cognition (*anumitipratibandhakatāvacchedaka*). In other words, according to the Naiyāyikas, if any valid knowledge stands as a hindrance to a given inference, then that given inference is considered as a case of *hetvābhāsa*. So *hetvābhāsa* need not be restricted to the defect of probans or *hetu*, though it might be one. However, the etymology of the term *hetvābhāsa* is offered in terms of the falsity of the probans — *hetorābhāsaḥ* (the appearance of the probans) or *hetuvat ābhāsate* (that which appears as the probans but is not really so). Probably deriving hint from such etymological analysis, the Buddhists restrict *hetvābhāsa* only to those cases where the hindrance to an inferential knowledge is due to the defect of the probans. This becomes very clear when we take a look at Dharmakīrti's statement of the *hetvābhāsa* as — *tatra trayāṇāṁ rūpāṇām ekasyāpi rūpasyānuktau sādhanābhāsaḥ uktāvapyasiddhau sandehe vā pratipādyapratipādakayoḥ* । (*NB*, 3.55-56). That is, according to Dharmakīrti, an argument (*sādhana*) is fallacious under any of the following conditions :

1. Of the three characterizing features of the *hetu* some is **not expressed** in the premises.
2. All the characterizing features are expressed but some of these features is **not acceptable to some debater.**
3. All the characterizing features are expressed, but some feature is **dubitable according to some debaters**.

It can be seen that the basic principles of fallacies, according to Dharmakīrti, are insufficiency, non-acceptability and dubitability. This third condition also marks another important point of difference of the Buddhist view from the Nyāya one. As we have already seen the Naiyāyikas define *hetvābhāsa* in terms of having a valid knowledge that stands as a hindrance to the inferential knowledge. So for the Naiyāyikas, in the case of *hetvābhāsa* we always have a valid knowledge as the preventing agency. If the preventing knowledge itself is something doubtful, it cannot make the inferential knowledge incorrect. But for the Buddhists, even if there is any doubt in the minds of the debaters as to whether the characteristic features are really occurring or not, there would arise *hetvābhāsa*. So for the Buddhists, the whole concept of *hetvābhāsa* centres round the threefold characteristics of the probans.

The Buddhists, as we have already noted, made a distinction between two types of inferences — inference for oneself and inference for others. So the question arises, does *hetvābhāsa* occur in both kinds of inference or in any one variety? To answer this question let us take a look at *svārthānumāna*. It had been defined by the Buddhists as the cognition of *sādhya* that occurs to a person who sees the *hetu*. This cognition of the *sādhya* or the probandum is an intuition (*darśana*) generated by a *hetu*. The reliability of such intuition is determined by examining whether the probans (*hetu*) which generates the intuition, possesses the three constitutive features or not. The inferring agent may not be aware of each of the characterizing features of the *hetu* when he actually intuits the *sādhya*. But in the case of inference for others which is the communicative act of proving, the agent tries to show that the *hetu* possesses all the three characteristics of a good probans (*sadhetu*). In this sense it may be said that *hetvābhāsa* is more pertinent for *parārthānumāna* than to *svārthānumāna*; the whole purpose of communicating a fact to other will fail if the characteristic features of the probans are not satisfied. Accordingly we find that in an epistemological text like *Nyāyabindu*, discussion of *hetvābhāsa* is made in the chapter on inference for others after explaining the nature of a good probans.

Such inference for others (*parārthānumāna*) has also been termed by Diṅnāga as *sādhana*. This *sādhana*, according to Diṅnāga, consists of three elements, namely *pakṣa* (thesis), *hetu* (probans) and *dṛṣṭānta* (instance). Of these three elements, if anyone is defective the whole argument turns out to be defective. Accordingly Diṅnāga distinguished among *pakṣābhāsa, hetvābhāsa* and *dṛṣṭāntābhāsa* as different types of incorrect or fallacious inference (*sādhanābhāsa*). It may be noted that the notion of false reasoning was also admitted by Vātsyāyana in his *Bhāṣya*. Vātsyāyana mentioned the term *nyāyābhāsa* (false inference) as opposed to *nyāya* (inference) treating inferences which do not agree with what is obtained by perception or scriptural testimony as *nyāyābhāsa* (*pramāṇair arthaparīkṣaṇaṁ nyāyaḥ . . . yat punar anumānaṁ pratyakṣāgamaviruddhaṁ nyāyābhāsaḥ sa iti*).

In Dharmakīrti's system an inference for others consists of two elements, one stating the existence of the probans in the locus (*pakṣa*) or subject of inference and the other stating the invariable necessary relationship between the probans and the probandum. In such a model of inference the premise which states the characteristic of the probans as existing in the locus (generally known as *pakṣasattva*) is an observation-statement, while the second premise, namely the *vyāpti*-statement, expressed either in affirmative or negative terms, is not an observation-statement, but a necessary one based either on the relation of causality or essential identity. Though Dharmakīrti generally adds the instance as part to the statement of *vyāpti*, he feels that the separate mention of *dṛṣṭānta* as an element of *parārthānumāna* is redundant — *na pṛthak dṛṣṭānto nāma sādhanāvayavaḥ kaścit tena nāsya lakṣaṇaṁ pṛthag ucyate gatārthatvāt* (*NB* 3.121). Dharmakīrti also holds that the mention of the conclusion in the full argument is not needed because the conclusion by virtue of the semantic force of the premises (*sāmarthyād*) follows from them. It seems that in the inferential model Dharmakīrti wants to state the *pakṣa* or thesis first before the argument and the argument follows as if to provide justification/support for the thesis in the form of a proof. Thus in Dharmakīrti's model *pakṣa* was not included in the actual body of the proof (*sādhana*) but was kept aside, while according to Diṅnāga *pakṣa* was to be included as a part of the proof. Since for Dharmakīrti the proof or the *sādhana* consists of the premise alone which are actually statement of the threefold characteristic of the probans, *sādhanābhāsa* consists in the wrong statement or non-mention or dubitability of any of those three characteristics. It may be noted in this context that though Dharmakīrti does not feel that the thesis needs to be always stated in a proof, he admits that *pakṣa* is something that is intended to be proved by the debater himself and which is not already falsified (*svarūpeṇaiva svayam iṣṭo 'nirākṛtaḥ pakṣa iti NB*, 3.38), thereby suggesting that the statement of the *pakṣa* is to be presented before the proof. Thus an example of a correct *parārthānumāna* may be given thus:

> Sound is non-eternal
> Because sound is a product
> Whatever is a product is non-eternal;
> For example pot which is other than sound is both a product and non-eternal.

Dharmakīrti's analysis of *sādhanābhāsa* bears some resemblance with Diṅnāga's account, but also has difference in some important respects. Diṅnāga thinks that *sādhana* or inference is constituted by the three elements — *pakṣa, hetu* and *dṛṣṭānta*. But Dharmakīrti does not attach much importance to *pakṣa* and *dṛṣṭānta*, but gives much emphasis on *hetu* and discusses the *hetvābhāsa*s elaborately. In that respect for him *hetvābhāsa* and *sādhanābhāsa* become synonymous. Though Dharmakīrti does not regard *pakṣa* or the thesis as part of the inference, any defect in the thesis may lead the whole argument in a wrong direction. *Pakṣābhāsa* has a role to exclude an apparently absurd statement before actually commencing the proof. It was introduced in order to avoid useless investigation.

Pakṣābhāsa thus shows that there can be incorrect inference even when the *hetu* possesses the three characteristics, as for example, in the inference — word is not audible because it is produced by human effort like a pot. Accordingly prior to the discussion of *hetvābhāsa*, Dharmakīrti has presented an analysis of *pakṣābhāsa*.

Similar is the case with *dr̥ṣṭānta*. Dharmakīrti does not completely deny the importance of *dr̥ṣṭānta*s in an inference but admits its necessity in some cases. To quote from the *Pramāṇavārttika*:

> *tadbhāvahetubhāvau hi dr̥ṣṭānte tadavedinaḥ* ।
> *kyapyete, viduṣāṁ vācyo hetur eva hi kevalaḥ* ॥ — I.27

Since the probans is either the essence of the probandum or its effect, the invariable concomitance of the probans and the probandum is to be stated in a generally accepted fact, i.e. an instance, for those who are not acquainted with it. For those who have knowledge of this invariable concomitant relationship, the *dr̥ṣṭānta* is not necessary, only the probans has to be stated. That is, for the hearer who is not familiar with the invariable concomitant relationship the instance has to be mentioned in the inference. Accordingly for such hearer the defects in the instances may mislead him in apprehending the *vyāpti* relation. Hence along with *hetvābhāsa*, Dharmakīrti has discussed *dr̥ṣṭāntābhāsa*, though his emphasis was on the *hetvābhāsas*. *Dr̥ṣṭāntābhāsa* is a case of example which is not able to perform the function allotted to an example, *dr̥ṣṭāntavād ābhāsate iti dr̥ṣṭāntābhāsaḥ*. One should be aware that no *dr̥ṣṭāntābhāsaḥ* is the same as *hetvābhāsa*. A *hetvābhāsa* occurs if any of the validity-determinative condition of an inference is not fulfilled at all. Non-fulfilment of any of these conditions can make an inference invalid and no amount of appropriate *dṛṣṭānta* can make it valid. With this short introduction let us pass on to the different varieties of fallacies of inference — *pakṣābhāsa, hetvābhāsa* and *dṛṣṭāntābhāsa* respectively.

II

Pakṣābhāsa

Before enumerating the different varieties of *pakṣābhāsa* let us take a look at the definition of *pakṣa* presented by Diṅnāga once again. In the *Nyāyamukha,* Diṅnāga defined *pakṣa* as —

> . . . . *svayaṁ* ।
> *sādhyatvenepsitaḥ pakṣo viruddhārthānirākṛtaḥ* ॥
> — *Nyāyamukha,* verse 1

A thesis is that which the proponent himself intends to prove and which is not refuted by objects contradictory to it. In the *PS,* the thesis has been defined as that which the proponent himself intends to state just according to its nature and which is not refuted by perception, etc. — *svarūpeṇaiva nirdeśyaḥ svayam iṣṭo 'nirākṛtaḥ* । (*PS* III.2).

A thesis should not be refuted by perception, etc. More precisely, the property to be proved (*sādhyadharma*) should not be refuted with regard to the subject by what is obtained by perception, etc. A thesis which is refuted by perception, etc. is called *pakṣābhāsa.* In the *Pramāṇasamuccaya,* Diṅnāga enumerated four types of *pakṣābhāsa* along with examples —

1. A thesis which is refuted by perception (*pratyakṣa-nirākṛta*), for example, sound is not audible (*aśrāvaṇo śabdaḥ*).
2. A thesis which is refuted by inference (*anumānanirākṛta*), for example, a pot is permanent (*nityo ghaṭaḥ*).
3. A thesis which is refuted by trustworthy words

(*āgamanirākṛta*). For example, there are no *pramāṇas* which have cognizable things as their objects (*na santi pramāṇāni prameyārthāni*).

4. A thesis which is refuted by verbal convention (*śabdprasiddhaḥ-nirākṛtaḥ*). For example the moon is not called "Candra" because it exists (*acandraḥ śaśī sattvāt*).

According to Diṅnāga these are the cases of refutation of the nature of *dharma* (*dharmasvarūpanirākaraṇa*). He further added to the list other categories of *pakṣābhāsa* in terms of what is refuted —

1. refutation of the nature of *dharma* (*dharmasvarūpa-nirākaraṇa*).
2. refutation of a qualification of *dharma* (*dharmaviśeṣa-nirākaraṇa*).
3. refutation of the nature of *dharmī* (*dharmisvarūpa-nirākaraṇa*).
4. refutation of the qualification of *dharmī* (*dharmiviśeṣa-nirākaraṇa*).
5. refutation of the nature or qualification of both *dharma* and *dharmī* (*ubhayasvarūpaviśeṣanirākaraṇa*).

Since the first variety is already illustrated, Diṅnāga in his *PSV*, proceeds to provide examples of the remaining four of the above list:

2. *nānyo 'vayavī avayavebhyaḥ tulānativiśeṣagrahāt* ।
3. *nānyo 'vayavā avayavinaḥ, apratyakṣatvaprasaṅgāt* ।
4. *nāsti dravyaṁ guṇadravyāṇāṁ dravyādravyātvaprasaṅgāt* ।
5. *sarvaṁ vākyam anṛtam* ।

They are the examples of refutation asserted by Diṅnāga himself. For example, in the case of a refutation of a qualification on *dharma*, the Vaiśeṣika's thesis that the whole is different from the parts, is refuted. In the *Nyāyamukha*, however, Diṅnāga's analysis is a bit different. There he mentions five varieties of *pakṣābhāsa* thus:

1. A thesis which is refuted by one's own statement, e.g. *sarvam uktaṁ mr̥ṣā.*
2. A thesis which is refuted by *pūrvābhyupāgama*, e.g. *aulūkasya nityaḥ śabda iti sādhayataḥ.*
3. A thesis which is refuted by verbal convention (*śabdaprasiddha*), e.g. *acandraḥ śaśī sattvāt.*
4. A thesis which is refuted by perception, e.g. *aśrāvaṇaśabdaḥ.*
5. A thesis which is refuted by inference, e.g. *nityo ghaṭaḥ.*

Now let us pass on to Dharmakīrti's exposition of *pakṣābhāsa*. Dharmakīrti deals with *pakṣābhāsa* in *PV*, chapter IV. There he introduces the subject by first stating the objective of the *pakṣa* and then pointing out when does such *pakṣābhāsa* occur. To quote from *PV*, IV.91:

> *asiddhaḥ pramāṇābhyāṁ sa copāgama iṣyate* ।
> *sandigdhe hetuvacanād vyasto hetor anāśrayaḥ* ॥

The tentative acceptance which is not refuted by the two *pramāṇa*s is regarded as the thesis. Since the probans is stated with regard to something doubtful what is refuted by the two *pramāṇa*s cannot be the object of the probans. This verse makes it clear that the doctrine of *pakṣābhāsa* has the practical purpose of rejecting a clearly wrong proposition before actually stating the proof. The thesis to be proved has to be doubtful. Accordingly that which is already refuted by the *pramāṇa*s has no need of proof, nor does one that is already proved need to be proved again.

According to the number of *pramāṇa*s accepted in his system, Dharmakīrti initially enumerates the number of *pakṣābhāsa*s as two:

1. A thesis which is refuted by perception, and
2. A thesis which is refuted by inference.

Apparently this seems to be in disagreement with his master Diṅnāga's list. To remove this inconsistency Dharmakīrti clarifies his position in the subsequent verse:

> *anumānasya bhedena sā bādhakā caturvidhā* ।
> *tatrābhyupāyaḥ kāryāṅgaṁ svabhāvāṅgaṁ jagatsthitiḥ* ॥
> — *PV*, IV.92

That is, in accordance with the classification of inferences Diṅnāga mentioned four varieties of *pratyakṣābhāsa*s. Of them "trustworthy words" (*abhyupāya*) is the probans as effect (*kāryāṅgam*) and "verbal convention" (*jagatsthiti*) is the probans as essence (*svabhāvāṅgam*). Thus the thesis which is refuted by inference is sub-divided into three varieties :

2. (i) A thesis which is refuted by an inference which functions due to the force of reality (*vastubala-pravṛttānumāna*).
   (ii) A thesis refuted by trustworthy words (*abhyupāya*).
   (iii) A thesis refuted by verbal convention (*jagatsthiti*).

Dharmakīrti regards *abhyupāya* as *kārya hetu* and verbal convention (*jagatsthiti,* i.e. *śābdaprasiddha*) as *svabhāva hetu*. Thus they are all included in inference. These varieties thus correspond to what Diṅnāga said in his *Pramāṇasamuccayaḥ*. The additional variety mentioned by Diṅnāga as *svavacananirākṛta* in his *Nyāyamukha* has been included by Dharmakīrti in 2. ii, i.e. as a thesis refuted by trustworthy words (*abhyupāya*). According to Dharmakīrti *āpta* means a speaker himself as well as other speakers who utters something after having determined its truth. A person does not speak anything unless he considers it to be true. Similarly he does not investigate a treatise unless he accepts it as true. Thus a treatise and one's own statement are regarded as same in essence and can be considered under one head. Accordingly a thesis which is refuted by trustworthy words can be subdivided into two varieties:

2. ii (a) A thesis which is refuted by a treatise.

(b) A thesis which is refuted by one's own statement.

The whole list of *pakṣābhāsa*, therefore, turns out to be as follows:

1. A thesis which is refuted by perception.
2. A thesis which is refuted by an inference which functions due to the force of reality.
3. A thesis which is refuted by treatise/scripture.
4. A thesis which is refuted by one's own statement.
5. A thesis which is refuted by verbal convention.

The enumeration of *pakṣābhāsa* in the *Nyāyabindu* is as follows:

(i) *pratyakṣanirākṛta*, e.g. *aśrāvaṇaḥ śabdaḥ* ।

(ii) *anumānanirākṛta*, e.g. *nityaḥ śabdaḥ* ।

(iii) *pratītinirākṛtaḥ*, e.g. *acandraḥ śaśī* ।

(iv) *svavacananirākṛtaḥ*, e.g. *nānumānaṁ pramāṇam* ।

In the text *Pramāṇaviniścayaḥ* also, Dharmakīrti deals with *pakṣābhāsa*. But his enumeration there is the same as one given in the *Pramāṇavārttika*, and so there is no need to mention it again. Thus Dharmakīrti enumerates Diṅnāga's list of *pakṣābhāsa* in accordance with the two types of *pramāṇa* admitted in Buddhist epistemology.[1]

III

Hetvābhāsa

Of the three types of fallacies of inference, the most vital one is the *hetvābhāsa* which arises because of the violation of the threefold characterization of the probans. In the third chapter of the text *Nyāyabindu*, Dharmakīrti remarks that the fallacies which should be demonstrated for refuting an argument are really *hetvābhāsa*s or fallacies of the probans. These are the fallacies of deficient probans, namely *asiddha, anaikāntika* and *viruddha*. The exposure of any one of them is sufficient for refutation. It is for this reason that Stcherbatsky reserved the term "logical fallacies" for *hetvābhāsa*s only. Let us now consider each of these varieties of *hetvābhāsa* in a detailed manner.

Asiddha

The fallacies based on falsity or dubitability of the first characterizing feature of the probans, are known as *asiddha*. The first characteristic may be violated, according to Diṅnāga, in two ways — either when the subject of the statement does not exist or when, though it exists the *hetu* is not predicated of it. On the basis of these two possibilities, *asiddha* is classified under the heads *āśrayāsiddha* and *svarūpāsiddha*. The fallacy of *āśrayāsiddha* occurs when the subject does not exist and *svarūpāsiddha* occurs when the subject exists but *hetu* is not predicated of it. It may be noticed here that though the term

1. For detailed discussion on pakṣābhāsa, vide, M. Irani, "On *Pakṣābhāsa*" in *Studies in the Buddhist Epistemological Tradition*, ed. by E. Steinkellner, 1991.

svarūpāsiddha is not used by Diṅnāga to denote any *hetvābhāsa*, his example of *ubhayāsiddha* tallies with the popular example of *svarūpāsiddha*. The only distinction seems to be that in *ubhayāsiddha*, the context of debate is taken into account, while in *svarūpāsiddha* it is not. In addition to these two varieties, Diṅnāga admits a third variety which he calls *sandigdhāsiddha*. This fallacy is based on the dubitability of the first step. In the *Nyāyamukha* Diṅnāga enumerates four varieties of *asiddha hetvābhāsa* — *ubhayāsiddha hetvābhāsa, anyatara-asiddha, sandigdha-asiddha-hetvābhāsa* and *āśrayāṣiddha hetvābhāsa*. Example of *ubhayāsiddha hetvābhāsa* is — "Sound is non-eternal because it is perceived by the eyes." This fallacy is so called because neither the disputant nor the opponent is supposed to accept the given probans "being perceived by the eyes" in the context of the subject "sound." The *anyatarāsiddha* variety of *hetvābhāsa* occurs when the probans is not recognized to be existent in the subject by the opponent only. An example of this kind will be "Sound is non-eternal because it is a product," for a person while arguing with a philosopher who believes in the eternity of sound. In this example the opponent is supposed to believe only in the manifestation of sound, but not in its creation or production. Therefore the probans "because it is a product" cannot be considered by him as existent in the subject. Therefore, this is known as *anyatara-asiddha-hetvābhāsa*.

It may be noted here that these two types of *hetvābhāsa*s are significant only in the context of a debate and in this sense may be called contextual fallacy. The principle that governs these two types is neither falsity nor dubitability but the principle of acceptance. The fallacy called *ubhayāsiddha* is committed when the first step of *parārthānumāna* is asserted by some debaters, but is not accepted by the two parties of the debate, namely by neither the proponent nor by the opponent. The fallacy called *anyatarāsiddha* is committed when the first step is not accepted by one of the debaters. Thus the principle behind these fallacies is that in the debate-context any debater can make a good inference only if its premises are accepted by both the parties. We shall see that similar contextual fallacies can arise with regard to the second and third features as well. It may be noted that the contextual fallacies are relative fallacies — in a changing situation the argument which is contextually fallacious in one context can be contextually sound in another context.

The third variety of fallacy that Diṅnāga considers with regard to the first feature of probans is *sandigdhāsiddha*. This fallacy arises when the existence of the probans in the locus is subject to doubt. For instance, when a doubt arises concerning smoke that has been seen, yet one proceeds to infer that there is fire because smoke has been seen. If we are not sure that the smoke we are seeing is really smoke, and we doubt that it may be vapour, smoke cannot be taken as the probans. Thus *sandigdhāsiddha* is evidently based on the dubitability of the first step.

The fourth variety, viz. *āśrayāsiddha*, arises when the subject is not proved. Such a fallacy arises when someone discussing with the Buddhists argues that the *ātman* is all-pervading, because it produces in every individual the feeling of joy. This argument is fallacious since for the Buddhists the subject *ātman* is not proved at all. Thus Diṅnāga's analysis of *āśrayāsiddha*, which is designated as *asiddha svabhāva* in the *PS*, refers to "unproved subject of thesis" and not to "undoubtedly absent subject of the thesis." Diṅnāga's example thus differs fundamentally from the popular Navya-Nyāya example of *āśrayāsiddha* namely "The sky lotus is fragrant because it is a lotus" which is based on the non-existence of the subject and thus on the falsity of the first step.

So, basic to the analysis of *asiddha hetvābhāsa*s we can identify the following alternative possibilities —

1. Both the *hetu* and the *pakṣa* are existent by themselves, but *hetu* is not predicated of the *pakṣa*. In other words *hetu* is predicated of some subject other than the *pakṣa* and some other predicate is predicated of the *pakṣa* but not the *hetu*. This is the case with *svarūpāsiddha.*
2. *Hetu* exists but *pakṣa*-subject does not. Therefore, the predication is false. This is the case with *āśrayāsiddha.*
3. *Hetu* exists, the *pakṣa* also exists. But whether the *hetu* exists or not is a matter of doubt. This is the case with *sandigdhāśraya.*

Let us now pass on to Dharmakīrti's analysis of *asiddha hetvābhāsa.* We find that his analysis is also close to Diṅnāga's account, though he spells it out in a more analytic way:

1. The existence of the *hetu* in the subject (*pakṣa*) is not accepted by both the debaters. This is known as *ubhayāsiddha.*
2. The existence of the *hetu* in the subject is not accepted by the opponent; this is called by him *prativādyasiddha.*
3. The existence of the *hetu* in the subject is not accepted by the proponent or arguer himself. This is described by Dharmakīrti as *svayaṁ vādino 'siddhaḥ.*
4. The *hetu* is doubted to exist (*svayaṁ sandigdhāsiddha*).
5. The *pakṣa* subject is doubted to exist, (*sandigdha āśrayāsiddha*).
6. The existence of the *pakṣa* is falsified. This is known as *āśrayaṇāsiddha.*

Of these six, it can be easily seen that the second and third varieties are subdivision of Diṅnāga's *anyatarāsiddha.* And the fourth and fifth varieties are the sub-types of Diṅnāga's *sandigdhāsiddha*. Let us now consider the examples given by Dharmakīrti. The example of the first variety is the same as that of Diṅnāga:

1. Sound is non-eternal because it is visible.
2. Trees are conscious because they die by changing their bulks. This is a fallacy for those who mean by death cessation of consciousness as in that case the *hetu* does not exist in the subject.
3. Example of the third variety is: Feelings of pleasure and pain are unconscious because they are impermanent or they have origination. This probans is unacceptable to the arguer *Sāṁkhya* himself.
4. Example of the fourth variety is the same as has been mentioned by Diṅnāga.

   There is peacock in that bush for we can hear its sounds. Now as that place is surrounded by many bushes, it is quite doubtful whether the sound is coming from that particular bush. So, it is a case of *āśrayaṇāsiddham* (. . . *yasmād deśādāgacchati kekāyitam/tasya vibhrame vyāmohe satyayam āśrayāsiddhaḥ/nirantareṣu vahuṣu nikuñjeṣu satsu yadā kekāyitāpātanikuñje vibhramaḥ kimasmān nikuñjāt kekāyitam āgatam āhosvid any asmāditi tadāyamāśrayaṇā-siddha iti*, — *NBT*, on 3.64).
5. The self is all-pervading, because it is apprehended everywhere.

Here the fallacy arises because the *dharmī*, namely the self, is not admitted as existent and real by the Buddhists. Thus the locus being non-existent, the probans cannot exist in the locus.

The Buddhist exposition of the *āśrayāsiddha* is interesting because it points out that the locus or the subject may be put to challenge by the opponent, though the proponent thinks it all right. If we take for example the argument *ākāśaṁ dravyam guṇāśrayatvāt* (ether is a substance because it is the locus of properties), we find that when the opponent is a Buddhist or a Cārvāka, he will challenge the locus itself because he does not recognize ether as a real object at all. Hence the proponent will be challenged to establish the reality of ether. The direction of the debate will be then turned towards a new problem. In this respect the Buddhist analysis of *āśrayāsiddha* fares better than the example of the Naiyāyika who normally illustrates this fallacy by taking as locus of the inference such fictitious objects as sky-lotus or golden mountain, etc. Such locuses are too absurd to be considered seriously as objects of debate. But in the Buddhist account the opponent will block the argument at the very outset by challenging the proposer to prove the ontological status of the locus.

Anaikāntika

The fallacies of *hetu* based on the falsity or dubitability of the second and/or third characteristic of the probans, constitute the *anaikāntika* variety of *hetvābhāsa*s. Diṅnāga classifies this *anaikāntika* fallacy under three varieties — *sādhāraṇa, asādhāraṇa* and *viruddhavyabhicārin* on the basis whether the predicate as expressed by the reason is either too narrow or too general or antinomic. Of these three, by *sādhāraṇa anaikāntika* Diṅnāga meant a *hetu* which exists both in *sapakṣa* and in *vipakṣa.* If the *hetu* resides in *vipakṣa* then it fails to satisfy the third characteristic of the probans. On the other hand, *asādhāraṇa anaikāntika hetu* is one which resides neither in *sapakṣa* nor in *vipakṣa.* If *hetu* does not reside in *vipakṣa* then it possesses the third feature. But if *hetu* does not reside in any part of the *sapakṣa* it fails to possess the second character. Thus *asādhāraṇa anaikāntika* implies the falsity of the second step. *Viruddhavyabhicārin* variety of fallacy means a strong signifying analogy which proves the opposite thesis. This variety of fallacy consists in offering two *hetus* which in spite of being equally strong analogies "prove" mutually contradictory conclusions. Let us take the example cited in Śaṅkarasvāmin's *Nyāyapraveśa*:

1. Sound is non-eternal because it is a product like a jar.
2. Sound is eternal because it is knowable by ears like soundness.

Though Diṅnāga includes both these arguments in the fallacy and adds that both the *hetus* are collectively *anaikāntika*, it seems that any debater who commits this fallacy makes only the first argument, while the other debater who points at this fallacy makes the second argument. It can be seen from this example that there is no logical opposition as far as the premises of the first argument and the premises of the second argument are concerned. Though the premises of the two arguments are compatible with each other, their conclusions are contradictory to each other. Secondly, it should be noticed that in case of this fallacy, both the *hetus* are asserted to possess all the three characteristic features. In spite of the fact that both the *hetus* satisfy the triple characteristics of the probans, we are prevented from concluding that both the arguments must be sound, because the conclusion of the two arguments are contradictory to each other. The admission of this *viruddhāvyabhicārin* type of fallacy by Diṅnāga indicates that he must have been aware of the fact that the account of the triple characteristics of the probans which he gave was not perfect so as to guarantee the truth of the conclusion. So, Diṅnāga had to go out of the way and declare a new fallacy of the probans called the *viruddhāvyabhicārin*. Dharmakīrti could observe the drawback of Diṅnāga's system of inference and so he tried to remove it well. Before going to discuss Dharmakīrti's exposition of the *anaikāntika* variety of *hetvābhāsa*, we may mention that Śaṅkarasvāmin in his *Nyāyapraveśa* added three more varieties to Diṅnāga's list of *anaikāntika hetvābhāsa*. These additions are *sapakṣaikadeśavṛttivipakṣavyāpī, vipakṣa-ikādeśavṛtti sapakṣavyāpī* and *ubhayapakṣaikadeśavṛtti*, depending on the fact as to whether the *hetu* resides in a part of the *sapakṣa* and in the whole *vipakṣa*, or whether the *hetu* resides in a part of the *vipakṣa* and also in the whole *sapakṣa* or whether the *hetu* resides in a part of the *sapakṣa* and *vipakṣa* respectively. Though these additions are not explicitly admitted by Diṅnāga as separate from the standard varieties of *anaikāntika hetvābhāsa* they have all been considered by Diṅnāga in his *hetucakra*. So, it seems that Diṅnāga included all of them under *sādhāraṇa-anaikāntika* type as these forms correspond to the way in which *hetu* can reside in both *sapakṣa* and *vipakṣa*, but Śaṅkarasvāmin thought *sādhāraṇa-anaikāntika* to be that *hetu* which resides in the whole *sapakṣa* and whole *vipakṣa*, which is actually a sub-type of Diṅnāga's *sādhāraṇa anaikāntika*. It is due to this difference in outlook that Śaṅkarasvāmin made such addition to the type of *anaikāntika hetvābhāsa*.

In Dharmakīrti's analysis of *parārthānumāna* there are two premises, one premise asserting the *pakṣadharmatā* feature, namely the existence of the probans in the locus of inference and the other premise stating the *vyāpti* relation between the probans and the probandum. Fallacies based on the falsity or dubitability of *vyāpti* statement are the *anaikāntika* and *viruddha* varieties. To quote from the text *Nyāyabindu* —

> *tathaikasya rūpasyāsapakṣe 'sattvasyāsiddhāvanaikāntiko hetvābhāsaḥ* । . . . *sarvatraikadeśe vā vartamānas tathāsyaiva rūpasya sandehe 'pyanaikāntika eva* ।
>
> (*NB*, 3.66-68)

same as that of Diṅnāga, but his exposition of *asādhāraṇa anaikāntika* variety is somewhat different. According to him though the non-availability of empirical evidence for *sapakṣa sattva* does not falsify the *vyāpti* statement, still it can show that the *vyāpti* statement is uncertain. And thus the uncertainty or dubitability of the *vyāpti* statement can amount to the fallacy. For Diṅnāga the *asādhāraṇa anaikāntika* fallacy consists in the falsity of the second step, for Dharmakīrti the fallacy lies in the doubt about the truth of the second step. Dharmakīrti describes this fallacy as one which is discovered by raising doubt about both *anvaya* and *vyatireka* between *hetu* and *sādhya*.

Dharmakīrti discusses another variety of fallacy which raises doubt about the *vyatireka* but not the *anvaya*. The *anvaya* or the *vyatireka* are to be taken in the sense of *sapakṣa sattva* and *vipakṣa sattva* respectively. The intention of Dharmakīrti is to suggest that if either *sapakṣa sattva* or *vipakṣa sattva* is dubitable, the universal *vyāpti* itself is dubitable. The example cited by him is — Mr *X* is not omniscient because he speaks. In such an example, we can find instances where both the probans and the probandum are co-existent, but can anyone get a case where the *hetu* and the *sādhya* are co-absent? For a doubt can always be raised regarding someone's being omniscient. The spirit of this example lies in the fact that if the *vyāpti* statement is true, the *vyabhicāra* must be impossible. In this case, though the *vyabhicāra,* viz. a speaking person who is omniscient, is not clearly discovered by us it cannot be shown to be an impossibility. Between "being omniscient" and "being a speaker" there is neither empirical inconsistency nor logical contradiction.

This variety of fallacious inference may be considered as *kevalānvayī* variety of inference recognized by the other schools of Indian philosophy, since here the inference is made simply on the basis of positive instances and no instance is available sharing the negative analogy between Mr *X* and some omniscient person. Dharmakīrti's discussion throws light on the fact that even an inference based on *anvaya* alone is sometimes fallacious, when the necessary *vyāpti* relation is in question.

Viruddha

The *viruddha* fallacy arises, according to Diṅnāga, when the *hetu* does not reside in any part of *sapakṣa*, but resides in the *vipakṣa*, partially or wholly. *Hetu* does not reside in any part of *sapakṣa* means, if anything other than the *pakṣa* or subject has the *hetu* resident in it, then it does not have *sādhya*. *Hetu* resides in *vipakṣa* means that there is something which does not have the *sādhya* or the property to prove, has the *hetu*. Thus *viruddha* fallacy implies the falsity of the second and third characteristics of the probans. To state explicitly, the *viruddha* variety of *hetu* is fallacious because the *hetu* can be used to prove the absence of *sādhya* when it is being wrongly used to prove the *sādhya*. The example cited to demonstrate the *viruddha hetvābhāsa* is: sound is eternal because it is a product. Just as we can conceive of different varieties of *sādhāraṇa anaikāntika* on the basis of the *hetu*'s existence in the *sapakṣa* and *vipakṣa*, in the case of *viruddha* also, we can conceive of variations on the basis of the alternative situation of the existence of *hetu* in the *vipakṣa*. The *viruddha* kind of *hetu* may exist in a part of the *vipakṣa* or in the *vipakṣa* as a whole. Accordingly we can conceive of two different types of *viruddha hetvābhāsa* — *vipakṣaikādeśavṛtti* and *vipakṣavyāpī* respectively. Diṅnāga in his *hetucakra* has referred to both these varieties.

Śaṅkarasvāmin in his *Nyāyapraveśa* adds three more to the list of *viruddha hetvābhāsa*. These are (i) *dharmaviśeṣaviparītasādhana*, (ii) *dharmisvarūpaviparītasādhana*, and (iii) *dharmiviśeṣa-*

viparītasādhana. The first one refers to the case where the *hetu* proves the negation of some implicit characteristic of *pakṣa*. The second one refers to the case where the *hetu* proves the negation of the subject and the third one refers to the *hetu* that proves the negation of some implicit characteristics of the *pakṣa* subject. Of these three the first and the third one prove the negation of the thesis intended by the debater, but not explicitly expressed by him in verbatim. In a particular debate context when a doubter *A* argues for a thesis *P* with the help of the *hetu M*; another debater *B* may be aware of the intended thesis *P* of *A*. But *B* may show that the probans *M* which *A* has provided for proving *P*, at the same time proves the negation of *P*. Thus, the *hetu* is defective. These two fallacies are in a peculiar way significant only in a debate context and are different from the external fallacy of *viruddha*. The difference between the two lies in the fact that in case of the external fallacy of *viruddha* that the thesis is contradicted by the *hetu*, is accepted by the debater while in case of the above-discussed fallacies, the *hetu* proves the opposite of the intended thesis.

Dharmakīrti's discussion of the fallacy called *viruddha* is almost the same as Diṅnāga. He does not differ much from Diṅnāga as far as the basic nature of the *viruddha hetvābhāsa* is concerned. According to both Diṅnāga and Dharmakīrti a *hetu* commits the *viruddha hetvābhāsa* when it is predicated of at least some *vipakṣa*-subjects but not predicated of any *sapakṣa*-subject. Dharmakīrti in his *Nyāyabindu* holds that *viruddha hetvābhāsa* occurs by violating the two characteristics of the probans, viz. existence of the probans in the similar instances and non-existence of the probans in the dissimilar instances — *dvayo rūpayor viparyayasiddhau viruddhaḥ* (*NB*, 3.81). The example cited by him is "word is eternal because it is a product or because it is produced by human effort." In the two examples we find that the probans "being product" does not exist in any instance of "eternity," on the other hand it is existent in all the instances of non-eternal entities. Similar is the case with the other probans, "being produced by human effort." Since the two probanses are opposed to the probandum "eternity," they are regarded as *viruddha.*

Dharmakīrti mentions another variety of *viruddha hetvābhāsa*, which he terms as *iṣṭa-vighātakṛt*, where the *hetu* is contrary to the intended probandum. The example of such *hetvābhāsa* is — "The sense organs are useful for something else because they are combinations of atoms just like bed, chair, etc. which are combinations of atoms and are useful for the person who uses them." Here the existence of self is the intended probandum. But the probandum stated in the argument is not self but "something other than the sense organs." When the arguer proves "something" he proceeds to claim that it is nothing but the permanent soul. The difficulty with this inference is that the *hetu*, viz. being a combination of atoms can at the most imply the existence of some other combination of atoms for the sake of which this combination is used. Thus the person also is a combination of atoms for the sake of which bed, chair, etc. are used. Therefore, the *hetu* is contrary to the implicit *sādhya*, viz. the self which is not a combination.

Now the question arises whether this variety of fallacy is to be considered as a special case of *viruddha hetvābhāsa* or can be included within *viruddha hetvābhāsa* in general. Diṅnāga is in favour of the first alternative while Dharmakīrti opts for the second one, since in his opinion the intended *sādhya* need not be differentiated from the stated explicit *sādhya* because both are expected to be proved. *Na hyamābhāṁ sādhyaviparyayasādhanatvena bhidyate* (*NB*, 3.91). To quote Dharmottara — *yasmād ayamiṣṭavighātakṛdābhyāṁ hetubhyāṁ sādhyaviparyyayasya sādhanatvena na bhidyate* । *yathā tau sādhyaviparyayasādhanau tathāyam apti yuktaviparyyayaṁ tu sādhayatu vā mā vā kiṁ uktaviparyyayasādhanena* । *tasmād anayor evāntarbhāvaḥ* । — *NBT*, on 3.91.

IV

Dṛṣṭāntābhāsa

Fallacies regarding the example of an inference have been regarded by the Buddhists as *dṛṣṭāntābhāsa*. In the *Nyāyamukha*, Diṅnāga has defined the example as one which "expresses that the reason is followed by the probandum, and that, wherever the probandum is absent the reason also is absent." In other words, for Diṅnāga examples are of two varieties — affirmative and negative depending on the affirmative and the negative application of the two predicates. Any other example which does not satisfy these conditions will be regarded as a case of fallacy of example.

Diṅnāga mentions ten cases of fallacy of examples, three regarding the *anvaya*, three regarding *vyatireka*, and one each regarding *viparītānvaya*, *viparīta vyatireka*, *ananvaya* and *avyatireka*. Let us try to explain each of these ten cases —

ANVAYA

(1) Where the probans is absent. Sound is eternal because it is immaterial as the atoms.

(2) Where the probandum is absent. Sound is eternal because it is immaterial as *karman*.

(3) Where both the probans and the probandum are absent. Sound is eternal because it is immaterial as a pot.

VYATIREKA

(1) Where the probans is found in *vipakṣa* case. Sound is eternal because it is immaterial as *karman,* viz. whatever is non-eternal is material, as *karman.*

(2) Where the probandum is found in *vipakṣa* case. Sound is eternal because it is immaterial as the atoms, viz. whatever is non-eternal is material, as the atoms.

(3) Where both the probans and the probandum are found in *vipakṣa* case.

Sound is eternal because it is immaterial as ether, viz. whatever is non-eternal is material as ether.

VIPARĪTĀNVAYA

Where the order of the probans and the probandum has been changed. The lightning is eternal because it is not the effect of some effort, as a pot. Whatever is non-eternal is the effect of some effort as is the case with a pot.

VIPARĪTAVYATIREKA

Where the absence of the probandum and the absence of the probans has been altered. The lightning is eternal because it is not the effect of some effort, as ether. Whatever is not the effect of some effort is eternal as ether.

ANANVAYA

Where the relation between the probans and the probandum is not present. The lightning is eternal because it is not the effect of some effort, as a pot. Whatever is the effect of some effort is non-eternal as a pot.

AVYATIREKA

Where the *vyatireka* relation is not present. The lightning is eternal because it is not the effect of some effort, as ether. Whatever is not the effect of some effort is eternal, as ether.

We may now take a look, at a post-Diṅnāga manual of Buddhist logic, the *Nyāyapraveśa* attributed to Śaṅkarasvāmin. In this book also we find a more or less same list of *dṛṣṭāntābhāsa* as is found in the *Nyāyamukha.* Examples have been classified under two heads — *sādharmya-dṛṣṭānta* and *vaidharmyadṛṣṭānta.* The former has been defined as one in which the probans is stated to be present only in the *sapakṣa.* For example, "whatever is produced is seen to be impermanent, like a pot." *Vaidharmyadṛṣṭānta,* on the other hand, is one in which the probans is stated to be absent wherever the inferable property is absent. For example, "whatever is permanent is seen to be a non-product, like space." In accordance with these two types of examples, *sādharmyadṛṣṭānta* and *vaidharmyadṛṣṭānta,* the fallacies of examples have also been classified under two heads — homogeneous and heterogeneous. In respect of homogeneity the pseudo example may be one of the following:

(1) Where the property of the probans is lacking (*sādhanadharmāsiddha*).

(2) Where the property of the probandum is lacking (*sādhyadharmāsiddha*).

(3) Where the properties of both the probans and the probandum are lacking (*ubhayadharmāsiddha*).

(4) Where the invariable connection between the probans and the probandum is lacking (*ananvaya*).

(5) Where there is a reverse connection between the probans and the probandum (*viparītānvaya*).

In respect of heterogeneity the pseudo examples (*vaidharmyena dṛṣṭāntābhāsa*) are:

(6) That which is not heterogeneous from the absence of the probans (*sādhanavyāvṛtta*).

(7) That which is not heterogeneous from the absence of the probandum (*sādhyavyāvṛtta*).

(8) That which is not heterogeneous with the absence of both the probans and the probandum (*ubhayavyāvṛttaḥ*).

(9) That showing an absence of disconnection between the probans and the probandum (*avyatireka*).

(10) That showing an absence of reverse disconnection between the probans and the probandum (*viparīta-vyatireka*).

Following *Nyāyapraveśa* let us try to give examples of each of these varieties.

(1) *Sādhanadharmāsiddha*: Sound is eternal because it is incorporeal, that which is incorporeal is eternal like the atoms. Here "the atoms" is the example. But it is such that though the *sādhyadharma* (the property of the probandum) is present, the *sādhanadharma* (the property of the probans) is not present, for atoms are considered to be corporeal.

(2) *Sādhyadharmāsiddha*: Sound is eternal because it is incorporeal, that which is incorporeal is eternal like intelligence. Here "intelligence" is the example. But it is such that though the attribute of probans is present, the property of the probandum, viz. eternity is not present as intelligence is not considered to be eternal.

(3) *Ubhayāsiddha*: Sound is eternal because it is incorporeal, that which is incorporeal is eternal like the pot. Here "the pot" is the example. But it is such that in it neither the property of the probans nor that of the probandum is present. So this is not a proper instance but a pseudo one.

(4) *Ananvaya*: Sound is non-eternal because it is a product, that which is a product is non-eternal like a pot. Here the example cited, viz. "pot" is not a proper one but a pseudo one. For a pot is considered to be the locus of productivity and non-eternity. It merely indicates that there is co-existence between the two. The possibility remains that there might be no invariable connection between them. So the case of pot cannot be considered as a proper exhibitant of invariable connection between the probans and the probandum and as such it is a pseudo example.

In the *Nyāyapraveśa* this variety of *dṛṣṭāntābhāsa* has been described as one which merely indicates the co-existence of the probans and the probandum without showing any connection between them.

(5) *Viparītānvayaḥ*: Sound is non-eternal because it is a product and that which is non-eternal is a product like a pot. Here the example is defective because it states the inverse of the invariable concomitant relation. In this case the *vyāpti* should be stated as "whatever is a product is non-eternal." Instead of stating the *vyāpti* in this way, it has been said as "whatever is non-eternal is a product." The convention is that the property of the probans is to be stated first and then the property of the probandum, here this convention is not followed and the relation is reversed. So there

is the fallacy. In the *Nyāyapraveśavṛtti* this is described as *nyāyamudrā-vyatikramaḥ,* i.e. exception to the accepted convention. However this is not the only fallacy. There is a counter instance to such an inverse relation, viz. "whatever is non-eternal is a product as in the case of lightning." (Product means that which is produced by some effort. Lightning is non-eternal, but it is not a product in the sense of being produced by some effort.)

(6) *Sādhyavyāvṛttaḥ*: Sound is eternal because it is incorporeal. That which is non-eternal is corporeal like atoms. Here the example is a wrong one for though in atoms there is absence of the probans, there is no absence of the probandum, as atoms are not non-eternal, but are eternal. In other words, the example is not heterogeneous with the opposite of the major term.

(7) *Sādhanavyāvṛttaḥ*: Sound is eternal because it is incorporeal and that which is not eternal is not incorporeal like activity. Activity cannot be regarded as a proper example for though it is concomitant with the absence of the probandum, there is no such concomitance with regard to the absence of the probans. Activity does not exclude the property of being incorporeal.

(8) *Ubhayavyāvṛttaḥ*: Sound is eternal because it is incorporeal; that which is not eternal is not incorporeal such as space. As space itself is such that it does not possess either the absence of eternity or the absence of incorporeality, it cannot be regarded as a proper example. In fact, schools like the Nyāya-Vaiśeṣikas regard space as eternal as well as incorporeal.

(9) *Avyatirekaḥ*: This type of fallacy arises where the negative concomitance is not stated but only the absence of the *sādhya dharma* (property of the probandum) and the *sādhana dharma* (property of the probans) are said to belong to the example. For instance, in the argument sound is eternal because it is incorporeal like the jar, instead of saying that which is not eternal is not incorporeal like the jar, we are saying that in the jar non-eternity and corporeality are present. This is regarded as a case of *avyatireka dṛṣṭāntābhāsa* for the example lacks the *vyatireka vyāpti*. *Vyatireka vyāpti* requires that it must be shown that the absence of the probandum is concomitant with the absence of the probans. In the present case this sort of concomitant relation is not taken into consideration, an example is just cited.

(10) *Viparītavyatirekaḥ*: This type of fallacy occurs where the order of the *vyatireka vyāpti* is reversed. Let us consider the argument — word is eternal because it is incorporeal. Here the *vyatireka vyāpti* proper should be "that which is not eternal is not incorporeal" *yadanityam tanmūrtam*. But if we say instead *yadamūrtam tadanityam* that will be the case of *viparītavyatirekaḥ*, for the *vyatireka vyāpti* occurs when the absence of the probandum is concomitant with the absence of the probans and not the other way round. As in this inference the *vyāpti* is not stated in the proper way it cannot be regarded as a proper case of inference.

A look at this list of pseudo examples shows its close similarity with the list provided by Diṅnāga in his *Nyāyamukha*. In fact, (1), (2), (3), (6), (7) and (8) are the same as the three erroneous *anvaya* and three erroneous *vyatireka* cases recognized by Diṅnāga. Truly speaking, these six cases only are absolutely wrong because the very formulation has been defective, but this is not the case with the remaining four. Though they are invalid in the cases of inference for others (*parārthānumāna*), they are quite valid for inference for one's own self (*svārthānumāna*). The *ubhayāsiddha* and *ubhaya vyāvṛtta* refer to cases in which both the *sādhya* and the *sādhana* are respectively unproved in the positive example and non-excluded by the negative example.

Dharmakīrti in his *Nyāyabindu* makes an elaborate discussion on the fallacious instances. Fallacious instances may be of the following types:

(1) Where the property of the probandum is lacking (*sādhya-vikalaḥ*).

(2) Where the property of the probans is lacking (*sādhana-vikalaḥ*).

(3) Where the properties of both the probans and the probandum are lacking (*ubhaya-vikalaḥ*).

(4) Where the property of the probans is in question (*sandigdha-sādhya-dharma*).

(5) Where the property of the probans is in question (*sandigdha-sādhana-dharma*).

(6) Where the properties of both the probandum and the probans are questionable (*sandigdhobhaya-dharma*).

(7) Where there is simply the possibility of the co-occurrence of the probans and the probandum, but there is no proof regarding their invariable concomitant relation (*ananvayaḥ*).

(8) Where in spite of the occurrence of the concomitance between the probans and the probandum, the relation is not shown (*apradarśitānvayaḥ*).

(9) Where the concomitant relation is stated in a reverse order (*viparītānvayaḥ*).

All these nine fallacies occur in respect of homogeneous feature, so they are regarded by Dharmakīrti as *sādharmyeṇa dṛṣṭāntadoṣaḥ*. Just as fallacies can occur in respect of instance exhibiting homogeneous feature, similarly with regard to instance about heterogeneous feature there are also fallacies. These are also nine in number and are as follows:

(10) Where there is no negative concomitance with the probandum (*sādhya vyatireka*).

(11) Where there is no negative concomitance with the probans (*sādhana vyatireka*).

(12) Where there is no negative concomitance with either the probans or the probandum (*ubhaya vyatireka*).

(13) Where the negative concomitance with the probandum is questionable (*sandigdha-sādhana-vyatireka*).

(14) Where the negative concomitance with the probans is in question (*sandigdha-sādhya-vyatireka*).

(15) Where the negative concomitance with both the probans and the probandum is questionable (*sandigdhobhaya-vyatireka*).

(16) Where the negative concomitance between the probans and probandum is not established (*avyatireka*).

(17) Where the negative concomitance between the probans and the probandum is not exhibited (*apradarśita-vyatireka*).

(18) Where the contrary of the negative concomitance between the probans and the probandum is established (*viparīta vyatireka*).

Let us try to explain each of these varieties with suitable illustrations after Dharmakīrti:

(1) Where the property of the probandum is lacking — Sound is eternal, because it is incorporeal like activity. Here in this inference the probandum is eternal (*nitya*) and the property is *nityatva* or eternity. Now such a property is lacking in the instance "activity." Therefore, this sort of inference is not possible. So activity or *karma* is an instance of *sādhyavikalaḥ*.

(2) Where the property of the probans is lacking — sound is eternal because it is incorporeal like the atoms. Here the atoms is the example. In this example though the property of the probandum, viz. *nityatva* is present, the property of the probans, viz. incorporeality is absent. Therefore, this instance being a case of *sādhana vikala* cannot be regarded as a proper one.

(3) Where the properties of both the probans and the probandum are lacking — Sound is eternal because it is incorporeal like a jar. Here the instance is "a jar." But as a jar is neither eternal nor incorporeal, it lacks the properties of both the probans and the probandum. Therefore, it is a fallacious one being a case of *ubhaya-vikalaḥ*.

(4) Where the property of the probandum is in question — This person is compassionate because he has the capacity to speak like the man on the chariot. In this inference "the man on the chariot" is the instance. But just because he is a person, it cannot definitely be said that he is compassionate. In fact, whether he is compassionate or not is doubtful. "Being compassionate" is the probandum. As the probandum is doubtful in this instance, this argument is a case of *sandigdha-sādhya-dharma*.

(5) Where the property of the probans is doubtful — This person is mortal because he is compassionate like the man on the chariot. In this inference, "the man on the chariot" is the instance. But simply on the ground of his being a person it cannot be said definitely that he is compassionate. In fact, whether he is really compassionate or not is doubtful. So this instance like the former one is fallacious, the fallacy here being that of *sandigdha-sādhana-dharma.*

(6) Where the properties of both the probans and the probandum are questionable.

"This person is not omniscient because he is compassionate like the man on the chariot." In this inference "the man on the chariot" is the instance. But just from the fact that someone is a person it is not possible to say with certainty that he is not omniscient, nor that he is compassionate. So the properties of both the probans and the probandum are questionable in this instance. So the instance is a wrong one being a case of *sandigdhobhayadharmaḥ.*

(7) Where there is no invariable concomitance between the probans and the probandum.

This variety of fallacy occurs with those instances which cannot properly demonstrate the invariable concomitance between the probans and the probandum. This may be possible in either of the two ways — either there is no *vyāpti* relation and so the instance cannot demonstrate it, or there is the *vyāpti* relation but the instance itself is incapable of exhibiting it. Accordingly this sort of fallacy may be of two types. One type is where the possibility of the co-occurrence of the probans and the probandum is observed but the probans is not invariably concomitant with the major term.

(8) The same fallacy can occur in another way also, where the invariable concomitance between the probans and the probandum is present, but it has not been exhibited in the instance.

Thus in both the cases of *ananvaya* or *apradarśitānvaya* the instance fails to perform its normal function of relating the *sādhya* with the *pakṣa.* So they are wrong. The difference between the two types of fallacies will be made clear if we take two cases. Let us first take the inference — this man is compassionate because he is a speaker, whosoever is a speaker is compassionate just as the desired man. Let us take another inference — sound is non-eternal because it is a product, whatsoever is a product is non-eternal like the pot.

From these two instances it is clear that the *dṛṣṭānta vākya* or the statement exhibiting the invariable concomitant relation is not the same in the two cases. In the first one the connection between the probans and the probandum is only an accidental one (*saṁbhavamātram*) and there is no invariable concomitance between the two. But in the second case there is an invariable concomitance between the two terms but that concomitance is not exhibited in the instance. So though both the instances share the same feature of not properly showing the *vyāpti* relation, the mode of expression is different in the two cases and so there are two different varieties of the same fallacy. In other words, Dharmakīrti is admitting a distinction between stating and showing.

(9) Where the invariable concomitance between the probans and the probandum is reverted.

This is also considered to be a case of mistaken instance. For example, sound is a product because it is non-eternal, whatever is non-eternal is a product. In this inference the probans is "non-eternal" and the probandum is "being a product." It is indeed true that being a product is a reason for something to be non-eternal. So we can say that there is an invariable connection between being a product and being non-eternal. In other words, we can say "whatever is a product is non-eternal" and this holds unconditionally for everything. But the opposite is not universally applicable. That is, "whatever is non-eternal is a product" is not always true. As such, from the fact of something being a product we can infer that it is non-eternal, but from the fact that it is non-eternal we cannot infer that it is a product. A product means that which is produced by the effort of any agent.

One may argue that though from non-eternity we cannot have knowledge of productivity since the two are not invariably related, in reality productivity is invariably related to non-eternity. So why is it that we cannot have such apprehension? In reply, it has been said that though in reality productivity is invariably related to non-eternity, that the reverse is not always true has not been taken into consideration by the speaker. It is by mistake that he takes the invariable relation to be so. Thus though the intention behind the argument may not be defective, it is because of the defect in the speaker's mode of presentation that the argument has become defective. Durveka Miśra in his sub-commentary *Pradīpa* tries to explain the point with an example. An axe has the nature of cutting objects. But if an agent takes it and simply puts it on the ground, it will not be able to perform its act of cutting. In such a case the purpose of the axe will not be served. However this failure is not due to any sort of impotency on the part of the axe, but due to the agent. Similar is the case with the instance where the invariable relation has been reverted. Here also the fallacy is due to the mistake on the part of the speaker and not on the argument itself. In the case of inference for others (*parārthānumāna*) mistake on the part of the speaker also constitutes fallacies.

These nine are cases of fallacies which arise mainly regarding the similarity of the probandum. So, they fall under one group which Dharmakīrti designates as *sādharmyeṇa dṛṣṭāntadoṣaḥ*. As the Buddhists believe that the *vyāpti* relation occurs in two ways — through the joint occurrence in presence (*anvaya*) of the probans and the probandum as also through the joint occurrence between them in respect of negation (*vyatireka*), we have to provide instance for both the positive and negative occurrences. Accordingly, just as there may arise defect in the case of instances of positive occurrences, there may arise defect in the negative occurrences also. Dharmakīrti describes them as the defects of instances due to dissimilarities (*vaidharmyeṇa dṛṣṭāntadoṣaḥ*).

These fallacies like the former group are also of nine types. Of them the first three are those where there is no negative concomitance in respect of the probandum or probans or both. If we say, "sound is eternal because it is incorporeal like the atoms" that will be the case of *sādhya vyatirekī*. For the invariable relation here would be "whatever is non-eternal is not incorporeal" and atoms in spite of their corporeality do not possess the property of non-eternity and as such they are not proper instances for such an inference. To avoid the fallacy, if we drop "atoms" as the instance and put "activity" in that position the inference will take the following shape — "sound is eternal because it is incorporeal like activity." This inference though free from the charge of *sādhya vyatirekī* will become a case of *sādhana vyatirekī,* for the instance "activity" does not possess the absence of incorporeality. Again if we replace the instance with "space" the argument will still be invalid, because space lacks both the features — absence of non-eternity and absence of incorporeality. Therefore, it will be a case of *ubhaya vyatirekī.*

Just as in *sādharmya dṛṣṭānta* we noticed that fallacies occur not only in cases where the probans or the probandum or both are lacking but also in those cases where any of them is doubted, in the *vaidharmya dṛṣṭānta* also the same thing happens. That is, if there is any doubt regarding the absence of the probandum or the probans or both, the argument will be wrong. Let us explain each of these alternative cases with suitable examples.

Sandigdhasādhyavyatirekaḥ: "Kapila and others are non-omniscient or non-authoritative, for they do not possess the proof of ominiscience or authoritativeness like the knowledge of astronomy. Those who are omniscient or authoritative are persons who possess and preach the knowledge of astronomy as did Ṛṣabha or Vardhamāna and others." In this inference Ṛṣabha and Vardhamāna are cited as instances for the negative concomitance between the probans and the probandum. But this example is not a proper one for it is quite questionable whether any Buddhists regarded Ṛṣabha, Vardhamāna and others as omniscient and authoritative. So this is a case of *sandigdhasādhyavyatirekaḥ.*

Sandigdhasādhanavyatirekaḥ: "This intended person is not to be admitted as authoritative by any brāhmaṇa well-versed with the three Vedas, because he is passionate. Whoever is admitted as authoritative by any brāhmaṇa well-versed with the three Vedas is not passionate like Gautama, or the authors of different Śāstras like Dharmaśāstra. In this inference the probans is "being passionate" and "Gautama and other authors of different Śāstras" is the instance. Whether Gautama and others were really free from passions or not is not an accepted fact for the Buddhists, but it is quite in question to them. So citing them as an instance to establish the invariable concomitant relation is not possible. This instance is a fallacious one, the fallacy is termed *sandigdha-sādhana-vyatireka*.

Sandigdhobhayavyatireka: Sages like Kapila, etc. are not dispassionate because of their eagerness of possession. Those who are dispassionate are persons who do not have any eagerness for possession like Ṛṣabha and others. In this inference "not dispassionate" is the probandum and "eagerness for possession" is the probans and "Ṛṣabha and others" is the instance. To establish such an inference it is necessary to have an invariable concomitant relation, and as such an invariable concomitance cannot be established in the positive the relation is stated in negative terms as "wherever there is absence of the probandum there is absence of the probans." Absence of the probandum, viz. absence of the negation of dispassion, and absence of the probans, viz. absence of eagerness for possession, are not considered as established facts by the Buddhists in the case of Ṛṣabha and others, but is quite questionable. Therefore this instance is not a proper one.

Avyatireka: "This person is dispassionate because he is a speaker. Those who are not dispassionate are not speakers like stone, etc." In this inference "being dispassionate" is the probandum and "being a speaker" is the probans. Indeed it is true that a stone is not an object which is not dispassionate and at the same time is not a speaker, still such invariable concomitance between the absence of the probandum with the absence of the probans cannot be established. Therefore, the instance under consideration cannot serve its proper function and so is defective. The fallacy here is called *avyatireka.*

Apradarśita vyatireka: "Word is non-eternal because it is produced like sky." In this inference "non-eternal" is the probandum, "being produced" is the probans, "sky" is considered to be the instance. It is an instance of the invariable relation in the negative way. It may be argued that this inference is a proper one as it possesses the absence of the probans as well as the absence of the probandum. So why is it regarded as a fallacy? In reply it has been said that the inference has been defective because the probans has been presented simply as possessed of the *vyatireka* but it does not show the invariable concomitance relation or *vyāpti* between the probans and the probandum. That the probans is invariably related with the probandum has to be shown by either an affirmative or a negative statement, otherwise that which is going to be proved cannot be proved. The invariable concomitance between the probans and the probandum either in terms of similarity or in terms of dissimilarity is to be shown by the instance. In the present argument the instance, viz. the sky does not show the negative concomitance between the probans and the probandum. Therefore, the argument is defective and the fallacy is known as *apradarśita vyatireka.* This fallacy is due to the defect of the speaker.

"Sound is non-eternal because it is produced. Whatever is not produced is eternal." In any argument the probans is said to be invariably connected with the probandum. Such invariable concomitance can be shown with the help of *anvaya vyatireka* relation. That is, if it can be shown that where the probans is present the probandum is present we have to show also that in the absence of the probandum the probans is absent. Only then we can be sure of the *vyāpti* relation between the probans and the probandum. If it is not shown that the absence of the probandum is invariably related with the absence of the probans, it is quite possible that even in the presence of the probans there can be the absence of the probandum. In that case the probans will not be apprehended as invariably connected with the probandum. Therefore, the absence of the probandum should be invariably related to the absence of the probans. In the case of *viparīta vyatireka* the reverse is the case, i.e. the absence of the probans is said to be invariably related to the absence of the probandum and not the other way. Since the absence of the probans is invariably related to the absence of the probandum, in the absence of the latter the former should not be possible. As wherever there is the absence of the probandum there is necessarily the absence of the probans, without the probandum the probans cannot exist. Otherwise the probans will not be invariably related to the probandum and so it will be wrong. In the above argument we find that from the fact of an entity being a non-product, its eternity is inferred. It means that whatever is a non-product is eternal. That is, the invariable connection has been conceived to be between "absence of productivity" and "the presence of eternity." But the fact is that though non-productivity is always related to eternity, eternity is not invariably related with the absence of productivity. This argument is a case of *viparīta vyatireka*. Like the previous one, here also the fallacy is due to the mistake of the speaker and not of any other thing.

After explaining with suitable examples the different varieties of fallacies of the instance, Dharmakīrti tries to find out the reason responsible for such fallacies. In any argument the instance or *dṛṣṭānta* is cited to show that the probans is invariably related to the probandum. The general characteristic of the probans is to show that it exists in all the similar instances (*sapakṣa*) and does not exist in any of the contrary instances (*vipakṣa*). In the case of fallacious instances this general feature of the probans is not observed with certainty.

If it is argued that the general characteristic of the probans is to be judged not by itself, but only in the context of some special ones, Dharmakīrti's reply would be that, that alternative also is not able to remove the fallacy of instances. His argument is like this. Since the particular cases fall under the general characteristics of the probans, therefore if we are able to prove something in the particular cases, it will suffice to apprehend it in general. That is, if in any particular case it can be shown that the probans exists in all similar cases and in all the contrary cases it is absent, then the probans will be true for that particular case. Once it is proved to hold in the particular case, it is able to show it in the general case. Unfortunately we are not able to provide anything in the particular case. Therefore, it follows that the feature of the probans cannot be stated in the general form.

It is thus clear that in the fallacious instances neither the general feature nor the particular characteristics of the probans can be found. So they cannot be considered as instances proper, but rather as *dṛṣṭāntābhāsa*.

Apparently it seems that Dharmakīrti has made a more subtle analysis of the fallacies of examples than it had been done by his preceptor Diṅnāga. But a close look at the lists of fallacies recognized by Diṅnāga and Dharmakīrti will reveal that there is virtually no difference between them. The first three fallacies associated with *anvaya* are mentioned by Dharmakīrti as *sādhya vikalaḥ, sādhanavikalaḥ,* and *ubhayavikalaḥ.* Similarly the three fallacies in connection with *vyatireka* have been admitted by Dharmakīrti as *sādhya vyatirekī, sādhana vyatirekī* and *ubhaya vyatirekī.* The *viparītānvaya* and the *viparīta vyatireka* fallacies are mentioned by the same name in Dharmakīrti's list. What Diṅnāga has recognized as *ananvaya* or as *avyatireka* have each been split into two by Dharmakīrti depending on whether the relation between the probans and the probandum has been stated or shown. The subtle distinction that Dharmakīrti draws between stating and showing is not noticed in Diṅnāga. Diṅnāga simply considers as fallacious that case where the relation between the probans and the probandum is absent. Dharmakīrti makes analysis of such an absence and shows that it may occur in either of the two ways, where there is simple co-occurrence between the two without there being any invariable connection, or there is no occurrence at all. What we find additional in Dharmakirti's list are *sandigdha sādhya-dharma, sandigdha sādhana dharma, sandigdhobhaya dharma, sandigdha sādhya vyatireka, sandigdha sādhana vyatireka* and *sandigdhobhaya vyatireka.* Actually the recognition of these additional six may be found to be due to such a thought that where the presence of the probans or the probandum or both is doubtful, there can arise fallacy in the same way as it can occur when they are absent. In an argument the conclusion can follow from the premises only when we have certain knowledge about the *avinābhāva* relation. In cases where either of the probans or the probandum is put into question we cannot have such a certain knowledge. Accordingly it would be a case of fallacy. Though Dharmakīrti has not explicitly stated this in the context of *dṛṣṭāntābhāsa*, that he has such a thing in mind becomes evident from the words of Dharmottara stated in the context of *hetvābhāsa* — *na kevalam anuktāvuktāvapyasiddhau sandehe vā*. If we understand Dharmakīrti in this light it will not be very difficult for us to hold that Dharmakīrti has not at all deviated from his preceptor, rather he has tried to make explicit what has been implict in Dīṅnāga.

We may wind up our discussion by taking a cursory glance at the reason why the Buddhist scholars felt the need of admitting a separate variety of fallacy as *dṛṣṭāntābhāsa* in addition to the well accepted class of *hetvābhāsa*. In the Nyāya tradition we do not find any discussion on *dṛṣṭāntābhāsa*. In fact they were regarded as fallacious in relation to the other members of syllogism. For instance, the argument "Word is non-eternal because it is a product like the pot" which has been considered to be a case of *ananvaya* by the Buddhists, will be included under the *savyabhicāra* or *anaikāntika* case of *hetvābhāsa*. For the probans "being a product" does not exist in all the *sapakṣa* cases as it does not exist in lightning. Lightning, though non-eternal, is not the result of a conscious effort of any agent. The *hetu* being non-existent in a *sapakṣa* case will be regarded as erroneous. The fallacy here is on the part of the probans and so is regarded as *anaikāntika*.

The reason for such a difference of opinion amongst the Buddhists and the Naiyāyikas may be found in the way *hetvābhāsa* has been conceived by the two schools. For the Naiyāyikas *hetvābhāsa* is regarded as the object of a correct knowledge of the impediment to an inference. In other words, the fault of a *hetu* is that something which being known frustrates or impedes the emergence of a correct inferential cognition. It may create hindrance to an inference either directly or indirectly. The hindrance is direct in the case of *bādhita* and *satpratipakṣa* when they directly prevent passage to a correct inferential conclusion. The hindrance is indirect in the case of *viruddha, savyabhicāra* and *asiddha* when they prevent the means of correct inferential conclusion by preventing the emergence of a correct *parāmarśa*.

The Buddhists, on the other hand, regarded *hetvābhāsa* to be any case where any of the three characteristic features of the *hetu* is lacking. It has further been explained that if the *hetu* is found to be unproved or doubtful for either the proponent or the opponent, it will be regarded as a case of *hetvābhāsa* in spite of the fact that the *hetu* has been mentioned. As *hetvābhāsa* has been restricted to the error of *hetu* or probans only and not to the defects of any other members of the argument, the Buddhists had to recognize fallacies of other members in addition to the fallacy of *hetu*. This is the reason for their admission of *dṛṣṭāntābhāsa* and *pakṣābhāsa* in addition to *hetvābhāsa*. Such a need was not felt by the Naiyāyikas since they defined *hetvābhāsa* as the object of any valid cognition creating an obstacle to an inference. So it is not confined to the defects of probans only, it can be defect with regard to any of the members of syllogism. It is such a difference of outlook towards *hetvābhāsa* that is responsible for the admission of a different type of fallacy for one school and not for the other.

15

Prasaṅgānumāna

THE problem of how to establish a universal proposition on the basis of observation of certain discrete individual cases has troubled logicians of all schools. While the Nyāya school tried to establish *vyāpti* between the *hetu* and the *sādhya* on the basis of their joint occurrence in presence and absence, the Buddhists held that it is to be based on the relation of causality and essential identity. Causality along with essential identity constitutes the basic principle of valid pervasion between the probans and the probandum; and such causality is to be inductively understood through positive and negative perception. However, in some instances, especially in the case of probans as essence (*svabhāva hetu*), the *vyāpti* between the two terms cannot be demonstrated through such positive and negative perceptions. As for instance the *vyāpti* between "being a *śiṁśapā*" and "being a tree" can be established by *pratyakṣa* and *anupalambha*, but the one between "existence" and "momentariness" cannot be so established. It is in such cases that the Buddhist logicians take recourse to *prasaṅgānumāna*. *Prasaṅga* may be regarded as a hypothetical negative reasoning which attempts to bring out an absurd undesirable conclusion on the basis of a universal statement already established by a proof.[1]

1. *pramāṇaprasiddha-vyāptikena vākyena parasyāniṣṭatvāpādanāya prasañjanam prasaṅgaḥ* I — *Bauddha Tarkabhāṣā*, p. 26.28-29.

It may be noted in this context that the Buddhist logicians are not unanimous in respect of admitting *prasaṅga* as a proof or as aid to a proof. For instance Vasubandhu in his *Tarkaśāstra* defended *prasaṅga* as a proof formulation while Diṅnāga, the father figure of Buddhist logic, did not admit such *prasaṅga* in his logical system. The case is different for Dharmakīrti. In the logical system of Dharmakīrti we find a transition regarding the admission of *prasaṅga* as a proof. At the earlier phase where he conformed to Diṅnāga's formulation of inference-for-others (*parārthānumāna*), *prasaṅga* was not considered as a proof by him. But this attitude changed in his later works. There he employed *prasaṅga* and *prasaṅgaviparyaya* as an aid to establish the *vyāpti.* In this chapter we propose to trace the development of Dharmakīrti's philosophy regarding the employment of *prasaṅga* as a proof.

Although Diṅnāga's formulation of the threefold characteristics (*trairūpya*) of a probans (*hetu*) was based on Vasubandhu's *Tarkaśāstra,* still he criticized the notions of *avīta* and *prasaṅga* as admitted by the Sāṁkhya philosophers. In his opinion *prasaṅga* cannot be considered as a proof (*sādhana*), it is rather a variety of a logical refutation (*dūṣaṇa*). In the *Pramāṇasamuccaya* he considered *prasaṅga* as a *jāti.* The reason for his not offering the status of proof to *prasaṅga* lies in the formulation of the characteristics of the probans. When a person *A* tries to inform some other person *B*, through an inference, the first thing required is that *A* must have knowledge of the existence of the probans in the locus of the inference. The probans in the *prasaṅga,* however, is a hypothetical one and hence cannot be realized in the locus. Therefore, *prasaṅga* cannot be considered as a valid proof. So far as Dharmakīrti conformed to Diṅnāga's formulation of *parārthānumāna* or inference for others, *prasaṅga* was not considered as a proof by him. In the *Pramāṇavārttika* and also in the *Pramāṇaviniścayaḥ*, Dharmakīrti followed Diṅnāga's notion of inference-for-others, viz. that an inference is an information on the object which is realized in the proponent's cognition. But the hypothetical object of *prasaṅga* is cognized only by the opponent. Thus it cannot be regarded as a proper inference. However, Dharmakīrti introduced *prasaṅga* as a semi-inference on the basis of essential identity in the *Pramāṇavārttika* in the later chapter. In his later works, for example, in the *Hetubindu* or in the *Vādanyāya* he admitted *prasaṅga* as a proper proof capable of determining the essential relation (*svabhāva-pratibandha*) in the case of inference aimed to establish the destruction of objects (*vināśitvānumāna*). In other words, the nature and status of *prasaṅga* has undergone several major changes in the different works of Dharmakīrti himself. Following him, later Buddhist logicians Ratnakīrti and Śāntarakṣita have made different uses of *prasaṅga* inference in their works. For instance, Ratnakīrti employed *prasaṅga* to establish the momentary character of all objects. Śāntarakṣita and his disciple Kamalaśīla also applied *prasaṅgānumāna* in the text *Tattvasaṁgraha* several times on different occasions, indicating that for them also *prasaṅga* had been a proof or *sādhana* and not a *dūṣaṇa*. But the major discussion on *prasaṅga* is found in the commentary *Prasannapadā* of Candrakīrti on Nāgārjuna's *Mūlamadhyamakaśāstra*. This, in fact, gave birth to a split between the two groups *svātantrika* and *prāsaṅgika* within the Mādhyamika School.

In the chapter on inference-for-oneself in the *Pramāṇavārttika* and in his auto-commentary on that chapter, Dharmakīrti did not offer any formulation of *prasaṅga* as a proof, though the term *prasaṅga* and its variants like *prasaṅgāt* or *prasajyate* have been used at least 102 times in the context of indicating that self-contradiction follows as a consequence from the hypothesis, which is actually the negation of the statement to be established. In this sense *prasaṅga* may be regarded as a hypothetical negative reasoning. *Prasaṅga* as a hypothetical negative reasoning has been only employed in this chapter to establish the essential relation.[2] That is, if there were no essential relation then there cannot be ascertainment of either affirmative necessary relation or negative necessary relation. The understanding is that, as there has been ascertainment of affirmative relation or negative relation, therefore, there has to be essential relation. That is, here *prasaṅga* has been used as a hypothetical negative reasoning similar to the *Modus Tollendo Tollens* of Western formal logic. Analogous application of the hypothetical negative reasoning can be found in the formulation of essential relation in its negative exemplification —

> *kāraṇam nivartamānam kāryam nivartayati, anyathā tat tasya kāryam eva na syāt* ı *siddhas tu kāryakāraṇabhāvaḥ svabhāvaṁ niyamayatīti ubhayathā svabhāvapratibandhād eva nivṛttiḥ* ı *anyathaikanivṛttyā, anyanivṛttiḥ katham bhavet* ı
>
> — *PVSV*, 11.2-4

Negation of cause negates the effect. If that were not so, then it could not have been its effect. But it has been established that the relation of effect and cause determines that the essence (of the effect) is restricted by the essence of the cause; as such both the two probanses (probans as effect and probans as essence) are excluded in the case of the absence of the probandum by the essential identity relation. If there is no essential relation between the two, then how can the negation of the one imply the negation of the other?

---

2. *na hi asati pratibandhe 'nvayavyatirekaniścayo 'sti* ı *tena tam eva darśayan niścayam āha . . .* — *PVSV*, 7.10-11.

Not only these cases, but formulation of the probans as non-apprehension (*anupalabdhi hetu*) involves the application of such hypothetical negative reasoning also. The formulation of a typical probans as non-apprehension can be stated thus — "There is no pot here, because it is not perceived in spite of the presence of all the factors responsible for the perception of the pot which is by nature perceptible." If the condition "which is by nature perceptible" is taken away from the formulation, then non-apprehension can be regarded as hypothetical negative reasoning.

It is with the help of this hypothetical negative reasoning that the semi-inductive theory of *bahirvyāpti* admitted by Diṅnāga had been transformed into a hypothetical deductive system of *antarvyāpti* by Dharmakīrti. If negative necessity (*vyatireka*) can be determined without a real locus, the hypothetical negative reasoning can substitute empirical exemplification (*dṛṣṭānta*). And the positive necessity (*anvaya*) can be determined by the determination of negative necessity on the basis of equivalent necessity. Thus the view "the probans is absent in the case of absence of the probandum" paves the way for the complete *prasaṅga* admitted in the later texts of Dharmakīrti and which have been formulated as *sādhya-viparyaye-bādhaka-pramāṇa*.

Dharmakīrti's first explicit formulation of *prasaṅga* can be found in the verse 12 of the chapter on inference-for-others (*Parārthānumānaparicchedaḥ*) of *Pramāṇavārttika*. There it is stated as *parakalpitaiḥ/prasaṅgo dvayasambandhād ekabhāve 'nyahānaye*. *Prasaṅga* is deduced on the basis of opponent's conceptualization. It serves to negate the other term in the absence of the first term on the basis of necessary relation between the terms. This formulation of *prasaṅga* is based on the logical transformation of the positive logical necessity

$H \rightarrow S$, to its contraposition $\sim S \rightarrow \sim H$ in the opponent's hypothetical locus. Here H stands for the probans and S for the probandum. So far as the first formula is based on the essential relation *tie* (*svabhāva-pratibandha*) the second formula is to be considered as a proof-formation on the basis of consistent logical transformation of the two formulae. Here Dharmakīrti seems to stand on the boundary line between his new theory of essential *tie* and the triple characteristic *trairūpya* theory of Diṅnāga.

A hypothetical probans implies the hypothetical probandum. Hypothetical probans is realized in the locus. Since there is a necessary relation between the probans and the probandum, it will follow that when the hypothetical probans is in the locus and there is the probandum. Since the relationship between the probans and the probandum can be presented in a logical transformation, the negation of hypothetical existence of the probandum will imply the negation of hypothetical existence of the probans. So the hypothetical existence of the probans in the locus will imply the hypothetical existence of the probandum in the locus and the denial of the probans. There seems to be an ambiguity concerning the realization of the probans in this type of *prasaṅga*, because the hypothetical probans which is formally transformed by pure logical transformation still cannot be realized in the hypothetical locus. As such Dharmakīrti had to substitute a new inference regarding momentariness for the original inference regarding destruction (*vināśitvānumāna*). For this, i.e. for proving the momentary existence of worldly objects, Dharmakīrti replaced his form of *prasaṅga* by a complex one. This new formulation of *prasaṅga* operates on the possibility of two hypothetical properties which are based on the Law of Excluded Middle in the reversed hypothetical locus. The negation of the hypothetical locus implies affirmation of the proper locus. These two loci are regarded as properties of a more basic locus. In the second chapter of his *Pramāṇaviniścayaḥ* Dharmakīrti proves the momentary character of all objects thus — what is capable of causal efficiency is regarded as truly existent. Non-momentary things (*akṣaṇikas*) are therefore non-existent because of contradiction involved in the successiveness and simultaneity of their activities.[3] Let us present the argument in the form of a proof:

Thesis: Existence defined in terms of causal efficiency is momentary.

Proof: Let us assume that non-momentary things are causally efficient. That is, if there are non-momentary things then they also are causally efficient. A thing which is causally efficient can exhibit this efficiency either simultaneously or successively. Hence, a non-momentary thing can exhibit its efficiency simultaneously or successively. To say that a non-momentary thing exhibits efficiency simultaneously implies self-contradiction, since in the second moment it has nothing to show its efficency. Again to say that the non-momentary thing exhibits causal efficiency successively involves self-contradiction for it means that it goes on producing the same thing repeatedly. Thus a non-momentary thing cannot be regarded to be causally efficient. But it had been assumed that non-momentary thing is causally effective. Thus, it follows that a non-momentary thing is effective and non-effective at the same time and this is contradiction. Therefore, we have to deny the existence of non-momentary things. In other words, we have to say that everything existent/real is momentary.

---

3. *arthakriyāsamartham yat tad atra paramārthasat* । *asanto 'kṣanikaḥ tasmāt kramākramavirodhataḥ.*

Let us present the proof formally —

E = existence defined as causal efficiency, M = momentariness, S = succession, $>$ = pervasion, such that $A > B = B$ is pervaded by A.

Thesis to be proved : $E \rightarrow M$ $[L_1 = E, M]$

Prasaṅga 1: Hypothetical thesis: $\sim M \rightarrow E$ $[L_2 = \sim M, E]$
Prasaṅga 2: $(S \,\&\, \sim S) > E$

$E \rightarrow (S\, v\, \sim S)$

Now, $(\sim M, S) \rightarrow$ Contradiction

Again, $(\sim M, \sim S) \rightarrow$ Contradiction

Therefore, $\rightarrow \sim M \rightarrow \sim E$

Prasaṅga-viparyaya: $L_2 = \sim M, E \,\&\, \sim E$

Therefore, $\sim L_2 = M \rightarrow [L_1, \sim L_2] \rightarrow [L_1 = E, M]$ Therefore, $E \rightarrow M$.

In this proof, we find that in order to prove the formula $E \rightarrow M$, its counterpositive formula $\sim M \rightarrow \sim E$ is hypothetically assumed. That is, if the term E is negated in the reversed formulation (*viparyaya*) of the hypothetical term M, by *prasaṅga* 2, the *prasaṅga* 1 deduces *prasaṅga-viparyaya* 1. This is what has been described as *sādhya-viparyaye-bādhaka-pramāṇa*. This *prasaṅga* not only implies the presence of self-contradiction in the opponents's presupposed properties, but also excludes the opponent's locus. The *bādhaka-pramāṇa* is based on self-contradiction between two essential properties which are presupposed in the opponent's locus. Two contradictory properties cannot occur in the identical locus. Hence, the locus is being excluded and so the original thesis gets established.

The negation of the hypothetical locus and property by this new complex *prasaṅga* formula (*prasaṅga* + *prasaṅga-viparyaya*) is therefore regarded as proper proof. The *bādhaka-pramāṇa* as self-contradiction of essential properties in a hypothetical locus is the determinant of the validity of *prasaṅga* proof, i.e. it changes the direction of the formulation from *anvaya* to *vyatireka*. In the *Vādanyāya*, Dharmakīrti observes that with regard to the proof of *vyāpti* or necessary connection in the context of *svabhāva hetu*.[4] In the case of essential property as probans, a proof of pervasion is the demonstration of a valid cognition which negates the probans in the contradictory/ opposite of the argued property. The reason why Dharmakīrti adopts this complex *prasaṅga* formula as a proof might be that he was interested in explaining the notion of *svabhāva-pratibandha* as the theory of internal determination of logical necessity. This explanation could not be offered without bringing in a change in the existing logic of external determination of *vyāpti* (*bahirvyāptivāda*). As such Dharmakīrti formulated a new type of hypothetical complex proof by combining the *prasaṅga* with the *prasaṅga-viparyaya.*

Manorathanandi in his commentary on the verse 12 of *Pramāṇavārttika* chapter IV, discusses the question whether the probans used in hypothetical negative reasoning *prasaṅga hetu* can be considered as a proper probans or not. The first answer here is that it cannot be considered as a proper probans (*pāramārthika hetu*), since it does not possess the three characters of a proper probans. Though not a probans in the ultimate sense, still it can be considered as a probans to prove something indirectly. Where the probans and the probandum are related by invariable concomitant relationship then on the basis of

---

4. *atra vyāptisādhana viparyaye bādhakapramāṇopadarśanam* ।
— *VN*, 6.5.

that relation, by denying the probandum the probans is found to be refuted. The example given by Manorathanandi is *sāmānyasya paropagatānekavṛttitvād anekatvam āpādyate.* It follows absurdly that the universal is several since the opponent admits that the universal resides in several different things. The *viparyaya* or absurdity is "The universal is not present in several different things because it is not several." The *viparyaya* or absurdity holds because here "presence in several different things" implies "being itself many." The contraposition of this general statement figures in this *viparyaya* and consists in the principle that what is not itself several different things is not present in several different things. "In the absence of the first" is a true statement that must be accepted; it is the *hetu* of the *prasaṅga-viparyaya,* i.e. "not being itself several things." The opponent's conceptual construction (viz. the universal's being present in several different things) is in effect the statement that leads to the absurdity (viz. the universal's being several things). It is thus the second term that is negated in the absence of the first. Thus the refutation of the probandum implies the absence of the probans. Hence truly speaking the proper proof is not the *prasaṅga* but the *prasaṅga-viparyaya,* i.e. the contrapositive reversed formula which operates on the basis of the *pramāṇa* that apprehends the invariable concomitant relation between the probans and the probandum.

Śāntarakṣita in his *Tattvasaṁgraha* has employed *prasaṅgānumāna* to refute the Mīmāṁsaka view that "the Vedas are eternal and self-evident truths as they are not the handiwork of any human being." Śāntarakṣita points out that the Vedas would become devoid of meaning, if they were independent of an author, as the truth or falsity of any statement is relative to the veracity or mendacity of the speaker, and the speaker being absent, the truth or otherwise of the Vedic statements would become impossible of ascertainment. Kamalaśīla in his *Pañjikā* points out that this argument of Śāntarakṣita is actually a *prasaṅgasādhana* and not any *svatantra* or independent proof, for the conclusion assumed here, viz. the Vedas are devoid of meaning is contrary to experience (for the Vedas have a determinate meaning) and the reason "without being made by any agent" (*akṛtakatva*) is not approved by both the parties. And these two contingencies are found in any *prasaṅga* argument.

Dharmottara in his commentary on *Pramāṇaviniścayaḥ* holds that the *prasaṅga-viparyaya* seems to be more prominent but nevertheless the *prasaṅga* "is a proof (*sādhana*), although it merely shows the *vyāpti*, e.g. 'whatever exists in many things is manifold [i.e. not unitary]' because it implies an invalidating valid cognition [*bādhaka-pramāṇa*]." The main function of *prasaṅga* is to introduce the *prasaṅga-viparyaya* — "As the logical reason is imagined only by the opponent to exist in the *dharmin* the *prasaṅga sādhana* is not formulated in an independent way, as the *hetu* is not established as existent in the *dharmin*." It is formulated rather to show what the *prasaṅga-viparyaya* is aimed at. Kamalaśīla in his *Madhyamakālaṁkārapañjikā* holds "that one can prove only *prasaṅga*s in the case of unacknowledged entities imputed by non-Buddhists." In his *Madhyamakāloka*, however, seemingly under the influence of Dharmottara, he argues for the use of a *svatantra sādhana* in such cases, although he does not find fault in the use of *prasaṅga*. For example, in the *Madhyamakāloka* it is said that, on the one hand it is not sufficient to refute *ātman, pradhāna,* etc. by just *prasaṅga*s but these pseudo-entities should also be refuted by *svatantra liṅgas*. Their unreality can be proved by both *prasaṅga* and *svatantra* methods without any difficulty.[5]

---

5. For details see H. Tauscher, "Phya Pa Chos Klyi Seng Ge's Opinion on *Prasaṅga*" in *Dharmakīrti*'s *Thought and its Impact on Indian and Tibetan Philosophy,* ed. S. Katsura.

The Naiyāyikas, however, did not accept such a respectable attitude towards *prasaṅga*. In fact, they did not recognize *prasaṅga sādhana* as a logically justifiable form of argument. They are insisting that the *probans* must be a real datum, attested by experience and approved by both the parties, and not a mere hypothetical entity. Otherwise there would have been the fallacy of unproven thesis (*asiddhatā-doṣaḥ*). The Nyāya attitude towards *prasaṅga* has been reflected in the following verse of Jayanta Bhaṭṭa where he says:

> *tatraitat syāt prasaṅgasādhanam idam, prasaṅgaś ca paraprasiddhyā parasyāniṣṭānipādānam ucyate . . . naitad evam prasaṅgasādhanam nāma nāstyeva paramārthataḥ* । *tad dhī kuḍyam vinā tatra citrakarme 'va lakṣyate* ॥ *na hi nabhaḥkusumasya saurabhāsaurabhavicāro yuktaḥ* । — *Nyāyamañjarī*, pp. 102–04.

Prasaṅga means the demonstration of a defect in an opponent's position by means of the data accepted by the latter. But this cannot be approved. Because *prasaṅga sādhana* is a form of argument which is not ultimately real. It is as unreal as the fresco-painting on a wall which does not actually exist. Certainly a judgement on the fragrance or non-fragrance of sky-lotus cannot be a justified one.

Thus it can be felt that *prasaṅga sādhana* has been considered as a potent logical weapon in the determination of the controversies during the medieval period and had been regarded as the only acceptable form of proof by the Mādhyamika School of Buddhism. Whatever be the logical merits of it as a valid syllogistic reasoning, the historical importance of *prasaṅga sādhana* cannot be under-rated by any student of Indian philosophy. What the Buddhists call as *prasaṅga* has been designated by different names like *ūha, tarka, mīmāṁsā, aniṣṭāpatti* by other Indian schools of thinkers. Several definitions have been proposed as its nature. For the

Naiyāyikas and the Mīmāṁsaka thinkers *tarka* cannot be considered as a *pramāṇa,* though it is an aid to *pramāṇa. Tarka* is considered by them to be an aid to *pramāṇa* because in a debate when there arises a doubt regarding the truth of a particular position, *tarka* shows us which particular position is provable and which is not. Thus it helps *pramāṇa* by directing it towards the right object of proof. Those who regard *tarka* to be *pramāṇa* belong to two groups. According to one group represented by the Mādhava Vedāntin like Vyāsatīrtha and the Vaiśeṣika philosopher Śrīdhara Bhaṭṭa *tarka* is a type of *anumāna,* while the other group of philosophers namely the Jainas regard *tarka* to be a separate *pramāṇa* through which *vyāpti* is known. Now whether *tarka* is a *pramāṇa* or not may be a matter of controversy among Indian logicians, but that *tarka* or *prasaṅga* plays an important role in asserting the relation of *vyāpti* has been recognized by all.

Let us now take a look at the question how far such *prasaṅga* proof of the Buddhists can be regarded as comparable to the indirect proof or *reductio ad absurdum* proof. In Western logic, indirect proof, generally known as *reductio ad absurdum* proof operates in the following way. An argument can prove a proposition *A* by showing that the denial of *A* together with accepted propositions B_1, B_2, . . ., B_n leads to a contradiction. Strictly speaking, this fails to prove the truth of *A,* since one of the previously accepted premises may be false. The force of this proof rests on using premises that are far better established than the denial of *A* so that the denial of *A* will be rejected and *A* accepted. Barwise and Etchemendy in their book *The Language of First Order Logic,* state the essence of this *reductio* proof very briefly thus — "To prove not-*S* using this method, assume *S* and prove some sort of contradiction." There are two ways in which we can prove "some sort of contradiction." The first one is that if *S* is added to a number of premises *P*, . . ., *R*, then the conjunction of *S*, *P*, . . ., *R* would lead to a contradiction. In that case if *P*, . . ., *R* are all true, *S* must be false and hence non-*S* must be true. The point to note in this proof is that when we want to prove the truth of not-*S*, we must accept the truth of *P*, . . ., *R*, otherwise the absurdity cannot be proved. The second way of presenting the *reductio* proof is that we can reason that the conjunction of *S* & *P* & . . . & *R* leads to a contradiction and is in that sense internally inconsistent, but none the less, we are not willing to say which of the conjoined statements are true and which must be negated. A number of things can happen here. The contradiction can consist in a new statement *T* and not-*T*. Or it can consist in the fact that the conjunction *S* & *P* & . . . & *R* besides of course implying itself also implies the negation of the conjunction, i.e. not-(*S* & *P* . . . & *R*). In either case, however, we are only prepared to say that *S* & *P* & . . . & *R* implies some contradiction and hence not-(*S* & *P* & . . . & *R*) is the case. As contrasted with the first one this version of the *reductio* can be described as the method of "internal inconsistency without commitments." To be specific, the *reductio* method proceeds to prove the internal inconsistency of a set of propositions, either by way of committing oneself to the truth of some proposition or without any commitment at all.

In the light of this notion of the *reductio ad absurdum* proof let us see whether the Buddhist account of *prasaṅga* as offered and employed by different logicians like Dharmakīrti, Śāntarakṣita, Candrakīrti, Bhāvaviveka, can be fit into any one of these two versions. If we look minutely at the analysis of Dharmakīrti as found in his *Pramāṇaviniścayaḥ*, *Vādanyāya*, and even in his *Pramāṇavārttika*, we find that he is advocating a sort of *reductio* in its first variety, i.e. where he shows *viparyaya* or inconsistency in the opponent's thesis and thereby establishes his own position. That is, he is showing the internal inconsistency in the opposed alternative from his own commitment to a particular philosophical position. As for instance, when he tries to prove the *vināśitva* feature or the *kṣaṇikatva* feature of all created objects by showing the *viparyaya* or inconsistency in the alternative that non-momentary objects are causally efficient, he himself is committed to the doctrine of momentariness of all worldly objects. It is this commitment which leads Dharmakīrti to employ the *prasaṅga-viparyaya* or *viparyaye bādhaka-pramāṇa* as a *sādhana* in his late works. This method is thus for him an aid to establish the universal or necessary relationship between existence and momentariness which is not easy to establish in the positive direction. Arcaṭa in his commentary on *Hetubindu* remarks that the *prasaṅga-viparyaya* actually is the prover of the identity relation (*tādātmyaprasādhakam*) between "being produced" (*kṛtakatva*) and "momentariness" (*kṣaṇikatva*) which is not possible to show in any other way.[6] Same is the case with his commentator Manorathanandi, who applied the *prasaṅga* to show the internal inconsistency that universal will have to be one and many at the same time in the opponents' thesis that universal resides in many instances. His application of *prasaṅga-viparyaya* is also out of the commitment that there are no universals. Later on, when Śāntarakṣita applied the *prasaṅga* proof to refute the Mīmāṁsā view regarding the Vedas being the creation of God, he also had his commitment towards the atheistic trend of the Buddhists. The same thing is true for the Mādhyamika philosopher Bhāvaviveka also. Bhāvaviveka in his commentary

---

6. . . . *vināśaṁ prati viparyaye bādhakaṁ pramāṇaṁ tādātmyaprasādhakam uktaṁ tat prasaṅgamukhena kṛtakalakṣaṇasyaiva sattvasya tadāmatāṁ gamayati nānyasya iti darśayitum* । — *HBT*, 76.25-27.

Prajñāpradīpa accuses Buddhapālita of forming a bad *prasaṅga* since when contradicted, it yields a proposition which the Mādhyamikas cannot accept. Bhāvaviveka presents the *prasaṅga* argument in the context of refuting the Sāṁkhya view regarding the *satkāryavāda*. Let us formulate his argument in the form of a proof:

1. It is true that the production of an object has a point and has a termination, i.e. production cannot go on endlessly for ever.
2. If something is produced from itself, then it would be produced pointlessly and this production will go on and on.

   If we add to these two statements the Sāṁkhya view that

3. Things are produced from themselves, we get the absurdity —

The production of those things would be pointless and without an end.

That this is absurd becomes evident when we conjoin it with statement 1 that the production of a thing has a point, etc. Thus we see that in Bhāvaviveka's formulation of *prasaṅga*, the *viparyaya* occurs because he is committed to the view that a thing's production has a point and has an end. So, in all these statements or applications of *prasaṅga* we have actually a *reductio ad absurdum* proof of the first variety, viz. internal inconsistency with a commitment.

The typical example of internal inconsistency without commitments is found in the case of Candrakīrti. Candrakīrti, as is well known, holds that showing a contradiction in an opponent's position is enough to convince people who are not mad men (*unmattakāḥ*). The *prasaṅga* attempts to show the opponent that his position is simply illogical and contradicted by what he himself had accepted. Thus it is only the opponent who is linked to the contraposition of the absurd consequence, and not the proponent himself. It is because of this that the Mādhyamika can refute all the four alternatives that things are produced from themselves, things are produced from others, things are produced from both themselves and others, things are produced from neither, without himself getting indulged in any particular thesis of his own — *nāsti ca me pratijñā*. It is because of this lack of any particular thesis of their own that the Mādhyamikas cannot be charged with any fallacy while refuting the views of others. In effect Candrakīrti seems to be arguing that other Buddhist logicians including his fellow Mādhyamika friend Bhāvaviveka, have imposed upon themselves a type of the *prasaṅga* proof with the ensuing commitment to the truth of certain statements and hence have been involved in *siddhāntavirodha*; while he himself has only used *prasaṅga* in its pure, pristine form, i.e. deriving contradiction without having any commitment of his own. Because of this non-commitment he cannot be charged of committing any fallacy. Candrakīrti himself goes no further than to show that the conjunction of the statements accepted by the opponent yields a contradiction, but does not himself say which statements are actually true and which must be negated. He does of course, know what the opponent's possible reaction will be, and therefore he himself can stand back and assert no more than that *P* & *Q* & . . . *S* will imply also not — (*P* & *Q* & . . . *S*) or that *P* & *Q* & . . . *S* implies internal inconsistency (*P* & *Q* & . . . *S*) and not — (*P* & *Q* & . . . *S*); nothing more than that.

This sort of non-committal attitude towards the *prasaṅga* has been taken to show that all the empirical truths are loaded with some kind of inconsistency and hence cannot be accepted at all. The real truth, however, is something which cannot be described by any description at all. The only way to grasp the truth is to get rid of all sorts of propositions and enter the realm of silence. The same attitude is found in the writing of Wittgenstein — "What we cannot speak about we must pass over in silence." (*Tractatus Logico Philosophicus* proposition 7). It is because of this recognition of the indescribable nature of the ultimate truth that the Prāsaṅgika sect of Mādhyamika philosophers have applied *prasaṅga* or *reductio* proof in the true sense.

16

Absence

How it is Known?

ABSENCES or negative facts or negations have drawn the attention of Western philosophers since the time of Plato. Plato in his dialogue *The Sophist* has elaborately dealt with the topic of negation. In the twentieth century we find Russell in his *The Philosophy of Logical Atomism* and early Wittgenstein in his *Tractatus Logico Philosophicus* discussing the issue of negative facts. However, it would be wrong to say that the Western philosophers, i.e. the philosophers of Europe and America, alone were concerned with this problem. The traditional Indian philosophers like the Buddhists, the Naiyāyikas, and the Mīmāṁsakas have pondered over this question again and again.

The problem as envisaged by them may be stated as follows — suppose that I enter my study and look at my writing table. I find several items on it but I do not see my favourite flower vase on it. I then say that my flower vase is not there, or it is absent. The problem is — how do we know the absence of the flower vase? One possible answer, generally offered by the Bhaṭṭa school of Mīmāṁsā, is that we fail to perceive the flower vase. Though this answer seems to be what common sense will say, there are reasons for withholding it. To begin with, perception and inference are, in one sense, faculties or cognitive capabilities whereas the act of failing to perceive something is not. The second reason for rejecting non-apprehension of something as a means of knowing its absence is that something may be present, yet we may fail to perceive it. For instance, if the table is dumped with several big things and the room has insufficient light and the flower vase is of small size compared to others on the table, in such a situation we fail to perceive the flower vase, even though it might be very much present there on the table.

If we look at the texts of classical Indian tradition, we find four different approaches to the problem of negative facts — (1) they are correctly analysed as straightforward positive facts known through inference; (2) there are real negative facts, but they can be known only through inference; (3) knowledge of negative facts arises from perception of positive presences; and (4) we can directly perceive real negative facts.

In Indian philosophy though Kumārila Bhaṭṭa has been well known to be the first philosopher to deal with the problem of negation critically, Dharmakīrti, the Buddhist logician, must be considered to be his older contemporary in this regard. Dharmakīrti in his two texts *Nyāyabindu* and *Pramāṇavārttika* has held the view that one knows something when one correctly reports upon entering a room under the right condition that one's friend is absent in that room. But what one knows is not a negative fact and is not known by perception. Rather, what one knows is a simple positive fact and it is known by inference. Let us discuss the view of Dharmakīrti in detail to know the Buddhists' response to the question of knowledge of negative facts. Negative facts according to the Buddhists are known through *anupalabdhi*.

In the Buddhist epistemological tradition we find a good leap in the analysis of *anupalabdhi* between Īśvarasena (CE 580–

640) and his pupil Dharmakīrti (CE 600–660). While for Īśvarasena, *anupalabdhi* was nothing but absence of perception (*upalabhyabhāvamātra* or *darśanabhāvamātra*) Dharmakīrti offered a complex theory of *anupalabdhi*. He widened up the conceptual frame and distinguished between two basic types of non-apprehension (*anupalabdhi*), depending on the difference in the nature of things whose non-existence is going to be established. Thus the two kinds of non-perception are "non-apprehension of something imperceptible (*adṛśya*)" and a quantified non-perception or "non-apprehension of something perceptible (*dṛśya*)." The former results in negation of cognition, word and activity with reference to existence" *sajjñānaśabdavyavahārapratiṣedha*),[1] while the latter results in "certain cognition of non-existence" (*asanniścayaphalāpi sā*).[2] In the case of imperceptible objects, the non-apprehension of something imperceptible, does not produce the cognition of its non-existence (*na tu vyatirekadarśanādāv upayujyate saṁśayāt*).[3] In his epistemological texts like *Nyāyabindu, Pramāṇavārttika, PVSV, Pramāṇaviniścaya, Hetubindu, Vādanyāya*, Dharmakīrti's main concern is with non-apprehension of (situationally) perceptible objects to establish the negation or absence of such perceptible objects inferentially. In such inferences, the positive basis, for instance, an empty spot on the table, represents the logical subjects (*pakṣa*), the absence of the negatum, for instance the flower vase, represents the property to be established (*sādhya dharma*) and the non-apprehension of the perceptible object as the probans (*hetu*). The non-apprehension conveys that the negatum, which would be necessarily perceived in the pertinent situation if it existed, is not actually perceived in that situation.

1. *PVSVT*, 4.8.
2. Ibid.
3. Ibid., 5.5.

It may be noted here by way of reference that in the pre-Dharmakīrti Buddhist literature the term *anupalabdhi* had not been analysed in such a precise way. But that the notion of non-existence was related to that of non-perception can be found in the different dialogues of Lord Buddha. For example, in the *Kāśyapaparivartasutta* of *Śikṣāsamuccaya*, the non-existence of mind is established on the basis of non-apprehension — "Mind, Kaśyapa, when being searched for, is not found (*na labhyate*). What is not found, that is not perceived (*nopalabhyate*). What is not past, not future, not present, that is beyond the three times. What is beyond the three times, that is neither existent nor non-existent (*tan naivāsti tan nāsti*). . . . " A look at Buddhaghoṣa's *Viśuddhimagga* gives us the impression that there also *anupalabdhi* or non-apprehension did not directly establish the non-existence of anything, but had been offered as the reason for the non-existence. In the non-Buddhist literature, in the *Nyāya-Sūtra*s the term non-apprehension can also be found as implying non-existence, but not as meaning non-existence. In Pakṣilasvāmi's *Nyāyabhāṣya* it has been said that the cognition of non-existence is only to be derived from non-apprehension. Similarly clear is the passage of the early Mīmāṁsā school where the term *anupalabdhi* is represented by the term *abhāva* (non-existence), as one of the means of cognition (*pramāṇa*) for a non-existent fact (vide Vṛttikāra's definition in the Śabarasvāmin's *Bhāṣya*).

Let us now concentrate on Dharmakīrti's exposition of the probans as non-apprehension. As stated earlier the logical reason called non-apprehension, in Dharmakīrti's philosophy, can establish the absence of an object only under the condition that the object in question is *dṛśya* (perceptible) as opposed to *adṛśya* (imperceptible). The imperceptibility of an object is commonly understood as its natural condition which is given independent of time, place, or cognizing subject. Such an interpretation seems to be supported by the examples of distant objects (*viprakṛṣṭa*) which have been instantiated in post-Dharamakīrtian text, the *Tarkabhāṣā*, as the mount Meru, the future emperor Śaṅkha and Piśāca or demons.[4] These objects are such that they cannot be perceived by anybody, at any time, or in any place, due to their generic nature, or due to an inherent lack in certain qualities, which characterize being perceptible. Stcherbatsky in his *Buddhist Logic* has interpreted *viprakṛṣṭa* as "inaccessible." Following that tradition, later scholars like Steinkellner, Katsura have expressed it as "totally imperceptible" (Steinkellner) or "by nature beyond our ordinary perception." Tillemans has said that ". . . if the entity is not perceptible (*adṛśya*), that is if it is a type of thing, like a spirit (*piśāca*) which is not empirically accessible to ordinary beings, then merely not apprehending it does not prove its absence at all."[5] Thus if imperceptibility characterizes something which is never perceived, which is by nature not perceptible, by implication perceptibility is to be understood as the natural condition of things.

However, it must be very clearly borne in mind that with the help of non-apprehension as a logical reason when we are to establish the absence or negation, that absence is not any generic absence but situation-specific. To state precisely, we want to infer that "there is no flower vase here on this table now" from the fact of the non-perception of the flower vase here at present. The thesis of such inference can be explicated as "In a particular place p_1, at a particular point of time t_1, and for a particular cognizer c_1, an object o_1 does not exist." The

4. *deśaviprakṛṣṭe sumervādau kālaviprakṛṣṭe bhaviṣyacchaṁkha-cakravartyādau svabhāvaviprakṛṣṭe piśācādau . . .*

— *Tarkabhāṣā*, 16.14-15.

5. Tillemans, "Dharmakīrti and Tibetans on *Adṛśyānupalabdhihetu*" *JIP*, vol. 23, 1995.

need for such explication lies in the fact that it excludes those objects which are regarded as absent for wrong reason, like the damage of the cognizer's sense faculties.

With this background information we may concentrate on one of Dharmakīrti's paradigm examples of such inference based on non-apprehension.

There cannot be a particular jar in a specific location, since the jar is not apprehended in that specific location though it is *upalabdhi-lakṣaṇa-prāpta*.

The notion of *upalabdhi-lakṣaṇa-prāpta*, involved in the minor premise, is the most important factor of this type of logical reason. The technical term *upalabdhi-lakṣaṇa-prāpti*, which is the verbal form of this noun phrase, has been explained by Dharmakīrti in his *Nyāyabindu* as follows: "*upalabdhi-lakṣaṇa-prāpti* is the entirety of the additional causal factors for a perceptual cognition and also the specific essence of the object."[6] The specific essence of an object is such that when it exists, it is necessarily perceived provided the additional causal factors for the perceptual cognition are given. The commentators offer two different interpretations of the compound *upalabdhi-lakṣaṇa-prāpti* on the basis of their difference in understanding the meaning of the term *lakṣaṇa*. Though all of them understand *lakṣaṇa* as standing for the causal factors which are necessary for the production of perception, for Śākyabuddhi, the *lakṣaṇa*s are identified as all the causal factors except the object itself (*pratyayāntara*), but for the Sanskrit commentators like Śāntarakṣita, Dharmottara, the *lakṣaṇa* is the complete causal complex which produces a perception (*janikā sāmagrī*), that is, it involves both the

6. *upalabdhilakṣaṇaprāptir upalambha-pratyayāntara-sākalyaṁ svabhāvaviśeṣaś ca* । — *NB*, 2.13

additional causal factors and also the object itself.[7] Arcaṭa though does not analyse the compound *upalabdhi lakṣaṇa* but is a supporter of the latter view as he explains the term *lakṣaṇa* in the light of the Buddhist model of four *pratyayas* which include the object as *ālambana pratyaya*.[8] With regard to the second interpretation of the term of *lakṣaṇa* a problem arises concerning the issue of causality. If *upalabdhi-lakṣaṇa-prāpti* means that an object has attained the additional causal factors for its cognition, the question arises why these so-called causal factors do not actually produce the perception of the object as their effect, for after all it is the nature of the causal factors to produce the effect always. If on the other hand they are regarded as causal factors but do not have any role in the production of the perception of the object, then can they really be considered as causal factors with regard to perception? Moreover, if *lakṣaṇa* means complete causal complex of perception, then when this causal complex is given, the effect must by definition be produced immediately. In such a situation, the object, which is *upalabdhi-lakṣaṇa-prāpti* must be perceived and cannot be regarded as non-existent. So the basic objective of the probans as non-apprehension, viz. to ascertain the non-existence becomes useless.

Dharmottara in his commentary on *Nyāyabindu* tries to answer all these objections and provide a justification for the employment of the probans of non-apprehension for proving

7. *upalabdhir jñānam | tasyā lakṣaṇaṁ janikā sāmagrī | tayā hy upalabdhir lakṣyate | tatprāpto 'rtho janakatvena sāmagryantarbhāvāt |*
— *NBT*, p. 101.7-8

8. *upalabdhilakṣaṇaprāptiḥ — upalambhapratyayātarāṇāṁ samanantarādhipatipratyayasaṁjñitānāṁ sākalyam, ālambanapratyayasya svabhāvaviśeṣaś ca | yaḥ svabhāvaḥ satsvanyesūpalambhapratyayeṣu san pratyakṣa eva bhavati' ityevaṁrūpā śāstrakṛtā 'nyatra vyākhyātā naiyāyikavipratipattinirāsārtham* — *HBT*, 167.25–168.1.

the non-existence of object. His interpretation of the term *upalabdhi-lakṣaṇa-prāpti* combines a causal analysis of a given instance of perception based on the principle of necessary production of perception. There he argues that an object is called apprehensible (*dṛśya*) in a certain place even though it does not exist there because apprehensibility or *dṛśyatva* is superimposed upon it. The assumption is made that, if this object existed here it would have been perceived; under such a situation *dṛśyatva* is superimposed even though the object does not exist there. But for what object can such an assumption be made? The reply is that such an assumption can be made for an object, for which the additional causes for a perception with itself as an objective basis are present in entirety. But when are these additional causes to be understood as present in entirety — when another real entity which is associated in the same one cognition (*ekajñānasaṁsargin*) is perceptually cognized. To explain, two real entities which can be apprehended by a cognition that arises from the same sense faculty and at which the attention of the other sense organ is equally directed are regarded to be associated in one cognition with respect to each other. If both such objects exist, there is no cognition which is limited to only one of them because the capacity of both of them is non-different. Therefore, when one such object which is associated in one cognition is actually perceived, the other object which possesses the same complete collection of additional causes for its perception is assumed as "if the other object existed here, it would have to be perceived" and in this manner *dṛśyatva* is superimposed on the other object.[9]

---

9. *atha yo yatra nāsti sa kathaṁ tatra dṛśyaḥ? dṛśyatvasamāropād asann-api dṛśya ucyate* ı *yaś caivaṁ sambhāvyate — yady asāv atra bhaved dṛśya eva bhaved iti* ı *sa tatrāvidyamāno 'pi dṛśyaḥ samāropyaḥ* ı *kaś caivaṁ sambhāvyaḥ* ı *yasya samagrāṇi svālambanadarśanakāraṇāni bhavanti* ı *kadā ca tāni samagrāni gamyante* ı *yadā ekajñāna-* →

The basic argument of Dharmottara rests on the fundamental notion of co-cognizability or *ekajñānasaṁsargitva* feature of two objects. Two objects are co-cognizable when they are apprehensible in the same act or mode of cognition or by the same sense organ. The spot *S* and the jar, the absence of which is perceived at *S* are co-cognizable or co-perceivable since both can be apprehended by visual perception, by the same sense organ eye. So the same act of seeing which cognizes the empty spot *S* without any jar would also have cognized the jar if it were there. The other conditions necessary for the perception of *S* and for the perception of the jar, had that been at *S*, are the same as *S* is perceived. Therefore, the other conditions necessary for the perception of *S* are satisfied. Since these other conditions are also the necessary conditions for the perception of the jar, had it been there at *S*, we can say that the other conditions necessary for the perception of the jar are satisfied. But still the jar is not perceived and hence the jar is non-existent there at *S*.

From Dharmottara's explanation, it is clear that the conditional statement he employs for expressing non-apprehension is hypothetical rather than counter-factual in the sense that the acceptability or truth of the antecedent "if the object existed . . ." is not yet determined. The conditional therefore serves to introduce a known state of affairs, the existence of the object inevitably and immediately produces its perception into the present situation, to the effect that the cognizer can state "I am not sure whether a pot exists or not,

→ *saṁsargivastvantaropalambhaḥ* । *ekendriyajñānagrāhyaṁ locanādi praṇidhānābhimukhaṁ vastudvayam anyonyāpekṣam ekajñānasaṁsargi kathyate* । *tayor hi sator naikaniyatā bhavati pratipattiḥ* । *yogyatāyā dvayor apy aviśiṣṭatvāt* । *tasmād ekajñānasaṁsargiṇī dṛśyamāne saty ekasmin itarat samagra-darśana-sāmagrīkaṁ yadi bhaved dṛśyam eva bhaved iti saṁbhāvitam dṛśyatvam āropyate* । — *NBT*, 101.9–102.3

but I have seen that additional causal factors are actually instantiated." Such an instantiation is given when a second object with identical causal factor is actually perceived. The two objects in question, the one which is determined to be absent and the other which is actually perceived require identical additional causal factors for their perception. Accordingly, two such objects are termed co-cognizable or associated in one cognition.

The explanation that we find here in *Nyāyabindu* is based on the causal conditions which are required for the cognition of an object especially on the co-cognizability aspect. But a second way of defining *anupalabdhi*, emphasizing on the psychological side of the individual is found in Dharmakīrti's *Hetubindu*. There he presents the definition of *anupalabdhi* as —

> *tasmād anyopalabdhir anupalabdhiḥ vakṣitopalabdher anyatvāt.*[10]

> That is, **non-apprehension is a perception other than the perception of the negatum.**

That is — it is the perception of the positive basis because, it is other than the perception which is meant/intended (*vivakṣita*). Steinkellner translates the term *vivakṣita* as *intendiert* and brings out the speciality of *anupalabdhi* in the following manner[11] — if the cognition disappoints the expectation of the cognizing person, because it is other than the cognition that was intended, it is, insofar as it is not this cognition, referred to as "non-cognition." The term expectation generally involves a

10. *HB*, p. 21.21.

11. Wenn die Erkenntnis die Erwartung der erkennenden Person enttäuscht, weil sie anders ist als die intendierte Erkenntnis, wird sie, insofern sie nicht diese Erkenntnis ist, als Nicht-Erkenntnis bezeichnet'. Steinkellner, *Dharmakīrti's Hetubinduḥ Teil II, Übersetzung und Anmerkungen, Wien,* 1967.

wish directed at the expected state of affairs, as for instance when a teacher tells her students "I expect you to do well in the examination," she is giving expression to her wish regarding her students' better performance in the examination. But there is another sense in which the term expected stands for, viz. as a synonym of probable, for example, when seeing dark cloud in the sky one says "I expect it will rain today." What one means is that it is probable that it will rain. It is in this sense of probability that the term expected is to be understood in the context of the definition of *anupalabdhi*. If we look at the definition of *Hetubindu* we will find that it assumes that negative cognition presupposes an expectation on the part of the cognizer in the sense of an intention directed at a cognition of the negatum by which is meant specially its perception. Since the negative cognition serves to disappoint this intention, it is believed to be something different from other cognitions.

Just as any intentional state contains two aspects — a psychological mode like believing, desiring, etc. and an intentional content expressed with a "that" clause, in the case of *anupalabdhi* also we can distinguish between two aspects. The intentional content generally serves to specify the fulfilment conditions. For instance, the wish that it would rain is fulfilled precisely when it rains. In the case of non-apprehension, however, the content of the negative cognition (. . . that a pot is absent) and that of the intentional state which precedes it (. . . that a pot is perceived) are mutually incompatible. The intentional state remains necessarily unfulfilled in a situation where a negative cognition takes place. The expectation that a pot is perceived remains unfulfilled in a situation where its absence is inferred. Provided that this is the case for all instances of negative cognition one might conclude that for Dharmakīrti each negative cognition serves to disappoint or frustrate a preceding intentional state. One desires to perceive X at locus Q; all the conditions are given that should X be present in locus Q, it would be perceived and yet X is not perceived. Hence, the desire to perceive X has been frustrated.

Let us now discuss another important question, viz. whether the inference drawn on the basis of non-apprehension can be considered as *pramāṇa* or not. As is well known in Dharmakīrti's epistemological framework the notion of epistemic validity is associated with the instigation of practical activities and the accomplishment of practical goals. A cognition is regarded as valid (*pramāṇa*) if it simultaneously indicates an object (*pradarśaka*), instigates activity with regard to it (*pravartaka*) and has the capacity to lead the cognizer to attain it (*prāpaka*). The problem is, how can negative cognition fit into this framework? Since there is no object it cannot indicate the object or instigate the activity of the agent and naturally no question of attaining the object arises. Dharmottara in his *Pramāṇaviniścayaṭīkā* tries to account for the validity of such negative cognition in the following manner. When a negative cognition occurs, it is the positive basis which is considered as the object of activity (*pravṛttiviṣaya*). Ascertaining that "here a flower vase is absent" we want to indicate that the spot is the bare spot on the ground as an object that is to be attained (*prāpya*). In a passage in *Īśvarapratyabhijñāvivṛttivimarśinī*, Abhinavagupta has shown more or less in the fashion of Dharmottara that the stipulation of a bare spot as that which is to be reached is conceptually linked with its function as realizing a goal (*arthakriyopayogin*). Thus the inference based on non-apprehension indicates the positive basis, instigates activity directed at it and is capable of leading the cognizer to reach it or rather to accomplish the goal it serves to realize in either of the two possible ways —

acquisition of what is desired or avoidance of what is to be avoided. Hence there is no difficulty in considering such inference to be a *pramāṇa*.

Moreover in Dharmottara's works non-apprehension has the function of excluding what is not intended which is logically presupposed by the determination of what is intended which in turn is presupposed by practical activity. This means that non-apprehension functions to ascertain the absence of an object at which from the viewpoint of the subsequently produced intentional state, no desire for attainment or avoidance is directed. On the basis of this, we can spell out the different steps involved in the cognitive process of non-apprehension —

a. Perception of a positive basis,
b. Ascertainment that the negatum is absent with respect to the positive basis,
c. Recollection of a practical effect of the positive basis,
d. Wish that the positive basis should be attained or avoided under the aspect of the remembered practical effect,
e. Activity directed at the positive basis, and
f. Attainment or avoidance of the practical effect = accomplishment of goal.

In conclusion it can be said that this analysis reveals the tendency of the Buddhist epistemology towards the accomplishment of human goals as responsible for an association of negative cognition with specific practical activities. The object represented by the logical subject in the negative cognition, which is regarded as its positive basis, is the object towards which the activity is directed. The focus of the negative cognition lies on this positive basis and not on the negatum or the absence. Herein lies the importance of the Buddhist analysis of *anupalabdhi* as a form of inference to know that something is not present at a particular place at a particular time.[12]

12. For details on the apprehension of negative facts, vide,

    1. "Levels of (Im)perceptibility : Dharmottara's Views on the dṛśya in dṛśyānupalabdhi" by B. Kellner in *Dharmakīrti's Thought & its Impact on Indian and Tibetan Philosophy*, ed. S. Katsura.

    2. "Negative Facts and Knowledge of Negative Facts", by Bredan S. Grllon in *Relativism, Suffering and Beyond : Essay in Memory of B.K. Matilal*, eds. by P. Bilimoria and J.N. Mohanty.

17

Testimony

A Separate Pramāṇa?

ONE of the most important topics that have drawn the attention of Indian epistemologists from time to time is *śābda-jñāna* or knowledge arrived at through linguistic means. The Nyāya as well as the Mīmāṁsā systems of Indian thought made very sophisticated and detailed analyses of the notion of *śabda-pramāṇa* or testimony as a means of valid cognition in order to provide rational arguments for accepting the authenticity of the *Śruti*. The Buddhists, on the other hand, in their insistence on admitting only two *pramāṇa*s found no need to accept *śabda-pramāṇa* or information obtained through words as an independent source of valid cognition, but reduced it to inference. Accordingly our proposed walk along the paths of Buddhist epistemology would remain incomplete if we do not take a look at the Buddhist response regarding *śabda-pramāṇa*.

To understand the Buddhist position, let us first state the position of the Nyāya school on *śabda-pramāṇa* in brief. *Śabda* or testimony has been defined by Gautama in his *Nyāya-Sūtra* as *āptopadeśaḥ śabdaḥ*; that is, testimony is the instruction of a reliable person. This definition has two implications. The first one is that the reliability of the statement or instruction depends on the reliability of the person who is making the statement. The second implication is that not simply any statement would be *pramāṇa* but only those that contain true information in the form of valid instruction are *pramāṇas*. Thus the whole question of the validity of the *śabda-pramāṇa*, that is whether a *śabda* can be regarded as a *pramāṇa* or not, centres round the question of the reliability or authenticity of the person who is giving the instruction. Accordingly, the Naiyāyikas proceed to explain the notion of "reliability" of the instructor thus: "A reliable person is one who has direct acquaintance of the *dharma*, i.e. righteousness or the moral order of the cosmos and who is urged by a desire to describe the object as he has seen. Reliability or trustworthiness consists in the direct acquaintance of the object and he who acts with such reliability is called a reliable person. Such reliability can be the common characteristic of a sage, an honourable man (that is one who leads an orthodox way of life following the Vedas) and the barbarians (that is, one who does not lead such an orthodox life). And it is a well-known fact that the activities of all beings in their practical life are carried out on the basis of such reliable knowledge."[1] This description thus highlights the fact that a reliable person must be *sākṣātkṛta-dharmā*, that is, he must have immediate experience of the true nature of things. He must be non-deceiving. He must not be guided by any intention to deceive his hearers, rather must have the desire to describe the object of his immediate experience truly to them. In the *Nyāya-Sūtra* it has further been pointed out that such reliable statements or *śabda* can be of two kinds according to whether the object it refers to is something manifest to the senses or not. While enumerating what is meant by the word *artha* the commentator explicitly

1. *āptaḥ khalu sākṣātkṛtadharmā yathādṛṣṭasyārthasya cikhyāpayiṣayā prayukta upadeṣṭā । sākṣātkaraṇam arthasyāptiḥ । tayā pravartata ity āptaḥ ṛṣāryamlecchānāṁ samānaṁ lakṣanam । tathā ca sarveṣāṁ vyavahārāḥ pravartanta iti.* Quoted from the *Nyāyabhāṣya* by Vittorio A. Van Bijlert in his *Epistemology and Spiritual Authority*, p. 17.

remarks that it should not be held that the instruction of a reliable person is a *pramāṇa* only with regard to the visible/ manifest objects as they are apprehended through the senses directly; it is also a *pramāṇa* even with regard to the unmanifest invisible objects since such objects can be apprehended by inference. With regard to the second kind of reliable words, the truth of the statement is completely dependent upon the trustworthiness of the speaker whereas the truth of the first statement is verifiable by direct perception.

According to the thinkers who accept the validity of testimony as a means of valid cognition, this testimony is admitted as different from sense perception since the object apprehended by it is beyond the reach of the senses. Nor can it be regarded as a case of inference, since it does not satisfy the three conditions prescribed for a valid probans. In the case of inference the object to be inferred (*anumeya*) is the subject as characterized by the probandum (*sādhya*). Such an inference is possible only when the probans is known to exist definitely in the locus. This condition known as *pakṣadharmatā* is not possible in the case of testimony. In the case of testimony the subject (locus) itself is the object to be proved, since that is what is expressed by the word. And unless the subject is established, how can there be any definite cognition of the probans as existing in such a subject/locus? Secondly, in the case of testimony, there is no possibility of concomitance between the probans, namely the word and the probandum, namely the object, since often the object spoken of does not exist at the place or at the time when the word exists. Hence we cannot think of any concomitance between words and the objects denoted by them, which is very much essential if we are to treat testimony as a variety of inference. On the basis of such arguments the advocates of the testimony thesis argue that testimony cannot be considered as a variety of either sense-perception or of inference. But the cognition that is generated by testimony with regard to such object as *agnihotra, svarga,* etc. is free from all sorts of doubt, and hence is valid. Therefore, we have to admit testimony as a separate means of valid cognition.

The Buddhists, however, do not accept testimony as a separate means of valid cognition or as *pramāṇa*. In the *Pramāṇavārttika* as also in his auto-commentary on the *Pramāṇavārttika,* Dharmakīrti discusses the Nyāya and Mīmāṁsā theories on testimony. Dharmakīrti thinks that there is no real connection between a word and its object; that is, no word can give us any information as regards a real object. Accordingly testimony does not communicate a reality. But he, as also Diṅnāga, have regarded Lord Buddha as *pramāṇabhūta* (he who is a means of valid cognition), and considered his words to be trustworthy even with regard to a thing beyond our control. This seems to be a dilemma — refuting the authenticity of testimony and at the same time admitting the words of Lord Buddha as authentic. Accordingly the views of the Buddhists with regard to testimony seem to be very interesting and deserve mention in any treatise on Buddhist epistemology.

Let us first state the Buddhist critique of the Nyāya and Mīmāṁsā theories. Dharmakīrti in his *Pramāṇavārttika* starts the discussion by holding that "since words do not have any inseparable relation (*nāntarīyakatva*) with the objects, so the words cannot establish the existence of the objects. They are only expressive of the intention of the speaker." His point is that words are not just as the things are, for if that were so, on the basis of the words, the nature of the objects could be ascertained. The force of the argument lies in the basic thesis of his epistemology, namely that we can prove the existence of an object on the basis of something only when there exists the *svabhāva pratibandha* relation between the latter and the former. The *svabhāva pratibandha* or inevitable relation, which has been renamed here as *nāntarīyakatā* is the force which can establish the connection of a sign with an object. In the case of *āgama*, the sign is the word, and there is no inevitable necessary connection between the word and the object. The absence of such necessary connection is proved by the fact that if there were such a connection, the nature of the object could have been ascertained from the word. But that is not the case. From the word "fire" simply we cannot ascertain the nature of fire. Here the existence of the object cannot be proved from words. In other words, testimony or *āgama* is not a *pramāṇa* with regard to the actual real object. From this, however, it would be wrong to conclude that *āgama* or testimony does not have any worth. The worth of testimony lies, according to Dharmakīrti, in expressing the intention of the speaker (*vaktrābhiprāyasūcakāḥ*). These words are produced on the basis of the intention (*āvivak*s) of the speaker. Since there is a causal relation between the words and the intention of the speaker, there is a necessary relation *nāntarīyakatābhāva* between the two. Thus being inseparably connected with the intention of the speaker, words can make only this intention known.[2]

But not every will of a person which is the basis of his intention corresponds to a reality as it is. In that case the speaker's intention which is based on such will, even when they are made known through words, would not be faithful to the real thing itself. After all, basically a thing, namely the word, being not connected by nature with another object, namely the reality, is not able to make the latter known. Therefore, words even though they form an *āgama*

---

2. *te hi vaktur vivakṣāvṛttaya iti tannāntarīyakās tāmeva gamayeyuḥ* ।
— *PVSVT*, 71.24-25.

fundamentally do not inform of a real thing.[3]

In the second chapter of the *Pramāṇavārttika*, Dharmakīrti elucidates this point. According to him, words by themselves do not express a thing; it is on the strength of a particular linguistic convention (*saṁketa*) that denotative words put in a meaningful sentence are made to express certain intentions or denote real objects by the speakers who use these words. The intentions of the speaker are meaningful constructions made out of concepts which are mentally derived from perceived real objects, momentary particulars (*svalakṣaṇa*). These concepts according to the Buddhists are "unreal"; they are not as real as the particulars from which they are derived. But these "unreal" concepts are very useful tools when they can impart information about real objects that produce useful effects. Such information is correct insofar as the hearer, on the basis of it, strives for and really acquires the desired effect-producing (*arthakriyākārī*) objects.

Apparently the view of Dharmakīrti that words do not reveal any real object, seems to be inconsistent with the observation made by the master logician Diṅnāga in his *Pramāṇasamuccayaḥ*. In that text he regarded *āgama* or testimony as a *pramāṇa*. His statement goes thus *āptavādā 'visaṁvāda-sāmānyād anumānatā*. Since the words of a reliable person generally do not disagree with reality, the knowledge based on such words is an inference. Again as inference is accepted as a *pramāṇa* by the Buddhists, it follows that Diṅnāga has regarded the knowledge based on the words of a reliable person to be an inference on the ground that both inference and testimony (knowledge based on the words of a reliable person) are *avisaṁvādaka*, that is, do not disagree with reality.

3. *na ca puruṣecchāḥ sarvā yathārthabhāvinyaḥ* | *na ca tadaprati-baddhasvabhāvo bhāvo 'nyam gamayati* | — Ibid., 71.25-26.

This means that for Diṅnāga *āgama* is a *pramāṇa* though it is not different from inference. But Dharmakīrti, as we have seen, has said that the words do not depict the nature of the object. So an inconsistency seems to occur between the views admitted by the two Buddhist logicians, Diṅnāga and Dharmakīrti.

Dharmakīrti himself resolves this inconsistency with reference to our practical behaviour. When Diṅnāga considered *āgama* to be an *anumāna*, his intention was not to describe the real authoritativeness of the *āgama*s but to highlight the fact that human behaviours are often dependent on the guidance of the *āgama*.[4] A person in this world cannot live without depending on the authoritativeness of the sacred tradition. This is because from the *āgama* he comes to know about the great blessings and the great misfortunes which result or do not result when one performs or does not perform some act, the consequences of which acts are not within the reach of one's present experience. At the same time the person has the conviction that the *āgama* is right, on the basis of the fact that we do not see a contradiction to this statement regarding acts and their future consequences, when a person actually is in a state of great blessing or great misfortune. So, when an act, positive or negative, has to be done, it will be better that the individual performs the act in a manner as prescribed by the *āgama*. By taking such practical considerations into account the teacher Diṅnāga regarded *āgama* to be a *pramāṇa* that is an *anumāna*.[5] The upshot of the entire discussion

---

4. *nācāryen bhāvikam prāmāṇyam kathyatā anumānatvam āgamasyoktam, api tu puruṣapravṛttim apekṣya* । — K. 390.20-22.

5. *nāyam puruṣo 'nāśritya āgamaprāmāṇyamāsituṁ samartho 'tyakṣaphalānām keṣāṁcit pravṛttinivṛttyormahānuśaṁsā 'pāyaśravaṇāt tadbhāve virodhādarśanāc ca* । *tatsati pravarttitavye baram evam pravṛtta iti parīkṣayā prāmāṇyam āha* । — *PVSVT*, 72.1-3.

is summed up by Dharmakīrti in the following verse:

> *āptavādāvisaṁvādasāmānyād anumānatā* ।
> *buddheragatyābhihitā parokṣe 'pyasya gocare* ॥
> — *PV*, vs. 219

Because the words of a reliable person generally do not disagree with our experience, the cognition based on *āgama* is considered by Diṅnāga as inference, even in those cases where the object of such *āgama* is beyond the range of any other means of knowledge; since in those cases there is no other possibility to explain it.

Before proceeding to present the justifications for viewing *āgama* as a type of inference, Dharmakīrti states the general properties of an *āgama* statement in the following verse:

> *saṁbaddhānuguṇopāyaṁ puruṣārthābhidhāyakam* ।
> *parīkṣādhikṛtam vākyam ato 'nadhikṛtam param* ॥
> — *PV*, vs. 217

That is, an *āgama* or a reliable statement is one (1) whose words are coherent, (2) for which there are means that are appropriate for attaining the desired end, and (3) which expresses what is useful to a human being. Such a reliable statement alone is made the subject of investigation as to whether it can be considered as a *pramāṇa* or not. A sentence, which does not possess these three characteristics, is not made the subject of investigation. Dharmakīrti also has explained wherein lies the trustworthiness of such *āgama* statements. According to him, the trustworthiness of such sentences about perceptible objects and imperceptible ones can be determined through the two *pramāṇa*s, perception and inference, on the basis of the fact that the information contained in such sentences is neither contradicted by perception nor by the twofold inference later on. This "twofold" inference has been explained by commentator Karṇakagomin as inference that operates through the power of a perceived real thing and inference that is based on tradition. In other words, for an *āgama* statement to be reliable or trustworthy two conditions must be fulfilled — first the information of the statement must have been obtained by the speaker through perception and inference, and secondly the information must not be contradicted by the subsequent perception and inference of the hearer.

Let us now have a look at the reasons why the Buddhist logician Diṅnāga regarded *āgama* as a type of inference. Dharmakīrti offered two arguments in support of it. Insofar as a statement of a trustworthy person (like Buddha, etc.) or in general (as in directly verifiable cases) is reliable and thus reveals an object in an indirect manner as does inference, Diṅnāga considers the knowledge generated by such statement, to be of inferential nature even in the case when the statement of the reliable person refers to an object which is not directly verifiable. So long as in the latter case no contrary results are perceived, there is no reason to deviate from the rule that the statement of a reliable person is like an inference. This first justification of Dharmakīrti may be stated in the form of an inference:

1. The non-disagreement of a cognition is inferred even with regard to an object inaccessible to perception or inference.
2. Since the cognition is based on the words of a reliable person like other cognitions concerning objects accessible to either perception or inference.

Therefore, this cognition of inaccessible objects though is produced by the words of a reliable person does not only inform us of the intention of the speaker rather informs us about the nature of reality. Accordingly, such cognition by virtue of its character of non-disagreement with reality is regarded as inference and not on account of its natural character of being composed of words.[6]

This first justification for considering the *āgama* as a sort of inference rests on the fact that the character of non-disagreement with object (*avisaṁvāda*) is shared in common by the statement as a *pramāṇa* and inference as a *pramāṇa*.[7]

The second justification that Dharmakīrti offers regarding testimony's being a variety of inference is as follows. We have known through our own power of perception and inference the correctness of the truth concerning the thing to be abandoned (i.e. suffering) and of the truth concerning the thing to be attained (viz. the avoidance of suffering) along with the causes of both, namely the causes of suffering and the causes for the removal of suffering or the eightfold path. All of these are the teachings of *āgama*. We see that these statements are true since they do not disagree with reality. So it can be concluded that the cognition originating from *āgama* with regard to other things beyond our control is an inference:

> *heyopādeyatattvasya sopāyasya prasiddhitaḥ* ।
> *pradhānārthāvisaṁvādād anumānaṁ paratra vā* ॥
> — *PV*, vs. 220

To state it elaborately, the fact that what is to be avoided, namely suffering, and what is to be attained, namely the removal of suffering, as also the causes of both suffering and

---

6. *tasyāsyaivaṁbhūtasyāptavādasya avisaṁvādasāmānyād adṛṣṭavya-bhicārasya pratyakṣāṇumānāgamye 'pyarthe pratipattes tadāśritatvāt tadanyapratipattivad avisaṁvādo 'numīyate* । *tataḥ śabdaprabhavā 'pi sati na śabdavadabhiprāyam nivedayatyevetyarthāvisamvādād anumānam api* । — *PVSVT*, 72.23-25

7. *anyathā 'ptavacanasyā 'visaṁvādād anumānatvam ucyate* । — *PVSVT*, 72.26

its removal, have all been taught to us by a reliable person, namely Lord Buddha; and these are not contrary to perception and inference of the hearer. Accordingly, the non-contrary character of such knowledge constitutes the trustworthiness of these objects. Since the above-mentioned main things taught by *āgama* serve the purpose of attainment of human end, they are worth utilizing. Again, since they are non-disagreeing with experience we will not be disappointed when we take it for granted that *āgama* or testimony is of such a quality even with regard to other objects beyond our knowledge. Moreover, such a trustworthy testimony has no defect and the author being so credible, does not intend to gain anything for himself by telling useless and untrue things with regard to an object beyond our cognition.[8]

Thus with the help of the above two different arguments Dharmakīrti tries to present justification in support of Diṅnāga's statement that *āgama* is a variety of *anumāna*. It may be noted that here *anumāna* means an inferential source (*anumānakāraṇa*) like *liṅga*. Karṇakagomin, for example elucidates that we should understand that *āgama* is an inferential source on account of its being the cause of an inferential cognition (*anumānakāraṇatvāt anumānam iti draṣṭavyam*). As it is impossible to explain in any other manner the authoritativeness of the *āgama* by considering our ordinary knowledge, when some act is going to be done it has to be admitted that it is certainly better to act according to our *āgama*. However, there is a word of caution. Since words do not have any inseparable connection with reality, in the context of *āgama*

---

8. *heyopādeyatadupāyānām tadupadiṣṭānām avaiparītyam avisaṁvādo yathā caturṇāmāryasatyānām bakṣyamāṇanītyā tasyāsya puruṣārthopayogino 'bhiyogārhasya 'visamvādāt viṣayāntare 'pi tathātvopagamo na vipralambhāya anuparodhāt niṣprayojanavitathābhidhānavaiphalyāc ca vaktuḥ* ı — *PVSVT*, 72.28–73.2

as inference the possibility of error cannot be eliminated. The authenticity of the *āgama* variety of inference depends on the authenticity of the speaker.

Though the Buddhists are ready to admit *āgama* as a variety of inference or as included in inference, they do not accept the nature of *āgama* as presented by the Naiyāyikas. According to the Naiyāyikas, a person endowed with such merits as the perception of an object as it is (*yathārthadarśana*), etc. is a reliable person.[9] The words of such a person is considered as *śabda* or testimony and is regarded as *pramāṇa*. In other words, for the Naiyāyikas the authenticity of testimony follows from the superior quality (*atiśaya*) of the *āptapuruṣa* (reliable person). The Buddhists reject this notion of the *āpta* advocated by the Nyāya philosophers on the ground that it is impossible for men to cognize him as being such a person who has the superior quality within, and so the examination of that person as *āpta* is impossible. Though the Buddhists are rejecting the Nyāya conception of *āptapuruṣa*, they do not disagree with the fact that ordinary people act with regard to an object beyond their control by depending on *āgama*. They at the same time admit the existence of a credible/trustworthy person who tells the truth and they try to prove his existence on the basis of the following arguments:

1. Ordinary human beings are possessed of virtues (*guṇa*) as well as faults (*doṣa*) which determine the rightness and wrongness of their behaviour.
2. All things which are sometimes inferior and sometimes superior, must have an opposite.
3. The faults have the quality of becoming inferior and superior (*nihrāsa* and *atiśaya*).

9. *yathārthadarśanādiguṇayuktapuruṣa āptaḥ* । — *PVSVT*, 73.6.

4. Therefore, there is an increase and decrease (*utkarṣa* and *apakarṣa*) of the faults by the influence from the opposite thing.
5. The faults are produced from ideas (*vikalpa*).
6. Therefore, even if a person has the material cause of all faults, these faults are decreased by means of the repeated practice of a certain virtue (which forms the *vipakṣa*) in the mind.
7. When this virtue attains a maximum, the faults are bound to be completely destroyed.
8. Therefore, it is quite possible that a person free from faults exists.

The question then naturally arises, how can we describe the person to be "free from faults" at all; for, even though his nature at present is free from all sorts of faults, is it not possible that these faults/defects might occur again? The Buddhists answer this question in the negative. Their point is that —

> The essential nature of mind which is beyond disturbance and has the truth as its objects cannot be removed by the opposing things even if the person has made efforts to remove it. It is because his mind is completely leaning toward such virtue.

To state precisely, it is not possible for the person consisting of the opposite of faults to have faults because he is beyond all disturbances. First he has given up all the faults, secondly, he is free from the suffering which is connected with the actual occurrence of anger, etc. or with future existence, and thirdly, he does not shrink from the taste of felicity in the perfect calmness. Moreover, all kinds of faults originate from *satkāya darśana* or the conception of "I," "min," etc. This is nothing but nescience or *avidyā*. So long as such nescience exists in human beings there is attachment to the self and mind; and from this attachment, hatred and other types of defects occur in the mind. Accordingly in some scriptures delusion or *moha* is described as the root cause of all faults and in some other, the *satkāya darśana* is regarded as the cause. When these two, namely *moha* and *satkāya darśana* are destroyed, the faults will disappear. The person who has apprehended the truth, knows that — It is not "I," "It is not mine" and becomes free from afflictions. Accordingly for such a person no hatred or other defects can occur. Since *moha* or *satkāya darśana* is considered as the root cause, for the person who has been able to set himself free from these defects originating out of *satkāya darśana* through the repeated practice of the theory of no-self *nairātmyavāda* there is no possibility that these defects will arise once again to him. Hence the contention of the opponents regarding the impossibility of a person's being free from defects or faults in future, stands refuted.

With this discussion on the *āgama pramāṇa* in background, let us now discuss the views of the Buddhists on the words of Lord Buddha. In a half-verse of the text *Pramāṇasamuccayaḥ*, Diṅnāga shows his respect to Lord Buddha by regarding him as a *pramāṇabhūta* (as a means of valid cognition) along with other epithets like striving for the welfare of the world, being teacher, being well-gone as well as being the saviour — *pramāṇbhūtāya jagadhitaiṣiṇe praṇamya śāstre sugatāya tāyine*. In this verse Diṅnāga tells us that Buddha is a *pramāṇa* on the ground that he possesses four other virtues. In the commentary Diṅnāga briefly explains the reason why he regards Buddha to be a *pramāṇa*, an authoritative speaker on religious matters. It seems that Diṅnāga is using the word *pramāṇa* in two different senses, the first one in a purely epistemological sense meaning the source of valid knowledge, and the second sense has a more general connotation where authority means right measure. If *pramāṇa* in both the senses is predicated of Buddha, it would mean that he has become an expert or authority on religious questions of ultimate concern to mankind and that his statements on religious matters could certainly be regarded as valid like the knowledge derived from perception and inference. According to Diṅnāga, Lord Buddha is a means of valid cognition or religious authority through his perfection in cause and effect, in order to produce reverence. The perfection in cause (*hetu*) and effect (*phala*) makes the Buddha, the religious authority that he is, makes him a *pramāṇa*. Here cause refers to the Buddha's striving for the welfare of the world (*jagadhitaiṣin*) and his being the teacher (*śāstrī*) while effect refers to the Buddha's being the well-gone (*sugata*) and his being the saviour (*tāyin*). Thus according to Diṅnāga, the last four qualities serve the purpose of describing the nature of Buddha's religious authority. The Buddha has perfected and saved himself, but he also saves others by teaching them the road to ultimate salvation, a road which he has travelled himself. This constitutes, according to Diṅnāga, the condition for Buddha's being a *pramāṇa*. Dharmakīrti in the first few verses of the second chapter of his *PV* deals specifically with the issue, in what sense Buddha can be regarded as a *pramāṇa*. In *PV* (II.1-6), Dharmakīrti deals with the definition of the term *pramāṇa* and in verse 7, the results of this discussion are applied to the doctrines of Lord Buddha to show that they are also *pramāṇa*.

As discussed earlier, for Dharmakīrti *śābda* or knowledge conveyed by words, refers to words used in a coherent, meaningful sentence which teaches suitable means and expresses what is useful to man. Coherently formulated sentences which refer to practicable methods to gain something and which, moreover, discloses a desirable human goal, can really communicate practical knowledge about real objects to the hearer, even though such statements do not reveal particular objects themselves as direct perception does. The trustworthiness of a meaningful statement is tested only afterwards when the hearer really perceives and acquires for himself the effect of the particular that was described in the statement. In the context of Lord Buddha, we find that the teachings of the Buddha constitute trustworthy knowledge and reveal to the hearer facts that were not known before him. Lord Buddha has pointed out to others the useful things that are to be realized and informed them of the truths which were so far unknown to them. Further Lord Buddha does not deceive others (*avisamvādayati*) with regard to the ultimate goals of human aspiration. Since Buddha's words are *avisaṁvādaka* and *ajñātārthaprakāśaka*, he can be considered as a means of valid knowledge. The trustworthiness of Buddha is proved by the extent to which a person really acquires for himself the objects taught by the Buddha. The teachings of Lord Buddha are found to be trustworthy when the hearer finds the objects which constantly produce desired useful effects (*arthakriyāsthitiḥ*). This is the trustworthiness with regard to visible objects, objects that are accessible to perception and inference of the hearer. The trustworthiness of Buddha regarding imperceptible objects can be inferred from his trustworthiness regarding perceptible, visible matters.

In verses II.145 of *PV*, Dharmakīrti summarizes the religious and epistemological authority of Lord Buddha thus:

> *tāyaḥ svadṛṣṭamārgoktir vaiphalyād vakti nānṛtam* ।
> *dayālutvāt parārthaṁ ca sarvārambhābhiyogataḥ* ॥

The Buddha has realized for himself the Supreme goal; he teaches the way to attain this goal in a reliable manner because he would not gain anything by making false statements, since there is not anything for him to attain. This disinterestedness is caused by his great compassion (*dayālutva*) and it is out of this compassion that the Buddha acts, lives and teaches (*sarvārambhābhiyoga*) in order to promote the supreme welfare to the whole world (*parārtham*).

This analysis of Dharmakīrti reminds us of a similar statement made by the Nyāya philosopher Pakṣilasvāmī while describing the characterizing features of an *āpta* speaker (*kiṁ punar āptānām prāmāṇyam sākṣātkṛtadharmatā bhūtadayā yathābhūtārthacikhyāpayiṣyati*) namely, having directly perceived the true state of affairs (*sākṣātkṛtadharmā*), compassion on living beings (*bhūtadayā*) and the desire to communicate the thing as it is (*yathābhūtārthacikhyāpayiṣā*). Both of them have regarded compassion to be the criterion of validity. Dharmakīrti more or less followed these three criteria stated by Pakṣilasvāmī but has given compassion priority over the other two in order to emphasize the speciality of the authority of Lord Buddha. For according to Dharmakīrti the first cause and the driving force behind Buddha's religious and epistemological authority is his compassion. Pakṣilasvāmī, on the other hand, emphasizes a temporal order of the criteria. The authoritative speaker first has perceived a thing or fact himself, then he is compassionate and out of compassion he seeks to correctly describe the thing or fact to others.

The real difference between Pakṣilasvāmī and Dharmakīrti seems to lie elsewhere. In Pakṣilasvāmī we do not get any explanation as to how or why the authoritative person has perceived the true state of affairs (*sākṣātkṛtadharmā*). The *āpta* simply has acquired his direct experience of higher things. Out of compassion, he relates his experience and knowledge to others and therefore his reliable statements are regarded as *pramāṇa*. Dharmakīrti, on the other hand, spells out the reason as regards how and why the *āpta par excellence,* the Buddha, has acquired his direct experiences of important religious facts. The Buddha was moved by *compassion* and therefore exerted himself to attain the state of complete cessation of suffering in order to teach others the way to the same goal. Before Buddha had reached the same goal himself, he had heard from the reliable tradition about the cause of suffering for the sake of teaching others the way to it.

The question immediately arises — how can the admission of testimony be harmonized with the general epistemological outlook of the Buddhists, specially of Diṅnāga and Dharmakīrti, which has its orientation towards *vastubala-pravṛttānumāna.* This problem is solved by the epistemological school in introducing three different types of objects, perceptible (*pratyakṣa*), imperceptible (*parokṣa*), and radically inaccessible (*atyanta-parokṣa*). The first sort consists of those things which are accessible to direct perception, like jar, book, etc. and the second group consists of things like impermanence, selflessness, etc. which can be proven through the usual *vastubala* variety of inference. To the third group, however, belong objects such as the different heavens (*svarga*) or the details of the law of *karma* which are inaccessible to direct perception and which cannot also be proved by citing some other state of affairs as probans. In short, it might be said that these objects are beyond the limits of ordinary rationality. It might be noted at this point that in the first two chapters of his *Pramāṇavārttika,* Dharmakīrti often uses the term *parokṣa* ambiguously to signify both the imperceptible and radically inaccessible variety though from what he speaks of in certain passages of the later chapters of the same text it is quite clear that Dharmakīrti himself did explicitly accept this threefold division of objects.

Thus, Dharmakīrti limits the scope of scripturally based inferences to cases where the objects are radically inaccessible and hence beyond the range of ordinary ratiocination. By such limitation he is able to preserve his theory of inferences being objectively grounded and at the same time maintain a distance from the Mīmāṁsā and Sāṁkhya schools who cite scriptural passages as a means of proof even in the context of ordinary properties like the impermanence of sound, etc. which can and should be decided by *vastubalapravṛttānumāna* since they are not beyond the scope of ordinary ratiocination.

To wind up, testimony or *āgama* or scriptural argumentation as applied to radically inaccessible object (*atyantaparokṣa*) can be considered as an inference — there is no need to postulate an additional *pramāṇa* called *śabda* as admitted by certain orthodox schools. It is, however, a rather special indirect case of inference because of the fact that it turns on inductive generalization which presupposes the use and correctness of direct perception and *vastubalapravṛttānumāna.*[10] The Buddhist view regarding testimony comes closer to the Nyāya view rather than to the Mīmāṁsā school. They do not admit testimony to be formed by eternal sentences like the Vedas, rather will be ready to admit that testimony consists in the words of a reliable person. Even in formulating the characterizing features that make a person reliable, the Buddhist logician follows the view of the Nyāya logician Pakṣilasvāmī. The important feature of the Buddhist account of testimony consists in its emphasis on the *intention* of the speaker. In the case of Lord Buddha, the intention was to help other people engulfed in the world of suffering, by

10 For detailed discussion please see the two articles "Dharmakīrti, Āryadeva and Dharmapāla on Scriptural Authority" and "How Much of a Proof is Scripturally Based Inference" by T. Tillemans in *Scripture, Logic and Language*, Wisdom Publications, Boston, 1999.

showing a way out, and as he had no other bad intention to deceive people in this regard, the Buddhists do not find any inconsistency in accepting the words of Buddha as a *pramāṇa*. This analysis of the Buddhist logician Dharmakīrti is a clear exposition of linking epistemology with their religious beliefs in a consistent and scientific manner. Herein lies the speciality of Buddhist epistemology — though it has a religious bias/ orientation, it does not give up its scientific spirit.

Conclusion

At the end of our walk through the trails of Buddhist epistemology, it is ripe time to assess the worth of our endeavour. That is, after discussing the different issues found in the main texts of Buddhist epistemological literature, let us try to evaluate the Buddhist theories in the light of contemporary debates in epistemology. At the outset we must remember that this sort of attempt may seem to be futile or not worth investigation, since to do this requires us to open a dialogue between the Buddhist logician and the contemporary Western epistemologists. And this dialogue happens to be a tilted one — on the one side we have very ancient literature written in the sixth century and guided mainly by definite religious commitments, and on the other side we have modern literature backed by reports of scientific researches going on since the first quarter of the twentieth century. Accepting this as a given fact we still want to engage ourselves in such a debate in order to ascertain the importance of Buddhist theories in the present day. It is indeed true that in the Buddhist literature we do not have any direct discussion of the questions raised by modern epistemologists. Still, on the basis of what has been said in the different Buddhist texts on the nature of knowledge, nature of inference, objects of perception, etc. we can reconstruct what would have been the response of the Buddhists to such epistemological queries. It is through such reconstructions that we can show the relevance of Buddhism in contemporary philosophy thereby refuting the opinion that Buddhism is a closed chapter in the book of philosophy.

Let us take a brief look at the important issues of the contemporary debates in Western epistemology:

1. Can skepticism be refuted?
2. What is knowledge?
3. Is the JTB definition an adequate and correct definition of knowledge?
4. Is truth the primary epistemic goal?
5. Does justified belief imply voluntary belief?
6. How can beliefs be justified?
7. Is Infinitism the only solution to the Regress problem?
8. What is immediate justification?
9. Is knowledge contextual?
10. Is there a priori knowledge?
11. Does perceptual experience have conceptual content?
12. Why is this preference for perceptual knowledge? What are we to say about other kinds of knowledge?
13. Is justification internal or external?
14. Is knowledge closed under known entailment?

Contemporary Western epistemology has off and on been threatened by the Cartesian evil demon. Accordingly, the important question that epistemologists all over the world across the centuries face is — can skepticism be refuted? In fact skeptics have challenged the very possibility of knowledge thus putting epistemology at stake. Skepticism has appeared in several forms from time to time. The absolute skepticism or radical skepticism, also known as philosophical skepticism, is formulated in terms of the possibility of knowledge. The philosophical skeptic does not claim merely that we in fact know a good deal less than we like to think, but rather that aspiring to knowledge is somehow, inherently problematic. Knowledge is impossible because we cannot even get to the point of having justified beliefs. Contrasted with this form of radical skepticism is relative skepticism or knowledge-specific forms of skepticism. According to this form of skepticism, in some cases, it is possible to hold that while we may have justified true belief, our justification falls short of the demand of knowledge. Skepticism that concedes the possibility of justification, but denies the possibility of knowledge is called knowledge-specific skepticism.

In Indian philosophy the skeptics have appeared again and again to challenge the possibility of having knowledge. Nāgārjuna, the famous Buddhist logician, has shown with his tetralemma that knowledge is not possible at all. So in his philosophy there is a form of absolute skepticism. Other than Nāgārjuna's philosophy, in most of the cases what we have is knowledge-specific skepticism. For example, when the Cārvākas endeavoured to show that inferential knowledge is impossible as it is open to doubt, they admitted that perception can give us knowledge that is indubitable and veridical. Faced with challenges from the skeptics, the Buddhist epistemologists tried to provide an account of knowledge which can refute such challenges. Knowledge, in the opinion of the Buddhists, is uncontradicted and reveals the nature of the object as it is. Such knowledge, for them, can be either perceptual or inferential in character. Perception directly reveals the object. Since the object is unique in character devoid of all sorts of properties, perception which reveals such object is also indeterminate, devoid of all varieties of conceptual content.

Accordingly, perceptual knowledge is free from all sorts of error and doubt. The other variety of knowledge is inference. It may be argued from the skeptic's point that even if we take for granted that perception provides us certain knowledge, doubt is possible in the case of inference. Since inferential cognition requires a universal premise and such universal premise cannot be established as true by any experience, inferential knowledge is open to doubt. From the Buddhists' standpoint, the challenge of the skeptic can be refuted even in the case of inferential knowledge, since they do not believe that the universal proposition is based on experience. According to them, such proposition is based on the logical principles of essential identity and causality. The universal proposition of the form "All cases of *S* are cases of *P*" becomes a necessary proposition for them and to deny such proposition involves self-contradiction. Accordingly knowledge which is based on such necessary proposition has to be regarded as certain and, hence, beyond doubt. In short, with their theory of perception as indeterminate cognition and their view of universal concomitant relation as based on the logical principles, the Buddhists are able to escape the clutches of the skeptics.

Like other systems, in Buddhism much emphasis has been laid on discussion of *pramāṇa* for a solid foundation for the philosophical doctrines. The Buddhist logician Dharmakīrti described *pramā* as *samyag jñāna,* that is *pramā* is non-contrary knowledge. The question obviously arises as regards how to judge that the cognition is expressing the proper nature of the object? Each cognition expresses some object or the other. So how can we determine that the object which is expressed by the cognition is not the proper object but a mistaken one? In reply the Buddhists hold that the truth or validity of a cognition is determined by the success of the voluntary action (*pravṛtti*). If the voluntary action which results from the cognition to attain the object, actually leads to the attainment of the desired object, the cognition will be regarded as a valid one. That property of cognition which leads to the success in the attainment of the object is technically regarded as *avisaṁvādaka*.

In the Western tradition knowledge is a belief or attitude that is true under some set of conditions or truth theory. As a belief or attitude, "knowledge" is dispositional and it therefore cannot be an act in itself. But on the account of Buddhist epistemological theory, *pramā* is the act (*kriyā*) of knowing indubitably that is constituted by a process involving the interaction of an agent, instrument and object of knowledge. This model requires that the action of knowing (*pramā*) is a cognitive event occurring in a particular person's mind within a particular set of circumstances.

To the question "Is truth the primary epistemic goal?" — the Buddhists' answer would be in the negative. The Buddhists in their epistemological hunt is guided by pragmatic motivation, viz. the attainment of human goal (*puruṣārthasiddhiḥ*). In the case of transcendental knowledge, the goal is the attainment of *nirvāṇa* and the removal of human suffering, and in the empirical level it is the attainment of the desired object (*upādeyasya grahaṇam*) and rejection of the unwanted one (*heyasya parihāra*). So mere validity or mere correspondence with the object cannot be the ultimate goal of knowledge. On the contrary, they believe that the validity of knowledge is determined by the fact whether that knowledge is capable of serving the purpose for which the knowledge is aimed at. If knowledge can lead to the success of the activity, then only knowledge will be regarded as valid. So the primary epistemic goal for the Buddhists is the attainment of human end. Since this goal can be achieved only when knowledge is valid or when knowledge reveals the object as it is, they investigate the question of truth or validity of knowledge. In other words, mere truth or truth as dissociated from pragmatic purpose has no meaning in Buddhist epistemology.

Another important issue of Western epistemology is — Is justified belief responsible belief? To answer this question from the Buddhist perspective, let us first note what this question actually means. To avoid the challenge of the skeptics and to distinguish knowledge from lucky guess, the epistemologists from the very beginning have highlighted the fact that a belief is not knowledge if it is only accidentally true. To enhance beliefs to the status of knowledge it is required that the beliefs should be justified, as Socrates says in Plato's *Meno* "knowledge should be *tied down*." The point is that true beliefs are useful only when they are stable. So we need the beliefs to be justified. There are two standpoints from which epistemic assessments of a belief can be made. In one standpoint, the person's entitlement to hold a particular view is focused, while in the other standpoint it is needed to consider whether the grounds on the basis of which the person is upholding the belief are adequate to establish the truth of his belief. In the former standpoint, emphasis is laid on the responsibility of the individual — whether the belief has been responsibly held/ formed. In this point of view, justified belief is what we get by living up to appropriate standards of epistemic behaviour. As distinct from the second approach where epistemic assessment is more impersonal, object-oriented, and hence may be regarded as providing "evidential justification," the former approach has been looking for "epistemic responsibility" or personal justification. The characterizing feature of the first approach is that epistemically responsible behaviour offers a kind of grounding — by behaving in an epistemically responsible way the knower himself increases the likelihood that the beliefs he forms are true. Thus the supporters of personal justification thesis point out that epistemic responsibility is an essential component of rationality and if we do not have any stake in rationality, we would have no interest in justification. But those who are in support of evidential justification hold that our fundamental interest is in having true beliefs which are essential for being successful in our undertakings. Hence evidences or groundings are more important as they make our beliefs true. In this debate there is a third alternative which tries to reconcile personal justification or epistemic responsibility with evidential justification. On this approach, one is epistemically responsible in believing a given proposition only if one's belief is based on adequate evidence. Prof Sibajiban Bhattacharyya in his essay "Knowing That"[1] points out that since our justified beliefs can be false in spite of our best efforts, the fact that I am right more often than not seems mysterious. To remove this mystery Descartes had to bring in the veracity of God, Leibnitz the principle of pre-established harmony, but not with much success. Goldman's reliability theory, on the other hand appears to be on the right track. This theory shows that the truth of the belief is dependent on the belief-forming or knowledge-yielding process. But this process must be a truth-guaranteeing process — a careful, cautious, safe, proven procedure which cannot but yield truth.

With this background we want to take a look at the Buddhist notion of valid knowledge or *samyag-jñāna*. Since like other schools of Indian philosophy the Buddhists believe that knowledge can be both valid and invalid, and as determination of valid knowledge is the main concern of their

---

1. *Doubt, Belief and Knowledge*, Indian Council of Philosophical Research in association with Allied Publishers, New Delhi, 1987.

epistemology, we will consider whether such valid knowledge involves epistemic responsibility or not. It may be noted here that the Buddhists in their epistemology did not prefer the idea of investigating knowledge for the sake of knowledge, but for the sake of some practical orientation — for the purpose of achieving some goal. The text *Nyāyabindu* starts with the declaration that "the attainment of human goal is preceded by valid cognition."[2] While specifying what they mean by the term "valid" it has been said that "it must reveal the object as it is" and also "it must reveal something new." In other words being uncontradicted by objective reality and being novel are the two distinguishing marks of valid knowledge. Now if we concentrate on the first feature, it will be seen that each variety of valid knowledge is grounded in objective reality. This seems to give rise to the idea that the Buddhists will be in favour of "evidential justification" approach which is not the whole story. According to the Buddhists, valid cognition has three dimensions — it is revealer of the object (*pradarśaka*), it is producer of voluntary action towards that object (*pravarttaka*) and it is the achiever of the object (*prāpaka*). So, being the revealer of the object does not constitute the sole feature of knowledge. Unless knowledge is able to lead the agent towards the attainment of the object the proper function of knowledge is not performed. In fact, whether knowledge is valid or not is judged on the basis of the fact as to whether the object indicated by that knowledge is achieved or not. When the object which has been shown by knowledge is attained and thus satisfies the purpose of the agent, knowledge is regarded as valid. Emphasis on this aspect of knowledge suggests that the Buddhists are not in favour of evidential justification simply, knowledge according to them involves epistemic responsibility also on the part of the agent. On the

2. *samyagjñānapūrvikā sarvapuruṣārthasiddhiḥ.*

basis of the evidences found there in reality, when one has valid knowledge of an object, one has the responsibility to attain the object through such knowledge. So it seems that the Buddhists' answer to the question — "Is justified belief responsible belief?" is more positive than it had been given by the Western epistemologists. Their answer is that if a piece of knowledge is valid, and in that sense justified by external evidences, it has to be rational. This sort of emphasis on the practical aspect of knowledge constitutes the beauty of the Buddhist epistemological theory.

Let us club the following questions in one single group — (1) Is Infinitism the solution to the regress problem? (2) Can beliefs be justified through coherence alone? Or are there immediately justified beliefs? In Western epistemological tradition coherence theory of justification has been proposed as opposed to the foundationalist theory of justification. The basic idea of coherence theory is that there is no question of a belief's being justified by itself as the foundationalists' basic beliefs are thought to be. To be justified, a belief must fit into a justified system and the system is more or less justified depending on how well the beliefs in it "hang together" "considered as a whole." This reference to a whole system of beliefs is crucial. Coherence theories do not claim merely that the epistemic significance of a given belief must always be assessed in the context of some further commitments. On the contrary, they hold that the justification of individual beliefs depends on certain properties of total belief systems. Coherence theories are thus radically holistic. However, this coherence theory has been faced with several problems. If someone puts forward a claim as more than a personal claim or as a report on how things seem to be, he might be asked to explain why. That is, he may be asked whether what he said is something that he assumes to be true or whether he really knows it to be the case. If he replies that it is something he knows, he may be asked — how he knows. In response, he will have to cite something in support of his claim — his evidence, his credential whatever. But with regard to these also, the same question can be asked — is what he cites in defence of his original claim something that he is just assuming or is it something that he knows? If the former, it will be of no help — one cannot base knowledge on mere assumption. If the latter, it will in turn, need to be backed up, and so on. Several alternative solutions have been proposed to this problem — (1) at some point one has to repeat something that one has already said; (2) at some point one can refuse to answer; and (3) one can keep trying to think of something new to say. The second alternative cannot be accepted, for that will make a dogmatic assumption. The first alternative is not acceptable either, as that will lead to the problem of arguing in a circle. The third alternative does not also prove better for that will lead to the problem of infinite regress. So, to avoid the circularity or the regress problem, if one goes on searching for something new one will be led to Infinitism. Infinitism, itself being a defect, cannot be considered as a solution to the regress problem. Hence to avoid all these problems it has been suggested by some epistemologists to take the Aristotelian position, viz. say that knowledge depends on self-evidence: anything we know must either be self-evident or deducible by self-evidently correct steps from self-evidently true premises. But, how can one find out what is self-evident? Why something's striking us as self-evident should be a guarantee of its correctness? If we ignore these questions, the skeptic will say that we are making dogmatic assumptions. If we try to find some further validation of intuitive self-evidence, we will be opening the possibility of regress once again. Perhaps the only alternative to solve all these problems is to say that there are some propositions which are not self-evident, but which are immediately justified.

An immediately justified belief is one which can be justified by reiteration. What justifies me in believing that I seem to have a headache is simply the fact that I seem to have a headache. Behind every immediately justified belief, as Chisholm has shown us, there is a self-presenting property which constitutes its sole justification. A property *F* is said to be self-presenting to a subject *S* at time *t* if *S* has *F* at *t* and necessarily if *S* has *F* at *t* then it is certain for *S* that he has *F* at *t*. The concept of the directly evident is wider than the concept of the immediately justified. *A* self-presenting proposition for *S* at *t* is one which is true at *t* and necessarily if it is true at *t*, it is evident to *S* at *t*. Hence it can be said that the proposition "I am thinking" expresses what is self-presenting for *S* at *t* if he is thinking at t and is immediately justified to *S*. For it is impossible for *S* to be thinking unless it is evident to him that he is thinking. And when it is evident to *S* that he is thinking the proposition "There is someone who is thinking" is also evident to him. But the latter proposition is not self-presenting or immediately justified. For it may be the case that there is someone who is thinking, but this fact is not evident to *S*. So, directly evident propositions are not necessarily self-presented ones.

These problems are not so crucial for the Buddhists, since they are not advocates of Coherence theory. They do not say that the epistemic justification of a certain proposition is to be found with reference to the whole system. On the contrary, they are supporters of correspondence theory. They hold that I can claim to know an object only when there is actually such an object in the outer world. So, whether any knowledge is valid or not is determined not by my system of beliefs but by the existence of the object. In other words, knowledge becomes immediately justified by the object. As the Buddhists are taking such a foundationalist stand, the problems associated with coherence do not arise for them. Since for the Buddhists perceptual knowledge is the best form of knowledge and this perceptual knowledge is justified by the actual existence of the particular object, they will be admitting a foundationalist approach where knowledge is founded on immediately justified beliefs.

Let us proceed towards another issue of the contemporary debate, namely, is knowledge contextual? To consider the Buddhist response to this issue, the main point of this debate needs to be highlighted. The above question refers to the debate between **contextualism** and **invariantism** in epistemology. The fundamental idea of contextualism is that standards for correctly attributing or claiming knowledge are not fixed but subject to circumstantial variation. Epistemic contexts are not exhausted by methodological and dialectical considerations: facts about the actual situations in which claims are made or beliefs are held are crucial too. This is because in claiming knowledge we commit ourselves to the objective well-groundedness as well. In this respect contextualism is opposed to both relativism and semantic invariantism. Semantic invariantism is the view that there is one single meaning to a sentence and that meaning remains the same in all contexts. Relativism, on the other hand, is the view that there is no fixed meaning of an expression — meaning is relative to the contexts in which the sentence is uttered. Relativism leads to the problem that we cannot speak of a single meaning to an utterance, which is independent of all situations. Hence, to understand the meaning of an expression requires the impossible task of knowing the meaning of an expression relative to all situations. To avoid the problem of both the theories contextualism has been offered, which holds that an expression has a single meaning, but in order to have knowledge of that expression we have to understand it as related to a particular context. Contextualism is the view that justification always takes place against a background of beliefs that are themselves in no way evidentially supported. The claims to knowledge are justified by excluding some relevant alternatives and these alternatives vary from one context of inquiry to another. Thus on the contextualist account of knowledge, sentences for knowledge claims do have complex context-sensitive semantics, so they will express truths by depending not only on what standards for ruling out are relevant but also depending on what restricted range of competitors are relevant. Both the standard and the range, as regards their relevance vary with the context. To explain this doctrine of contextualism let us take an example — John knows there is milk on the rug. When a speaker says this to a hearer, he means to state that among the propositions logically conflicting with "There is milk on the rug." John is in a position to rule out all those conflicting sentences that are relevant competitors according to the standard for relevance to the current context. For example, to know the above statement, John must be in a position to rule out such competitor, as "There is only some whitish water on the rug that looks like milk but is not milk." On the other hand, the invariantist account of the semantics of "know" holds that "*S* knows that *p*" will have as a logically necessary condition some such severe proposition as this "according to a single invariant standard for ruling out that can never be transcended, *S* is in a position to rule out as untrue all propositions that are logically incompatible with *p*." To put it simply, on the invariantist account there is one single meaning of *p* which remains the same in all contexts, and does not vary from context to context.

In the face of such a debate, let us try to explore in which side the Buddhist logicians would like to place themselves. Though we do not find the subtle points of contextualism in the writings of the Buddhist writers, still when we go through their logical texts, as for instance the *Pramāṇavārttika* of Dharmakīrti, we find support of contextualism. The basic point of the contextualist theory of knowledge as distinct from the invariantist theory is that — to say that "*S* knows *p*" *p* does not need to have a fixed meaning in all contexts, rather the meaning of *p* can vary from context to context. Accordingly the knowledge claim also will vary in different contexts. In the auto-commentary of *Pramāṇavārttika*, Dharmakīrti tells us that though an object is unique and indivisible in nature still the same object appears differently in the knowledge of different individuals. In other words, different individuals will have different knowledge regarding the same object, such difference being due to the difference in the mental make-up, life situation, and cultural upbringing of the concerned individual.[3] The example given by Dharmakīrti is that of the sight of a dead body of a woman. The sight of the same dead body gives rise to three different impressions, that of the impermanent character of worldly objects, that of sensuous enjoyment, and that of something to be taken as food, respectively in the minds of a saint, an individual filled with sex feeling, and a dog. The saint has the idea of the non-eternal, impermanent character of beauty, etc., the individual man who can think of nothing but sensual enjoyment has the idea of physical enjoyment, and the dog for which the body is nothing

3. *yadyapy aṁśarahitaḥ sarvato bhinnasvabhāvo 'nubhūtaḥ, tathāpi na sarvabhedeṣu tāvatā niścayo bhavati, kāraṇāntarāpekṣatvāt* । *anubhavo hi yathā vikalpābhyāsaṁ niścayapratyayān janayati* । *yathā rūpadarśanāviśeṣe 'pi kuṇapa-kāminī-bhakṣyavikalpāḥ* । *tatra buddhipāṭavam tadvāsanābhyāsaḥ prakaraṇam ityādayo 'nubhavāt bhedaniścayotpattisahakāriṇaḥ.* — *PVSV*, 20.29-21.1

but a lump of fleshes, has the impression of something to be consumed. Accordingly concerning the same object the three will have three different pieces of knowledge. In other words, it cannot be said that regarding a particular object, people will always have the same type of knowledge; on the contrary, knowledge of the object will vary from person to person and from situation to situation. Another example considered by Dharmakīrti is that of an approaching man. Seeing a man coming from a distance, a student has the knowledge "My teacher is coming," but his daughter has the information "My father is coming." When the daughter has the knowledge that her father is coming, that piece of knowledge rules out all other relevant alternatives possible in that situation, viz. the teacher is coming, my friend is coming, etc. as untrue. But the student's knowledge rules out as untrue the alternatives — my father is coming, my friend is coming, etc. So it may be considered as a case of contextualism. Thus the above passage of the *Pramāṇavārttika* gives us the permission to place Buddhist epistemologists on the contextualist side.

Another important issue in the debates of Western epistemology is regarding the possibility of a priori knowledge — Is a priori knowledge possible? The word a priori means generally "prior to or independent of experience." Accordingly a belief or claim is said to be justified a priori if its epistemic justification, the reason or warrant for thinking it true does not depend at all on sensory or other types of experience. Understood thus, the notion of a priori justification is essentially a negative one, specifying as it does what the justification of the belief does not depend upon, but saying nothing about what it does depend upon. Historically the main proponents of rationalism upheld the view that a priori justification derives from the intuitive apprehension of necessary facts. Traditional empiricists, on the other hand, believe that a priori knowledge is explained by truth-by-virtue of meaning. If one understands what it means to say that "2+2 = 4" one knows that it is true. To say of such a proposition "I know what it means, but it just doesn't seem very plausible to me" is a bad joke. There are, of course, many philosophers who deny that there is any such thing as "meaning-constituting." According to them, there is no reason to suppose that some propositions are true by virtue of meaning alone. Moreover, even if we admit that there are some propositions which are meaning-constituting, we do not have an explanation of a priori knowledge, because there is no automatic connection between a proposition's being meaning-constituting and its being true. For we can understand theories which are known to be false. In face of such difficulties, the foundationalists try to offer a different explanation of a priori knowledge. They hold that there are some terms which derive their meaning ostensively by correlation with what is directly presented in experience; on the basis of such primitive meanings other terms may be introduced. This may be by explicit term-by-term definitions; or it may be by rules for the use of whole sentences, rules that thus implicitly define the terms contained in the sentences. As "purely conventional" such definitions and rules are true in virtue of meaning alone; hence, these propositions can be said to be known a priori.

Let us now see what would be the Buddhists' answer to the question on the possibility of a priori knowledge. Apparently the Buddhists who uphold the theory of indeterminate perception, seem to be upholding a sort of foundationalism in their epistemology; but if we look seriously into their discussion of logical truths, especially those which establish the connection between the probans and the probandum, we can get an idea of their account of a priori knowledge. In the philosophy of Dharmakīrti it has been repeatedly said that the relation of invariable concomitance, technically known as *vyāpti* or *avinābhāva,* cannot be established by observation and non-observation of two phenomena, but on the basis of the principles of essential identity and causality. The examples offered by Dharmakīrti regarding such principles are — "All oaks are trees" and "All cases of smoke are cases of fire." One who understands the meaning of the word "oak" as "oak tree" understands the truth of the statement "All oaks are trees." In other words, one need not look for any extraneous fact to verify the truth of such a statement. So the knowledge of such propositions can be regarded as a priori. Similar is the case with smoke and fire. One who knows the meaning of the expression "smoke" as something which is produced out of fire, can know the truth of the statement "All cases of smoke are cases of fire." For the occurrence of such knowledge, information about conventions guiding the meaning is necessary, and nothing else is required. So this is also a case of a priori knowledge. This indicates that though the Buddhists would not admit all knowledge to be a priori, they would admit that in some cases knowledge does not need to depend on perceptual evidences. Such knowledge can therefore, be regarded as a priori. In other words, the possibility of a priori knowledge is not something inconceivable in their epistemological framework; they would not be in agreement with the rationalists in holding that all a priori knowledge is analytic. If the examples cited by them as necessary truths are considered, it will be noticed that some sentences like "All oaks are trees" are analytic while the others like "All cases of smoke are cases of fire" are synthetic. That is, for the Buddhists, there are both analytic a priori truths as well as synthetic a priori truths.

The obvious Buddhist response to the query — Does perceptual experience have a conceptual content? — seems to be negative. Perceptual experience, in the true sense of the term, is non-conceptual and hence devoid of all sorts of conceptual content. Perception has been conceived by the Buddhists as that type of knowledge which can apprehend the unique particulars (*svalakṣaṇa*). These unique particulars constitute the ultimate reality — they alone are real being causally efficient. Now each particular has its own unique character and is distinguished from all other objects of its own kind and those of another. Since there is no common characteristic, which is or can be shared by two particulars, the unique particulars are regarded as indescribable. Accordingly the knowledge, which apprehends such particulars, cannot be determinate. Perception, as such, has been defined by Diṅnāga, the master logician, as "that which is devoid of all sorts of conceptual construction," conceptual construction being identified by him as "the association of name, genus, etc." At this stage of epistemological thinking it was believed that all sorts of error arise only in the level of concepts; and so, Diṅnāga did not feel any necessity to add any other property to the definition of perception. Perception occurs only through immediate contact of the sense organs and their respective objects. Later on, the opponent group pointed out that errors occur in perception when the sense organs themselves are defective. With a defective sense organ when one apprehends an object, that perception cannot reveal the object as it is. In face of that criticism, later Buddhist logician Dharmakīrti, for example, added the epithet "non-erroneous" to the definition of perception retaining the non-conceptual character. Thus, for him, perception is knowledge which is free from conceptual construction and which is non-erroneous at the same time.

Apparently this view of the Buddhists, that perceptual experience does not contain any conceptual element, gives rise to some practical problem. We have seen earlier that the Buddhists believe knowledge to be worthwhile only when it serves some practical purpose. Perception being a variety of knowledge, therefore, has to serve some practical utility. But how can the object serve my purpose unless I identify it as so and so. For instance, at the moment of thirst I must identify the object presented to my senses to be water, so that I can use it to quench my thirst. That is, I must know the object as "water." But the moment I identify the object known as water, my knowledge will fail to satisfy the criteria of perceptual knowledge, viz. of being non-conceptual. So the problem remains, with their emphasis on the pragmatic utility of knowledge can the Buddhists claim that perceptual experience is free from conceptual content? The Buddhists themselves were aware of this problem. So, they tried to solve it by distinguishing between two levels of reality — empirical level and transcendental level. In the empirical level, where we are concerned with pragmatic utility, we have to admit conceptual contents in perceptual experience. But when one is able to transcend this empirical level and attain the ultimate level, he will have direct knowledge of the true nature of the object. The true nature of the object is its uniqueness, its indeterminate character. Accordingly such perceptual experience will be indeterminate, free from all sorts of conception. At that moment the individual will realize the falsity or futile character of empirical knowledge. But so long as one has not attained that ultimate stage, one has to admit the conceptual contents of perceptual experience. So the proper reply to the stated question is, perceptual experience, as it ought to be, is really free from conceptual contents; but the perceptual experience that we have in our empirical life cannot be free from conceptual contents.

Associated with this issue on perception there is another question — why is this preference for perceptual knowledge? What are we to say about other kinds of knowledge? The answer to them, from the Buddhist standpoint is that, since perceptual knowledge is rooted in objective reality and is free from conceptual construction, this perception or immediate apprehension of an object can give us true knowledge of the reality. And such truth is the guiding force in the attainment of the object. Accordingly the Buddhists show their preference for this variety of perceptual knowledge. As regards the other variety of knowledge, namely inference, the Buddhists are aware that we cannot have that amount of certainty as there is in perceptual awareness. Still we have to admit the truth or legitimacy of such conceptual knowledge for our pragmatic purposes. In our practical life we are guided in our activities towards the attainment of object through inference. So inferential knowledge is also accepted as true. But at the same time the Buddhists make it very clear that when we transcend this level of empirical reality, such inferential knowledge will have no worth while perceptual knowledge or immediate apprehension remains true even at that level.

The question that we are going to discuss next is — is justification always external according to the Buddhists, or, do they admit that justification can be internal as well? The — answer is positive and negative both. The Buddhists are supporters of external justification and internal justification both. In the case of perceptual knowledge, justification is external while in the case of inferential cognition justification is internal. Perceptual knowledge, according to the Buddhists, is that which directly represents the object as it is. Since the object is unique and is devoid of all sorts of attribute, perception is indeterminate. Thus the only way to justify perception is through the existence of the object. If the object is found to be as it has been exhibited in our perceptual awareness our knowledge is valid. The justification of our immediate knowledge, therefore, lies not in the knowledge itself but in something outside. In other words the justification is external. All the Buddhist scholars are unanimous in this regard. But regarding the justification of inferential cognition there is a difference of opinion among the Buddhist epistemologists. In the case of inferential cognition we pass from the knowledge of the probans to the knowledge of the probandum only through the knowledge of the invariable concomitant relationship between the probans and the probandum. Accordingly in the case of inferential cognition the whole question of justification boils down to the question of justifying the knowledge of the invariable concomitant relationship. Here at this point there is a difference in the views of Diṅnāga and Dharmakīrti. As Diṅnāga held the view that invariable concomitant relationship is established through observation of positive and negative instances both, it can be said that Diṅnāga was in favour of external justification in the case of inferential knowledge also. On the contrary, in the philosophy of Dharmakīrti there has been a new approach to the problem. Dharmakīrti did not believe in the idea that necessary concomitant relation can be established by observation and non-observation of two facts occurring together, but on the basis of the principles of essential identity and of causality. So anyone who understands these principles will be able to apprehend the truth of the proposition. Thus if one understands the principle of essential identity and understands that the essence of an oak consists in its being a tree, one will be justified in believing that all oaks are trees. For this justification there is no necessity to take note of the existence of oaks in the actual world. Similar is the case with the proposition concerning fire and smoke. When one realizes that fire is the cause of smoke and one realizes the principle of causality that the effect cannot occur without the cause, one will be able to apprehend the truth of the proposition — All cases of smoke are cases of fire. One need not depend on anything else for the justification of this proposition. This shows that for Dharmakīrti the justification of such necessary proposition lies not in anything outside, but in the concepts themselves, e.g. in the concept of oak, or in the concept of smoke. Accordingly he will be in favour of internal justification in the case of inferential cognition. As the Buddhist epistemologists believe in two different types of knowledge — one immediate or direct and the other mediate or indirect — they do not have any difficulty in admitting two different kinds of justification for two different types of knowledge.

Another important problem in Western epistemology is — Is knowledge closed under known entailment? The principle of Epistemic Closure under Entailment states that if S knows that p and he also knows that p entails q, then S also knows that q. We can express this principle of closure as subjunctive principle, abbreviating "knows that — as Kp and "entails" by the hook sign, thus —

$$(p)\,(q)\,[\,\{Kp\ \&\ K\,(p - q)\} \rightarrow Kq]$$

This principle assumes that knowledge is closed under known logical implication; that the operation of passing from something known to something else known to be logically entailed by the former does not take us outside the closed area of knowledge. In other words, known logical implications are, as a matter of necessity, known by us if we are already in possession of knowledge of the implicatum (that which implies). The sceptics have tried to show that under this closure principle we cannot claim to know anything and this claim has been refuted in different ways by different epistemologists.

Without entering into the details of the sceptics' argument or the epistemologists' answer let us see whether such a closure principle could be acceptable to the Buddhists in their epistemological framework. A look at the Buddhists' account of inferential cognition, will enable us to justify the claim that such a principle would have been acceptable to them. Inferential cognition presupposes that the cognizer is in possession of knowledge of the probans and also of the knowledge of invariable concomitant relationship between the probans and the probandum. Then, on the basis of such prior information or knowledge, he can proceed to have knowledge of the probandum which was so far unknown to him. We may rewrite the Buddhist inference pattern in the following form:

> *S* knows that *p* (*p* = probans)
> *S* knows that *p* is invariably related to *q* (*q* = probandum)
> Hence, *S* can validly infer *q*; that is *S* knows that *q*.

Since inference is a variety of knowledge, we can state the conclusion "*S* infers *q*" as "*S* knows that *q*." To show the similarity of this inference pattern with the closure principle, it is essential to show that the invariable concomitant relationship between the probans and the probandum is a relation of entailment — that the probans entails the probandum.

History of Buddhist logic tells us that though Diṅnāga showed that invariable concomitant relationship between two terms can be established on the basis of positive and negative instances indicating thereby that the relationship between them is not necessary rather contingent. This view changed during the tenure of Dharmakīrti. Dharmakīrti categorically asserted that the relationship between the probans and the probandum cannot be based on observation or non-observation of different instances but on the logical principles of essential identity and causality. Thus if it is known that the probandum constitutes the essence of the probans or that the probans is the effect of the probandum, then from such probans we can pass on to the probandum. Since essential identity and causality constitute the basis of the invariable concomitant relationship, this relationship is necessary. Hence, it can be said that the probans entails the probandum. As the agent must possess knowledge of this necessary concomitant relationship before hand, it can be said that the second premise of the Buddhist inference pattern is actually similar to the second conjunct of the antecedent of the closure principle. On the basis of this, it will perhaps not be wrong to claim that the Buddhists will have no objection in admitting the closure principle of knowledge, that is, they can say that knowledge is closed under known entailment.

To wind up, it can be said that though the Buddhist epistemologists did not directly discuss all the issues which have been raised by modern epistemologists, a thorough reading of their texts shows that it is not difficult to imagine their possible answers. The attitude that comes out from these answers is that of a foundationalist attitude, belief in something outside that justifies our direct awareness of such object. This feature of knowledge also accounts for its responsibility — that is, if the individual claims to have knowledge of an object, he will have the belief that being guided by such knowledge he will be able to get the desired object and satisfy his purpose. This pragmatic orientation gives the Buddhist epistemology a unique status. Along with a fascination towards externalism the Buddhists also keep space open for a priori knowledge where simply on the basis of the concepts involved we can get valid knowledge. In other words, the Buddhist view can be looked upon as providing another alternative solution to the issues raised in the contemporary debates in epistemology.

Bibliography

Primary Sources

Abhinavagupta, 1986, *Īśvarapratyabhijñāvimarśinī*, ed. K.A. Subramania Iyer & K.C. Pandey, Delhi: Motilal Banarsidass.

Arcaṭa, 1949, *Hetubinduṭīkā* in *Hetubinduṭīkā of Bhaṭṭa Arcaṭa with the Sub-commentary entitled, Āloka of Durveka Miśra*, ed. S. Sanghavi and M.S. Jinavijayji, Gaekwad Oriental Series 113, Baroda: Oriental Institute.

Dharmakīrti, 1934, *Sambandhaparīkṣā*, tr. Erich Frauwallner, *Wiener Zeitschrift für die Kude des Morgenlandes*, 41:261-300.

———, *svārthānumāna paricchedaḥ by Dharmakīrti*, ed. D.S.V. Malvania, Hindi Vishvavidyalaya Nepal Rajya Sanskrit Series, vol. II.

———, 1955, *Nyāyabindu with Dharmottara's Nyāyabinduṭīkā* and *Durveka Miśra's Dharmottarapradīpa*, ed. Dalsukh Malvania, Tibetan Sanskrit Works Series 2, Patna: Kashi Prasad Jayaswal Research Institute.

———, 1960, *Pramāṇavārttikam: The First Chapter with the Auto-commentary*, Serie Orientale Roma 23, ed. Raniero Gnoli, Rome: Instituto Italiano peril Medicoed, Estremo Oriente.

———, 1964, *The Pramāṇavārttika of Dharmakīrti*, tr. Satkari Mookerjee and Hojun Nagasaki, Patna: Nava Nālandā Mahāvihāra.

———, 1966, *Dharmakīrti's Pramāṇaviniścayaḥ : I Kapite! : Pratyakṣam*, Einleictung, Text der Tibetischen Übersetzung, Sanskritfragmente, Deutsche Übersetzung, ed. Tilmann Vetter, Vienna: Osterreichische Akademic der Wissenschaften . . .

———, 1967, *Dharmakīrtis Hetubinduḥ : Tibetische Text and rekonstruierter Sanskrit Text*, ed. and reconstructed Ernst Steinkellner, Vienna: Osterreichische Akademie der Wissenschaften.

———, 1972a, *Sambandhaparīkṣā*, in *Vādanyāyaḥ Sambandhaparīkṣā ca*, ed. Svami Dvarikadasa Sastri, Dharmakīrtinibandhavali 2, Baudha Bharati 8, Varanasi: Bauddha Bharati.

———, 1984, *Pramāṇavārttika of Ācārya Dharmakīrti with Manorathanandi's commentary*, ed. Svami Dvarikadasa Sastri, Bauddha Bharati, 3. Second Edition, Varanasi: Bauddha Bharati.

———, 1989, *The Pramāṇavārttika of Ācārya Dharmakīrti with the commentaries, Svopajñavṛtti of the Author and "Pramāṇavārttikavṛtti" of Manarothanandin*, ed. Ram Chandra Pandeya, Delhi: Motilal Banarsidass.

Dharmottara, 1994, *Nyāyabinduṭīkā* in Dharmakīrti (1994).

Diṅnāga, 1930, *Pramāṇasamuccaya* ed. and restored into Sanskrit with *Vṛtti, Ṭīkā* and *Notes* by H.R. Rangaswamy Iyengar, Mysore: Mysore University Publication.

———, 1982, *Ālaṁbanaparīkṣā and Ālaṁbanaparīkṣāvṛtti*, In "Diṅnāga's *Ālaṁbanaparīkṣāvṛtti*" ed. and tr. Fernando Tola and Carmen Dragonetti, *JIP*, 10,105–34.

Kamalaśīla, 1968, *The Tattvasaṁgraha of Ācārya Śāntarakṣita with the Commentary Pañjikā of Śrī Kamalaśīla*, ed. Svāmi Dvārikādas Śāstrī, Varanasi: Bauddhabhāratī.

Karṇakagomin, 1943, *Pramāṇavārttikasvavṛttiṭīkā: Ācārya Dharmakīrteḥ Pramāṇavārttikam (Svārthānumānaparicchedaḥ) Svopajñavṛttyā Karṇakagomiviracitayā Taṭṭīkayā ca sahitam*, ed. Rahula Saṁkrityayana, Allahabad: Kitab Mahal, reprinted, Kyoto: Rinsen Books, 1982.

Mokṣakaragupta, 1942, *Tarkabhāṣā of Mokṣakaragupta*, ed. with a Sanskrit Commentary E. Krishnamacharya, Baroda: Oriental Institute.

Nāgārjuna, 1960, *Madhyamakaśāstra* of Nāgārjuna with the commentary Prasannapadā by Candrakīrti, ed. P.L. Vaidya, Mithila Institute of Post-graduate Studies and Research, Darbhanga.

Nyāya-Tarkatīrtha, Tārānāth and Tarkatīrtha Amarendramohan, 1985, *Nyāyadarśanam with Vātsyāyana's Bhāṣya, Uddyotakara's Vārttika, Vācaspati Miśra's Tātparyaṭīkā & Viśvanātha's Vṛtti*, Delhi: Munshiram Manoharlal Publishers.

Prajñākaragupta, 1953, *Pramāṇvārttikabhāṣyam or Vārttikālaṁkāraḥ of Prajñākaragupta*, ed. Rahula Samkrityayana, Patna: Kashi Prasad Jayaswal Research Institute.

Ratnākaraśānti, 1910, *Antarvyāptisamarthanam* in *Six Buddhist Nyāya Tracts In Sanskrit* ed. M.M. Haraprasad Shastri, Kolkata: The Asiatic Society, reprint in 1989.

———, 2002, *Antarvyāptisamarthanam,* ed. Arun Mishra, New Delhi: ICPR.

Śaṅkarasvāmin, 1971, "A Sixth-century Manual of Indian Logic" ed. and tr. M. Tachikawa, *JIP,* 1; 111–29.

Śākyabuddhi, 1992, *A Study of the Pramāṇavārttikaṭīkā by Śākyabuddhi from the National Archives Collection, Kathmandu. Part I: Sanskrit Fragments Transcribed,* ed. M. Inami, K. Matsuda and T. Tani, *Studia Tibetica* 23, Tokyo: Toyo Bunko.

Śāntarakṣita, 1968, *The Tattvasaṁgraha of Ācārya Śāntarakṣita with the Commentary Pañjikā of Śrī Kamalaśīla,* ed. Svāmi Dvārikādas Śāstrī, Vārāṇasī: Bauddhabhāratī.

Śāntideva, 1960, *Bodhicaryāvatāra of Śāntideva with the Commentary Pañjikā of Prajñākaramati,* ed. P.L. Vaidya, Buddhist Sanskrit Texts 12, Darbhanga: The Mithila Institute of Post-graduate Studies and Research.

Siddhasena Divākara, 1909, *Nyāyāvatāra* : *The Earliest Jaina Work on Pure Logic* with Sanskrit text and commentary, ed. with notes and English tr. S.C. Vidyābhūṣaṇa, Kolkata: Indian Research Society.

Vasubandhu, 1970, *Abhidharmakośa and Bhāṣya of Ācārya Vasubandhu with Sphūṭārtha Commentary of Ācārya Yaśomitra,* Vārāṇasī: Bauddhabhāratī.

Vinītadeva, 1971, *Vinītadeva's Nyāyabinduṭīkā,* Sanskrit original reconstructed, from the extant Tibetan version, with English translation and annotations by Mrinal Kanti Gangopadhyay, Kolkata: Indian Studies, Past & Present.

Yaśomitra, 1970, *Abhidharmakośa and Bhāṣya of Ācārya Vasubandhu with Sphūṭārthā Commentary of Ācārya Yaśomitra,* Vārāṇasī: Bauddhabhāratī.

Yaśovijay, 1973, *Mahāmahopādhyāya Yaśovijaya's Jaina Tarka-Bhāṣā,* ed. with tr. and Critical Notes D. Bhargava, Delhi: Motilal Banarsidass.

Secondary Sources

Alcoff, L.M., ed., 1998, *Epistemology: The Big Questions,* Massachusetts, USA. Blackwell Pub.

Anacker, S., 1984, *Seven Works of Vasubandhu, The Buddhist Psychological Doctor*, Delhi: Motilal Banarsidass.

Bagchi, S., 1953, *Inductive Reasoning: A Study of Tarka and its role in Indian Logic*, Kolkata: Kolkata Oriental Press.

Bernecker, S. & F. Dretske, eds. 2005, *Knowledge: Readings in Contemporary Epistemology*, Oxford: Oxford University Press.

Bhatt, G.P., 1989, *The Basic Ways of Knowing*, Delhi: Motilal Banarsidass.

Bilimoria, P. & Mohanty, J.N., 1997, *Relativism, Suffering and Beyond: Essays in Memory of Bimal K. Matilal*, New Delhi: Oxford University Press.

Chakraborty, A., 1997, "Seeing Daffodils, Seeing as Daffodils and Seeing Things called, 'Daffodils'", in P. Bilimoria & J.N. Mohanty (1997).

Chatterjee Sastri, H., 1983, *Bauddhācāryasammata Svārthānumāner Saṁkṣipta Ālocanā* (in Bengali), Kolkata: Sanskrit College.

———, 1994, *Saugatadarśanam*, Part I, Kolkata: Sanskrit College.

Chi, R.S.Y., 1969, *Buddhist Formal Logic: The oldest Buddhist Text on Logic after Chinese and Tibetan Materials*, Heidelberg: Kommission by O. Harrassowitz, Leipzig.

Derose, K. & T.A. Warfield, eds., 1999, *Skepticism: A Contemporary Reader*, Oxford, New York: Oxford University Press.

Dhruva, A.B., ed., 1930, *The Nyāya Praveśa*, Part I, Sanskrit Text with Commentaries, Baroda: Oriental Institute.

Dreyfus, G., 1997, *Recognizing Reality: Dharmakīrti's Philosophy and Its Tibetan Interpretations*, Albany: Suny Press.

———, 2003, *The Sound of the Two Hands Clapping: the Education of a Tibetan Buddhist Monk*, Berkeley: University of California Press.

Dunne, J. D., 1999, "Foundations of Dharmakīrti's Philosophy: A Study of the Central Issues in his Ontology, Logic and Epistemology with particular attention to the *Svopajñavṛtti*," Ph.D dissertation, Harvard University.

———, 2004, *Foundations of Dharmakīrti's Philosophy*, Boston: Wisdom Publication.

Franco, E., 1986, "Once Again on Dharmakīrti's Deviation from Diṅnāga on *Pratyakṣābhāsa*", *JIP*, 14:79-97.

———, 1991, "The Disjunction in *Pramāṇavārttika*", *Prmāṇasiddhi* Chapter, Verse 5c, Steinkellner (1991): 339-51.

Funayama, T., 1999, "Kamalaśīla's Interpretation of "Non-Erroneous" in the Definition of Direct Perception and Related Problems", in Katsura (1999): 72–99.

Ganeri, J., 2001, *Philosophy in Classical India: The Proper Work of Reason,* London: Routledge.

Gillon, B. S., 1991, "Dharmakīrti and the Problem of Induction", in Steinkellner (1991): 53–58.

———, 1997, "Negative Facts and Knowledge of Negative Facts", in Bilimoria and Mohanty (1997).

Griffiths, P., 1986, *On Being Mindless: Buddhist Meditation and the Mind — Body Problem,* La Salle, Illinois: Open Court.

Gokhale, Pradeep P., 1992, *Inference and Fallacies discussed in Ancient Indian Logic with special reference to Nyāya and Buddhism,* Delhi: Sri Satguru Publications.

Hattori, M., 1968, *Dignāga on Perception, being the Pratyakṣaparicchedaḥ* of *Dignāga's Pramāṇasamuccaya for the Sanskrit Fragments and the Tibetan Versions,* Cambridge: Harvard University Press.

Hayes, R. P., 1987, "On the Reinterpretation of Dharmakīrti's Svabhāvahetu", *JIP* 15:319–32.

———, 1988, *Diṅnāga on the Interpretation of Signs,* Studies of Classical India 8, Dordrecht: Kluwer Academic Press.

Hayes, R.P., and B.S. Gillon, 1991, "Introduction to Dharmakīrti's Theory of Inference as presented in *Pramāṇavārttika Svopajñavṛtti,* 1-10" *JIP,* 19: 1–74.

———, 1997, "Whose experience validates what for Dharmakīrti", in Bilimoria and Mohanty (1997).

Iwata, T., 1993, *Prasaṅga and Prasaṅgaviparyaya bei Dharmakīrti and seinen Kommentatoren,* Wien: Universität Wien.

———, 2003, "An Interpretation of Dharmakīrti's *Svabhāva Hetu*", *JIP,* 31: 61–87.

Jayatilleke, J.N., 1963, *Early Buddhist Theory of Knowledge,* reprinted, Delhi: Motilal Banarsidass, 1980.

Kajiyama, Y., 1966, *An Introduction to Buddhist Philosophy,* Memoirs of the Faculty of Letters, Kyoto University, Kyoto.

———, 1989, "*Tripañcakacintā*: Development of the Buddhist Theory on the Determination of Causality", in Y. Kajiyama, *Studies in*

Buddhist Philosophy: Selected Papers ed. K. Mimaki, et al. Kyoto: Rinsen Book Co., 475-90.

Katsura, S., ed. 1999, *Dharmakīrti's Thought and its Impact on Indian and Tibetan Philosophy*: Proceedings of the Third International Dharmakīrti Conference, Hiroshima, November 4-6, 1997, Vienna: Österrichische Akademie der Wissenschaften.

———, 1979, "The *Apoha,* Theory of Diṅnāga", *IBK,* 28: 16-20.

———, 1983, "Diṅnāga on *Trairūpya*", *Journal of Indian and Buddhist Studies,* 32, 15-21.

———, 1984, "Dharmakīrti's Theory of Truth", *JIP,* 12: 215-35.

———, 1986, "*Svabhāvapratibandha* revisited", *IBK,* 69: 473-76, 26-29.

———, 1991, "Diṅnāga and Dharmakīrti on *Apoha*", in Steinkellner (1991a): 129-44.

———, 1992, "*Pramāṇavārttika* IV. 202-06 — Towards the Correct Understanding of *Svabhāvapratibandha*", *IBK* 40: 1047-1052 [35-40].

Kellner, B., 1997, *Nichts bleibt nichts, Die buddhistische Zuruckweisung von Kumārila abhāvapramāṇa, Übersetzung und Interpretation von Śāntarakṣitas Tattvasaṁgraha, vv.* 1647-690 *mit Kamalaśīlas Pañjikā, WSTB,* 39. Vienna: Arbeiskreis für Tibetische und Buddhistische Studien.

———, 1999, "Levels of (Im)Perceptibility: Dharmottara's View on the *dṛśya* in *Dṛśyānupalabdhi*", in Katsura (1999): 193-214.

———, 2001, "Negation — failure or success/remarks on an *Allegedly characteristic Trait of Dharmakīrti's* Anupalabdhi-Theory", *JIP,* 29:495-517.

Keyt, C.M., 1980, "Dharmakīrti's Concept of the *Svalakṣaṇa*", PhD dissertation, University of Washington.

Kraser, Helmut, 1991, *Dharmottara's kurze Untersuchung der Gultigkeit einer Erkenntnis : Laghuprāmāṇyaparīkṣā,* vol. I: Tibetan text and Sanskrit materials, Vienna: Österreichische Akademie der Wissenschaften.

———, 1995, "Dharmottara's Theory of Knowledge in his *Laghuprāmāṇyaparīkṣā*", *JIP,* 23: 247-71.

———, 2001, "On Dharmakīrti's Understanding of *pramāṇabhūta* and his Definition of *Pramāṇa*", *WZKS,* 45: 173-99.

———, 2003, "On the Ascertainment of Validity in the Buddhist Epistemological Tradition", *JIP,* 31:161-84.

Lasic, Horst, 1999, "Dharmakīrti and his Successors on the Determination of Causality", in Katsura, (1999), pp. 233-42.

———, 2003, "On the Utilization of Causality as a Basis of Inference: Dharmakīrti's Statements and their Interpretation", *JIP*, 31, pp. 185-97.

Matilal, B.K., 1971, *Epistemology, Logic and Grammar in Indian Philosophical Analysis*, The Hague: Mouton.

———, 1985, *Logic, Language and Reality*, Delhi: Motilal Banarsidass.

———, 1986, *Perception: An Essay on Classical Indian Theories of Knowledge*, Oxford: Clarendon Press.

———, 1998, *The Character of Logic in India*, ed. Jonardon Ganeri and Heeramon Tiwari, State University of New York, 1st Indian reprint by New Delhi: Oxford University Press, 1999.

Motilal, B.K., and D. Evans, 1986, *Buddhist Logic and Epistemology: Studies in the Buddhist Analysis of Inference and Language*, Dordrecht: D. Reidel Publishing Company.

Mohanty, J.N., 1984, "*Prāmāṇya* and Workability — Response to Potter", *JIP*, 12, pp. 329-38.

———, 1992, *Reason and Tradition in Indian Thought: An Essay on the Nature of Indian Philosophical Thinking*, Oxford: Oxford University Press.

———, 1993, *Essays on Indian Philosophy: Traditional and Modern*, Delhi: Oxford University Press.

Nyāyatarkatīrtha, Anantakumar, 1955, *Vaibhāsikadarśana*, Kolkata: Orient Book Co.

Oetke, Claus, 1991, "*Svabhāvapratibandha* and the Types of Reasons in Dharmakīrti's Theory of Inference", in Steinkellner, (1991), 243-68.

———, 1999, "The Disjunction in *Pramāṇasiddhi*", in Katsura (1999): 243-50.

———, 1999, "Clarifications", in Katsura, 1999 : 287-94.

Oki, Kazufumi, 1999, "*Pravṛtti* as an Action of a person", in Katsura (1999): 287-94.

Ono, Motoi, et al., 1996, *KWIC Index to the Sanskrit Texts of Dharmakīrti*, Lexicological Studies 8, Project on Lexicological Analysis, Institute for the Study of Languages and Cultures of Asia and Africa, Tokyo: Tokyo University of Foreign Studies.

Potter, Karl H., 1977, ed., *Indian Metaphysics and Epistemology: The Tradition of Nyāya-Vaiśeṣika up to Gaṅgeśa: Encyclopaedia of Indian Philosophy,* vol. II, Delhi: Motilal Banarsidass.

———, 1984, "Does Indian Epistemology Concern Justified, True Belief?", *JIP,* 12: 307-27.

Prets, Ernst, 1992, "On the Development of the Concept of *Parārthānumāna*" *WZKS,* 36: 195-202.

Randle, H.N., 1926, *Fragments from Diṅnāga,* London: Royal Asiatic Society, First Indian Reprint, Delhi: Motilal Banarsidass, 1981.

Rajendra Prasad, 2002, *Dharmakīrti's Theory of Inference : Revaluation and Reconstruction,* New Delhi: Oxford University Press.

Sen, Prabal K., 2006, "A Note on *svasaṁvedana*", paper presented at the International Seminar on *Knowledge of Knowledge* at the Dept. of Philosophy, Jadavpur University, Kolkata.

Shah, Nagin, J., 1967, *Akalaṁka's Criticisms of Dharmakīrti's Philosophy: A Study,* Lalbhai Dalpatbhai Series II. Ahmedabad: L.D. Institute of Indology.

Siderits, Mark, 1985, "Word Meaning, Sentence Meaning and *Apoha*", *JIP,* 13:133-51.

———, 1991, *Indian Philosophy of Language: Studies in Selected Issues,* Studies in Linguistics and Philosophy 46, Dordrecht: Kluwer Academic Publishers.

———, 1999, "*Apohavāda,* Nominalism and Resemblance Theories", in Katsura (1999): 349–62.

———, 2003, "Deductive, Inductive, Both or Neither", *JIP,* 31: 303-21.

Stcherbatsky, T., 1984, *Buddhist Logic,* vols. I and II, New Delhi: Oriental Books Reprint Corporation.

Steinkellner, Ernst, ed., 1991, *Studies in the Buddhist Epistemological Tradition: Proceedings of the Second International Dharmakīrti Conference: Vienna,* June 11–16, 1989, Vienna: Österreichische Akademie der Wissenschaften.

———, 1971, "Wirklichkeit und Begriff bei Dharmakīrti", *WZKS,* 15:179-211.

———, 1974, "On the Interpretation of the *Svabhāvahetu*", *WZKS,* 18: 117-29.

———, 1984, "*Svabhāvapratibandha* Again" *Acta Indologica* 6: 457-76.

———, 1991, "The Logic of the *Svabhāvahetu* in Dharmakīrt's *Vādanyāya*", in Steinkellner (1991): 311-24.

———, 1991, "Dharmakīrti on the Inference of Effect (*kārya*)", in *Papers in Honor of Prof. Dr. Ji Xianlin on the Occasion of his 80th Birthday* ed. Z. Li, et al. Peking.

———, 1994, "Śākyabuddhi's Commentary on *Pramāṇavārttika* I.3 and its *Vṛtti*", WZKS 38:379-87.

———, 1996, "An Explanation of Dharmakīrti's *svabhāvahetu* definitions", in *Festschrift Dieter Schlingloff* ed. F. Wilhelm. Reinbeck: Dr. Inge Wezler Verlag für Orientalistische Fachpublikationen: 257-68.

———, 1997, "Kumārila, Īśvarasena and Dharmakīrti in Dialogue, A New Interpretation of *Pramāṇavārttika,* I.33", in *Bauddhavidyāsudhākaraḥ: Studies in Honor of Heinz Bechert on the Occasion of his 65th Birthday* ed., P. Kieffer-pulz and J. Hartmann, Swisttal-Odendorf: 625-46 Öua.

———, 1999, "Yogic Cognition, Tantric Goal and Other Methodological Applications of Dharmakīrti's *Kāryānumāna*-Theorem", in Katsura, (1999): 349-62.

———, 1999, "Early Tibetan Ideas on the Ascertainment of Validity", in *Tibetan Studies,* vol. I (Buddhist Philosophy and Literature) ed. I. Shoren, & Y. Zuiho, Naritasan.

Tauscher, H., 1999, "Phya Pa Chos Klyi Seng Ge's opinion on *prasanga*", in Katsura, (1999).

Tillemans, Tom J.F., 1990, "On *Sapakṣa*", *JIP,* 18:53-80.

———, 1991, "More on *parārthānumāna* Theses and Syllogisms", *AS/EA,* 45:133-148.

———, 1995, "Dharmakīrti and Tibetans on *Adṛśyānupalabdhi*", *JIP,* 23.

———, 1995, "On the so-called, Difficult Point of the *Apoha* Theory", *AS/EA* 59/4 : 854-89.

———, 1999, *Scripture, Logic, Language: Essays on Dharmakīrti and His Tibetan Successors,* Studies in Indian and Tibetan Buddhism, Boston: Wisdom Publications.

Tucci, G., 1930, *The Nyāyamukha of Diṅnāga: The Oldest Buddhist Text on Logic, After Chinese and Tibetan Materials,* Heidelberg: Kommission by O. Harrassowitz, Leipzig.

———, *Minor Buddhist Texts,*

Tuske, 1998, "Diṅnāga and the Raven Paradox", *JIP*, 26.

Van Bijlert, Vittorio A., 1989, *Epistemology and Spiritual Authority, The Development of Epistemology and Logic in the Old Nyāya and the Buddhist School of Epistemology with an Annotated Translation of Dharmakīrti's Pramāṇavārttika II (Pramāṇasiddhi) vv 1–7, WSTB*, 20, Vienna: Arbeitskreis für Tibetische und Buddhistische Studien.

Vattanky, J., 2001, "Geṇeral Definiton of Fallacy", *Rabindra Bharati Journal of Philosophy*, vol. VIII.

Vetter, Tilman, 1964, *Erkenntnissprobleme bei Dharmakīrti*, Vienna: Östereichische Akademie der Wissenschaften.

———, 1990, *Der Buddha und seine Lehre in Dharmakīrti's Pramāṇavārttika, Der Abschnitt über der Buddha und die vier edlen Wahrheiten im Pramāṇasiddhi-Kapitel, WSTB*, 12, Vienna: Arbeitskreis für Tibetische und Buddhistische Studien. Second and revised, edition, First edition published in 1984.

Vidyābhūṣanṇa, S.C., 1920, *A History of Indian Logic, Ancient, Mediaeval and Modern Schools*, Kolkata, reprinted Delhi: Motilal Banarsidass, 1988.

Vora, P.R. and S. Ota, 1979, "The Memorial Verses Explanatory of Sources of Knowledge and the Author's Own Commentary" *Saga–Ryukoku Tanki Daigaku Kiyo*, no. 25.

Vyas, C.S., 1991, *Buddhist Theory of Perception with Special Reference to Pramāṇavārttika of Dharmakīrti*, New Delhi: Navrang.

Williams, M., 2001, *Problems of Knowledge: A Critical Introduction to Epistemology*, New York: Oxford University Press.

Yaita, H., 1985, "On Anupalabdhi: Annotated tr. of Dharmakīrti's Pramāṇavārttikasvavṛtti (II)", *Journal of Chisan Studies*, Taisho Universtiy, 48:1-14.

———, 1987, "Dharmakīrti on the Authority of Buddhist Scriptures (Āgama): An Annotated tr. of the Pramāṇavārttikasvavṛtti, adv. 213-17." *Journal of the Nanto Society for Buddhist Studies*, 58:1-57.

———, 1988, "Dharmakīrti on the Person Free from Faults: Annotated tr. of the Pramāṇavārttikasvavṛtti, adv. 218-23", Nanto Bukkyo Kenkyukai II. 433-445.

Zwilling, Leonard, 1976, "Dharmakīrti on *Apoha*", Ph.D dissertation, University of Wisconsin.

Index